IRAN

GLOBAL ENCOUNTERS: STUDIES IN COMPARATIVE POLITICAL THEORY
Series Editor: Fred Dallmayr, University of Notre Dame

This series seeks to inaugurate a new field of inquiry and intellectual concern: that of comparative political theory as an inquiry proceeding not from the citadel of a global hegemony but through cross-cultural dialogue and critical interaction. By opening the discourse of political theory—today largely dominated by American and European intellectuals—to voices from across the global spectrum, we hope to contribute to a richer, multifaceted mode of theorizing as well as to a deeper, cross-cultural awareness of the requirements of global justice.

Gandhi, Freedom, and Self-Rule, edited by Anthony J. Parel

Beyond Nationalism? Sovereignty and Citizenship, edited by Fred Dallmayr and José M. Rosales

Conversations and Transformations: Toward a New Ethics of Self and Society, by Ananta Kumar Giri

Comparative Political Culture in the Age of Globalization: An Introductory Anthology, edited by Hwa Yol Jung

Hinterlands and Horizons: Excursions in Search of Amity, by Margaret Chatterjee

New Approaches to Comparative Politics: Insights from Political Theory, edited by Jennifer S. Holmes

Comparative Political Philosophy: Studies under the Upas Tree, edited by Anthony J. Parel and Ronald C. Keith

Iran: Between Tradition and Modernity, edited by Ramin Jahanbegloo

Democratization and Identity: Regimes and Ethnicity in East and Southeast Asia, edited by Susan J. Henders

IRAN
Between Tradition and Modernity

Edited by
Ramin Jahanbegloo

LEXINGTON BOOKS
Lanham • Boulder • New York • Toronto • Oxford

LEXINGTON BOOKS

Published in the United States of America
by Lexington Books
An imprint of The Rowman & Littlefield Publishing Group, Inc.
4501 Forbes Boulevard, Suite 200, Lanham, Maryland 20706

PO Box 317
Oxford
OX2 9RU, UK

British Library Cataloguing in Publication Information Available

Library of Congress Cataloging-in-Publication Data

Iran : between tradition and modernity / edited by Ramin Jahanbegloo.
    p. cm.
    Includes bibliographical references and index.
    ISBN 0-7391-0529-9 — ISBN 0-7391-0530-2 (pbk.)
    1. Iran—Intellectual life. 2. Social change—Iran. 3. Islamic
modernism—Iran. 4. Islam and politics—Iran. 5. Secularism—Iran.
6. Culture conflict—Iran. 7. Globalization. I. Jahanbegloo, Ramin.

    DS318.82.I73 2003
    955—dc22   2003015174

Printed in the United States of America

♾™ The paper used in this publication meets the minimum requirements of American
National Standard for Information Sciences—Permanence of Paper for Printed Library
Materials, ANSI/NISO Z39.48-1992.

Contents

Part III: Intellectual Discourses of Modernity

Part IV: Modernization, Gender, and Political Culture

Acknowledgments

THIS VOLUME HAD ITS ORIGIN IN A 2001 Centre for Iranian Research and Analysis (CIRA) conference held at the University of Toronto and cosponsored by the Department of Political Science. Most of the contributors to this volume, with the exception of Sohrab Behdad, Mohamad Tavakoli-Targhi, Monica M. Ringer, and Majid Tehranian, were present at this conference. Subsequently, a book was developed, drawing on the best papers and adding several others to assure diversity as well as depth of coverage. To each of my colleagues who wrote for this volume and patiently revised their manuscripts, I express my gratitude and my sincere thanks.

As with all such projects, many were involved in making it a successful project. While I do not have room to thank all of them, several must be cited. Fred Dallmayr, who included this volume as part of his series *Global Encounters: Studies in Comparative Political Theory*, was supportive throughout the process. I am also particularly grateful to the National Endowment for Democracy, and especially to Sally Blair, Zerxes Spencer, and Marc Plattner, who were of a great help and kindness to me during my ten-month fellowship in Washington, D.C., a period during which I put together the present book.

Finally, I would like to thank Serena Leigh Krombach and Brian Richards from the Rowman & Littlefield Publishing Group and Lexington Books for taking this project seriously and bringing clarity, consistency, and better organization to this book.

Ramin Jahanbegloo
Washington, D.C.
September 2003

Introduction

FRIEDRICH NIETZSCHE PROPHESIZED with remarkable accuracy that the twentieth century would be marked by great wars fought in the name of philosophic ideas. What Nietzsche could not have anticipated was that at the ending years of the twentieth century there would be a revolution in the name of God, establishing an Islamic theocracy. Iran's Islamic Revolution of 1978–1979 was clearly one of the most important events of the twentieth century and a momentous development in the modern history of Islam. Carried forward on a wave of popular support, the Iranian Revolution toppled what was considered by many to be the pseudo-modernist monarchy of the Shah and instituted the Islamic Republic under the leadership of the late Ayatollah Khomeini. Defying all the myths of secular modernization and shattering all the political ideologies of modernity, the Islamic Republic became the first theocratic state in the modern world to have institutionalized the idea of Velayat-e-faqih, or the "Rule of the Jurist."

During the past twenty-five years, the Iranian Revolution has attracted a great deal of attention from scholars and intellectuals around the world, as well as interest among policy makers and journalists. Perceived by many as a revolt against the secular modernity of the West, the Iranian Revolution was welcomed by some Western thinkers, such as Michel Foucault, as a triumph of spiritual values over the profane world of capitalist materialism. By saying this, Foucault was actually observing the Iranian Revolution as a means of critically attacking aspects of Western culture of which he disapproved. For Foucault, the Iranian Revolution was a protest against the very political rationality of the modern era. Edward Said, who was in Paris at that time, remembers Foucault talking about the Iranian Revolution as a "very exciting, very strange and crazy" form of revolt. Foucault's analysis was that this revolt could also involve a radical change in subjectivity among the Iranian population. In hoping so, Foucault saw the Iranian Revolution in much the same way as Kant had seen the French Revolution 200 years before: despite the political violence into which it had escalated, it could be seen as a sign of progress toward modern emancipation and freedom. Although the concept of freedom was the invisible center of gravity of the Iranian Revolution, it remained invisible, since the idea itself was hardly ever institutionalized in the Iranian political system. On the contrary, the political system of the Islamic regime was intentionally designed to institutionalize the involvement and dominance of Islamic clergies in all aspects of the political process and government functioning. After nearly a quarter of a century of violent revolutionary upheavals, a bloody war with Iraq, and power struggles among the political groups in Iran, the Shi'i clergy that came to power in 1979 has been able to consolidate its hold over all the levers of power. Many consider this transformation of the Shi'i hierocracy from a political force to a ruling regime as a political exemplification of the historical tension between "tradition" and "modernity" in Iran. As a matter of fact, this tension has been a durable and influential factor in the political and cultural formation of Iranian society for the past 150 years. Yet this tension appears to be less an irreconcilable clash between "modernity" and "tradition" than a series of ontological and anthropological encounters between the two. These encounters, the major theme of this book, are too complex to be simply characterized as a monolithic conflict between the liberal and enlightened values of "modernity" on one side and the dark and backward forces of "tradition" on the other. As most of the chapters in this book suggest, Iranian intellectual and political history cannot be subjected to a binary "either/or" classification when considering the complexities and ambiguities of Iran's philosophical and political encounters with modernity and the West. As Hamid Dabashi reminds us in his chapter on Abdolkarim Soroosh, "Blindness and Insight: The Predicament of a Muslim Intellectual," "We can no longer think in those terms [tradition versus modernity]. The world has left that false opposition behind." Dabashi affirms that in the absence of secular intellectuals, silenced, exiled, or murdered, those who define themselves today in Iran as "religious intellectuals" are "busy de-historicizing 'Islam' in a mute dialogue with an absent interlocutor [modernity]." Yet, according to Dabashi, this appears to be a futile exercise because it fails to achieve its objectives. "This failure is less a matter of theoretical blindness than a measure of historical belatedness." What Dabashi affirms is that Iranian religious intellectuals such as Soroosh are dealing with an epistemologically imploded Western modernity, but they do not realize that the Islam that they have in mind "is a dialectical outcome of a conversation under duress with a modernity that no longer exists. . . . What Islam will emerge in a globalizing context where all binary oppositions have melted away is yet to be seen."

Religious or secular, for Iranian intellectuals the predicament of modernity is circumstantial to their peripheral situation. Ours is the modernity of the once semicolonized. Maybe that is why the same historical process that has taught us to accept and to cherish the positive values of modernity has also made us the victims of modernity. The crisis of modernity is also part of our heritage. Whatever its other promises, the delegitimation of modernity, not at the level of the efficacy of modern instruments but of the ultimate beneficence and morality of the project itself, has undoubtedly created a different agenda for a dialogue between "tradition" and "modernity." Our attitude toward modernity therefore cannot be other than deeply ambiguous. This is reflected in the way our experiences with modernity have taken place in the last 150 years, from mid-nineteenth-century Iran to contemporary Iran. This ambiguity does not stem from any uncertainty about whether to be for or against modernity. Rather, the uncertainty occurs because we know that to create a dialogue between our traditions and modernity, we need to have the courage not only to struggle for truth but to examine and question our old concepts and values. Today, in the age of the global village, perhaps the time has come once more to mobilize that courage.

Our historical experience with modernity entitles us to engage in a Socratic examination of our "fragmented selves." It was Socrates who taught us that the unexamined life is not worth living. He was an enlightener who spoke, not just *ad captum vulgi*, but to the circumstances of his day. Accordingly, our present-day situation in Iran shows us that the quarrel between the "antimodernists" and the "modernists" must be redefined as a form of schizophrenia. There are neither antimoderns nor moderns, and certainly no postmoderns in today's Iran, but only simulacra of our fragmented selves. The position of all antimoderns in Iran is ultimately modern and is a reproduction of a misunderstanding about modernity. In the same way as moderns, we are also part of a tradition and a past. That we cannot return to this past in no way cancels the fact that we have already been there, and so, as historical beings, are somehow still there. Time does not separate Iranian modernity from Iranian traditions at this level; it binds them together. To reject Iranian traditions entirely would be to reject our modernity as well. On the same basis, the meaning of a "return to tradition" is not clear either, and at the moment in Iran any kind of return to "tradition" is a modern claim. It is on the basis of such difficulties, but also of a dialogical process between "tradition" and "modernity" in Iran, that the reexamination of the Iranian imagination of modernity helps us to understand and to recognize in a better way what Mohamad Tavakoli-Targhi calls in his contribution to this volume entitled "The Homeless Texts of Persianate Modernity" "the heterotopic experiences." According to Tavakoli-Targhi

> By recovering the significance of heterotopic experiences in the formation of the ethos of modernity, the lands beyond Europe, instead of being the reverse image of Enlightenment and modernity, served as "laboratories of modernity," as sites of earliest sightings of "hallmarks of European cultural production". . . . [As a result] modernity can be viewed [as] a product of a global network of power and knowledge that emerged initially around the sixteenth century. The heterotopic experiences of crisscrossing peoples and cultures provided multiple scenarios of modernity and self-refashioning. Whereas Europeans constituted the modern Self in relation to their non-Western heterotopias, Asians and Africans redefine the Self in dialogic relations to Europe, their new significant Other.

What Tavakoli-Targhi criticizes is a form of historical thought among Iranian historians that by developing a fractured conception of historical time narrates "Iranian history in terms of the European past." In other words, "An eternally recurring Iranian premodernity [is thus] superseded by an already enacted 'Western' modernity."

The agonizing question is how to have an autonomous experience of modernity when dominated by a process of global modernity that brings to the Iranian the sentiment of superiority. This complex sentiment of inferiority mixed with that of the loss of the Iranian self through the global domination of the West has been the foundation for theoretical elaborations on the two concepts of tradition and modernity among four generations of Iranian intellectuals. Heavily and somehow uncritically influenced by the ideas of the European Enlightenment, the first generation of Iranian intellectuals of the late Qajar period (individuals such as Mirza Malkum Khan), called for nothing less than imitating and surrendering to Western modernity. For these members of the Iranian elite, this was the only way to fill in the gap that existed with the West and also the unique way to escape existing social ills in the Iran of the late nineteenth and early twentieth centuries. In the same manner as Malkum Khan, Taghizadeh, who could be considered one of the leading figures of the second generation of Iranian intellectuals, proposed the "unconditional acceptance and promotion of European civilization and absolute capitulation to European customs, education, sciences, industry and ways of life without any exception."[1] In his chapter "Iranian Society, Modernity, and Globalization," Jamshid Behnam gives the following account and analysis of the mindset of intellectuals such as Malkum Khan and Taghizadeh by suggesting that

From the nineteenth century onward, Iranian intellectuals responded variably to the issue of facing the West. Based on their ideological and philosophical stances, their responses ranged from idealizing to demonizing the West. The stages of "captivation," "emulation," "criticism," and even "rejection" emerged one after another and at times concurrently. The contradictory feelings of "fascination" and "hatred" toward the West made it difficult to find a proper position in dealing with it. Whereas Malkum Khan advocated unequivocal acceptance of Western civilization and culture, Seyyed Hassan Taghizadeh wanted the same with the condition that the Persian language be preserved. Ali Akbar Dehkhoda spoke of acquiring selective components of modernity. Mohammad Ali Jamalzadeh preferred a kind of "engagement" with Western civilization, and Mohammad Ali Furughi preferred the "contemporary civilization."

In addition to his analysis of the intellectual attitudes of the late nineteenth and early twentieth centuries in Iran, Behnam introduces a philosophical distinction between the two concepts of "modernity" as used in the West, and *tajaddod* in Persian, which was used by several generations of Iranian intellectuals to mean "renewal." According to Behnam, *tajaddod* is

> different from the meaning of the term in the West, where modernity is a sociological concept, and a philosophical idea conceived in a different cultural context. Iranian intellectuals' desire for *tajaddod* was derived from Iran's lagging behind and Western civilization's advancement, and *tajaddod* was intended to create the best incorporation of national culture with modern values and beliefs. In other words, one should define modernization in Iran as the desire for change and innovation, shaped by temporal conditions and national identity.

Unlike Behnam, who makes a clear distinction between the two concepts of "modernization" and "modernity," Monica M. Ringer, in her chapter "Negotiating Modernity: Ulama and the Discourse of Modernity in Nineteenth-Century Iran," tries to show that in late Qajar Iran "the conceptualization of a future modernity was part and parcel of the modernization process." Through her focus on Iran's first secular educational institutions such as Dar al Fonun, Ringer emphasizes the intellectual debates surrounding the modernization process that have been structuring much of the reform agenda and the ongoing tension between "tradition" and "modernity" in Iran for the past hundred years. According to Ringer, "The ulama played a unique role in these debates, both as actors (reformers and opponents of reform), and as the direct or indirect targets of many reform programs." And "because the ulama found themselves threatened by reform projects as a group, they are often portrayed as opponents of modernization and reform." For Ringer, the use of adjectives such as "conservative" and "progressive" contribute to confusion rather than clarity in our understanding of the intellectual ferment of nineteenth-century

Iran. Therefore, the correct historical and sociological approach is to treat the Ulama individually in terms of their position to the questions of modernization and Shiite intellectual traditions.

Sohrab Behdad's intellectual and political biography of Navvab Safavi, "Utopia of Assassins: Navvab Safavi and the Fada'ian-e Eslam in Prerevolutionary Iran," follows this pattern of thinking. For Behdad, "the historical significance of Navvab Safavi's thought is in the impact that he and his organization had on the development of the Islamic character of the Iranian Revolution." In Navvab Safavi's utopia, "what was Islamic was absolute and ideal, and what was not Islamic was servile and contemptible." Therefore his opposition against the impact of Reza Shah's reforms was mainly a protest against the dominance of secular ideals and values in the Iranian public arena. Reza Shah's modernization policies were adhered to by progovernmental intellectuals as well as those excluded from the polity. This made it more difficult for conservatives such as Navvab Safavi to develop strong ideological arguments against the modernization process and in favor of tradition. Perhaps this is one of the reasons why, according to Behdad, Navvab Safavi and Fada'ian-e Eslam's utopia took a terrorist shape. As Behdad clearly affirms: "In the decades between the political activities of Navvab Safavi and the formation of the Islamic Republic, much had changed in Iranian society. In the latter period Islam entered the political arena as a leading force riding on the powerful force of the revolution."

This time the question of Iranian national identity and cultural authenticity was placed at the center of intellectual debates concerning "modernity" and its impact on Iranian life.

The idea of abandoning Western modernity and returning to the "authentic" roots of Iranian culture that was elaborated in the 1960s and early 1970s by intellectuals such as Jalal Al-e Ahmad and Ali Shariati laid the ground for a critique of politics of modernization in Iran. Reevaluating the causes of the defeat of the nationalist and democratic movements in Iran and the role of Western imperialism in this defeat, Al-e Ahmad argued that Iranians have been forced to be servile consumers of Western products and to reshape their native culture to resemble a machine. He compared the process of modernization in Iran to a disease, "Occidentosis" (Gharbzadegi) that had infected the Iranian society and degenerated Iranian cultural subjectivity. Al-e Ahmad's critique of universal modernity also involved a relentless attack on the entire modern Iranian intellectual tradition of secularism. For Al-e Ahmad the antireligious orientation of Westernized Iranian intellectuals (either leftist or liberal) was simply an imitation of their Western counterparts and was not rooted in the authentic Iranian culture represented by Islamic identity.

Shariati began from where Al-e Ahmad had left off by criticizing those among the Iranian intellectuals who ignored the Islamic culture of Iran. But while Al-e Ahmad focused on the critique of modernization in Iran and its negative effects, Shariati concentrated more on elaborating an ideal Islamic ideology as an authentic return to Iranian roots. In the case of Shariati, the "authenticity" intellectual discourse was put together with a new Islamic revolutionary ideology founded more on the action of the true believers than on the role of Islamic jurists and scholars. As a result "Shariati concluded that Islam needed to be reformed both theoretically and organizationally."[2] The need for this reform was to create a new ideology that could produce not clerics, but anti-imperialist warriors and politically engaged intellectuals. Heavily influenced by Third World nationalistic and anticolonialist attitudes and sentiments, Shariati reshaped and enriched, through his critique of modern secularism and his instrumentalist view of Islam in politics, the defiant behavior of Iranian revolutionaries toward the West.

As Farzin Vahdat points out clearly in his chapter "Mehdi Haeri Yazdi and the Discourse of Modernity," "In contrast to someone like Ali Shariati, who considered human subjectivity as the privilege of the collectivity, Haeri has repeatedly endowed the individual as the beneficiary of modern subjectivity." Maybe this is one of the main reasons why the thought of Haeri Yazdi has a significant role to play in the current debates on the dialogue between modernity and tradition in Iran. "Haeri's crucial emphasis on the role of free human volition in his views on the philosophy of ethics, should be viewed as his nurturing of human subjectivity. It is in the last stage of his discourse, his thought on the social and political spheres, that this development yields very concrete results in establishing universal human subjectivity and its materialization in rights of citizenship." Haeri's nonideological approach toward Western philosophy and modernity and the search for reconciling what he calls the "methodology of Western philosophy"[3] with Islamic philosophy is a good example of a tolerant and democratic effort in creating the dialogical bridge between "modernity" and "tradition" in contemporary Iran. Yet, this passion has not been shared during the past fifty years by all Iranian clerics and intellectuals.

One of the most virulent antidemocratic and antimodernist thinkers of the postrevolutionary period is Reza Davari Ardakani. A well-read philosopher and a connoisseur of German and French philosophy, Davari was influenced, in the same way as Shariati, by some features of Heidegger's thought that he tried to translate in an Islamic idiom. Echoing Heidegger's critique of technology, Davari claimed that Western civilization was dominated by secularism and materialism, which were based on the separation of politics and religion and doomed to be destroyed by alienation and solitude. Inviting the Iranian intellectuals to face the West in its "unity" and in its "totality" and not through its particular individualities, Davari strongly advocated a total transformation of the modern foundations of the West and a full rejection of the West in its totality as the "other" of Islamic identity. Taking into consideration Davari's antimodernist account of the West, Mazyar Lotfalian takes a more precise look at his analysis of Western technology and science in chapter 2, "Keywords in Islamic Critiques of Technoscience: Iranian Postrevolutionary Interpretations." Lotfalian maintains that

> the emergent discourse of authenticity was an important turn in the appropriation of technoscientific identity prior to the Iranian Revolution and affected the intellectual understanding of science and technology. However, during the Cultural Revolution in Iran, there was a turning point in the understanding of what constituted authenticity. A new understanding had emerged. Davari Ardakani explained this differentiation in meaning by reflecting on how "Gharbzadegi" assumes an immunity from cultural invasion, especially technological invasion. . . . Davari's argument is compelling in that he points to a complex set of questions that have emerged in Iran since the beginning of the Iranian Revolution. His questions concern the nature of science and technology: Is there a new condition for science in the West? Does science have a solid foundation or are its foundations constructed and dependent on particular conditions of possibility? Davari carries on to argue that if the foundation of science is not on solid ground, as the postmodernists have argued, we then need to ask if this condition has anything to offer to us for the development of science and technology. This is a double bind that means that science is not dependent on the West as a place but as particular construct, rooted in Western modern epoch.

Through this analysis of Davari's view on science and technology, Lotfalian comes to the conclusion that his philosophical attempt is to overcome the "epochal understanding" of the West by increasing the possibility of a dialogue with the West. Yet, it seems that Davari's philosophical attempt is a complete disavowal of the modern principles that are considered the founding pillars of a pluralistic and democratic dialogical space. Maybe this line of reasoning can account for the basic change in the Iranian people's perceptions of the Pahlavi regime that caused them to follow the clerical opposition in 1979. The question to ask here is simply: How did dissatisfied Iranians accept the Islamic revolutionary ideology and organize to act collectively against the shah's regime? This could be followed by another question: How is it that a quarter of a century after the victory of the Iranian Revolution and the establishment of the clerical regime, the solution to Iran's economic, political, and social problems and growing discontent among the people is not yet another revolution?

Iran has never been more a country of paradoxes and contradictions than it is today. Many people in the West continue to see Iran as a truly radical Islamic country. But the truth is that Iran is a country in a painful transition to democracy, and maybe the only Muslim country where people are rapidly moving away from radical Islam. Iran is likely to be a very different country five to ten years from now. Islam will likely become less important as a governing principle and the society will become more pluralistic. If one has to look for a logic of continuity in Iranian history, one can always say with Majid Tehranian (chapter 12, "Power and Purity: Iranian Political Culture, Communication, and Identity") that "the cyclical patterns of Iranian history from excessive centralization to excessive fragmentation have resulted in conditions of perennial insecurity, mistrust, and adaptability. Every Iranian more or less bears the psychic imprint of the cyclical swings to political extremes producing a variety of defense mechanisms." For Tehranian these fluctuations have produced a set of dialectical response such as "power and purity, imperialism and conspiratorialism, mysticism and nihilism, heroism and opportunism, and messianism and fundamentalism," which form the pillars of Iranian political culture. Tehranian concludes that today in Iran

> the main challenge remains to be one of maintaining the creative tension between the moral vision of a free and just society from the practical politics of compromise in a pluralistic society. Centuries of dependency and decay in Iran have created psychohistorical pathologies that stand in the way of economic, political, and cultural modernization. As the nation achieves greater independence and self confidence, the wounds of impotence will be gradually healed while a political culture of tolerance and compromise emerges.

Many Iranians inside and outside the country share the optimism of Majid Tehranian concerning the political future of Iran. For many, the landslide election of Mohammad Khatami in 1997 set Iran on a winding and at times turbulent path toward democracy. Despite all the pressures coming from inside and outside and the onslaught of the religious Right, the reformers, screened by the regime itself, have been applying enormous pressure on the Islamic theocracy to modify its political behavior. Yet to those whose mental construct of a democracy is a society peopled by truly equal citizens, who have an equal voice in choosing their representatives and holding them accountable, the democratization process in Iran remains very shallow and governmental accountability remains weak. Yet, it seems as if the Islamic Republic has entered a gray zone without having any attributes of democratic life. We are dealing here with a revolutionary government attempting to reform itself in the face of increased popular appeals for participation and change and the pressure of the globalized world. As Nikki Keddie formulates correctly in the introduction of *Iran and the Surrounding World*: "Iran's resistance to the world race toward globalization and free trade has some positive aspects. Free trade in film, for example, could swamp Iran's film industry as it has those of many countries. On the other hand, no country today can be an island, and Iran's continuing economic crisis seems to guarantee continued efforts to improve relations with the outside world."[4] Iranian civil society survives today as a cultural space for the development of democratic values such as tolerance, pluralism, and a willingness to create channels other than political parties for the articulation, aggregation, and representation of different interests. For the past two decades, two social categories have played the most important role in the formation and empowering of civil society in Iran: women and intellectuals.

In the case of women, the chapters by Roksana Bahramitash, "Women's Employment in Iran: Modernization and Islamization," and Sussan Siavoshi, "'Islamist' Women Activists: Allies or Enemies?" are both very enlightening on the struggle of Iranian women against social exclusion and marginalization. Despite the ongoing process of Islamization of Iranian women's spheres of life since 1979, women's voices and actions have continued to be heard and seen in Iranian society. According to Roksana Bahramitash, "Iranian women have been able to push for improvements in spite of hardships. In fact, under the Islamist regime, a greater number of the female population was able to enter into the labor market." Also, "the extent and the persistence of women's political agitation constantly put pressure on the government to make changes to their initial policy of sending women back home."

As in the case of Bashramitash's chapter, Sussan Siavoshi's account of two Iranian Islamist women goes against the stereotypical images of Iranian women as "helpless victims who are objects of pity." Siavoshi concentrates more on the role of these women in the Iranian political arena rather than in the economic sphere. Challenging once again the dichotomy of modern versus traditional, she considers that "the attributes of many of the key players and leaders of the Revolution destroyed the neat boundaries between modern and traditional person, as depicted by modernization theorists, with relative ease. Among these players were many Islamist women such as Maryam Behrouzi, Zahra Rahnavard, Azam Taleghani, and Monireh Gorgi." What interests Siavoshi about the political roles played by both Rahnavard and Behrouzi is not their direct participation in the project of Iranian women's emancipation. "With their critique of liberalism and their conviction that religion should be mixed with politics," affirms Siavoshi, "these Islamists would be automatically placed, by modernization theorists, in the category of traditional and antiprogressive forces. Based on this judgment, there will be no reason for genuine supporters of women's right to contemplate any cooperative scheme with these women."

The point formulated here by Siavoshi could be extended to all levels of Iranian civil society. There is a disagreement among Iranian citizens as to whether any Islamist—man or woman—could or should be considered as part of a movement for the advancement of democracy in Iran. One way to answer this question is to be receptive to the multiplicity of different voices that exist today inside Iranian civil society. The appeal to the idea of pluralism is the only way for us to subordinate all powers to the respect of the freedom each individual and each group has to be a subject in Iranian society. This challenge is today that of the public intellectuals in Iran. Ahmad Sadri, in "The Varieties of Religious Reform: Public Intelligentsia in Iran," clearly shows us how this challenge has been taken by figures such as Abdi, Ganji, and Hajjarian. According to him, "it would be neither hyperbolic nor redundant to call them a 'public intelligentsia' since they straddle the fence between intellectual production and political agitation." For Sadri, the path to reform and democracy in Iran is clearly shown to us by these public intellectuals and those who use "decades-old rhetorical devices to confront the powerful discourse of the reform [show] their ideological bankruptcy."

Nader Hashemi seems to share Sadri's optimism on the force of the reform movement in Iran. His contribution, "The Relevance of John Locke to Social Change in the Muslim World: A Comparison with Iran," becomes more meaningful to the readers of this volume in the post–September 11 debate on Islam and democracy. In response to many in the West and especially scholars and politicians who accused Muslims of hating democracy and rejecting Western political values, Hashemi invites us to take a closer look at what appears to him as a similarity between present-day Iranian civil society and the society pictured by John Locke in seventeenth-century England. According to Hashemi

> In studying the political philosophy of John Locke at the end of the twentieth century, in light of the political and religious debates in the Muslim world, one is struck by the similarity of the two cases. This similarity is most pronounced in the Islamic Republic of Iran where, as a result of the 1997 presidential election, an open and vibrant political climate emerged that has significantly transformed the political culture. The proliferation of independent newspapers, journals, and magazines is the best measure of this change.

Against those who believe that the universal value of democracy as that of modernity belongs only to the West, Hashemi shows us that there are ways in Muslim countries, such as Iran, to reconcile the Islamic religion with democracy and that it is a matter of developing pluralism and tolerance on the ground.

There are fifty-five Islamic countries and none is democratic in the Western sense. For most of the Islamic believers of these countries, Islam answers questions about the individual and his responsibilities that no political philosophy can ever propose. They maintain that Islam is bigger than democracy. Yet it is a misconception to think that there is no such thing as a "democratizing" process in Islamic countries such as Iran. It is of course doubtful whether Iranians have truly internalized and accepted the democratic principle. But Iran has undergone a classic case of disillusionment by the innermost of its members as evident notably by the thoughts and actions of a new generation of Iranian intellectuals. The collapse of the intellectual models that dominated post–World War II understanding of politics and modernity in Iran gave a new currency to the ideas of democracy and democratization against ideology and ideologization of the tradition. The very notion of "ideology" has lost much of its coherence among the new generation of Iranian intellectuals, and it has accompanied the crisis of political legitimacy in Iran. This crisis was felt in Iran as a vacuum that was left by the ontological and political failure of creeds such as Marxist–Leninism and Islamic fundamentalism. This vacuum is filled today by the category of "civil society," which could serve as a conceptual and practical key to the democratic transition in Iran.

The concept of civil society is used today in the literature of the fourth generation of Iranian intellectuals not only as an institutional package but mainly as a particular mode of thinking and a special mode of political conduct. As a matter of fact, the category of civil society has a true significance for the new generation of Iranian intellectuals both as a critical tool and as a regulative principle for democratization in Iran. Taken at this level, the idea of civil society as it is discussed by the Iranian intellectuals today embodies the debate on Western modernity and raises questions about the significance of the historical experience of Western politics. The point here is not about the replicability of democratic practices and institutions, but about the possibility of identifying a common set of goals and purposes best described by the Iranian intellectuals by the idea of accountability and responsibility. The two concepts of "accountability" and "responsibility" can introduce a new complexity and sharpness to assessments of the difficulties facing the process of democratic transition in Iran, both in establishing preconditions and dealing with its consolidation. It is true that globalization could lead to the empowerment of civil society in many countries including Iran, and the new generation of Iranian intellectuals can influence the Iranian youth by helping them to understand how the world is changing. The process of democratization is not fully dependent upon the progress of globalization, but it does depend on the idea of "globality," which is linked to the idea of responsibility.

As we can see from their writings, the new generation of Iranian intellectuals do not identify their role as that of engaging in ideological politics, but of expressing critical views concerning the antidemocratic and authoritarian aspects of Iranian political and social traditions. The shock of the revolution and the reevaluation of political ideals have been part of a learning process that has generated a collective sense of responsibility among the younger generation of intellectuals in Iran and led them to opt for political pragmatism rather than ideological dogmatism. As a result, writings and publications of the fourth generation of Iranian intellectuals have become avenues of expression for those who think that the main task is not only to choose between systems of political ideologies but also to create an intellectual community with a well-developed understanding of such questions. The incessant attack on Iran's secular cultural producers is today ironically indicative of the fact that the new generation of intellectuals in Iran are validators of philosophical change and true democracy promoters. It is a fact that, among the Iranian intellectuals, a whole generation of democracy promoters base their arguments on the democratic transition in order to move to new intellectual frameworks, new debates, and eventually a new paradigm of political change. Today the new generation of Iranian intellectuals represent what can be considered the "Third Culture." The strength of the Third Culture is precisely that it is also a culture of horizontal accountability that is marked by the emergence of critical uncertainty, where solid traditions of authoritarianism give way to fragile traditions of authoritarianism. As a result of that, concerned with the political implications of uncertainty, the new generation of Iranian intellectuals have been critically defining the inner boundaries of democratization (the threshold between critical thinking and democratic transition) as well as its outer boundaries (the onset of democratic transition and its institutional formation through a permanent dialogical process between the tradition and the modern in Iran).

Today Iran is going through a cycle of erratic oscillations in which moments of democratic hope alternate with times of great despair. Yet this uncertainty is accompanied by the absence of a romantic view of the Iranian intellectual as an avant-garde guardian of an ideology and the demonizing traditionalist view of the intellectual as obstructer of national and religious traditions. Nearly a quarter of a century after the revolution, the distinctive contribution of the new generation of Iranian intellectuals to the Iranian democratic debate is not how to choose between morality and politics in a society where cynicism and confusion cover the voices of common sense and civility, but how to forge a politics of responsibility in the absence of which democracy would become a void concept. This is a form of philosophical reflection on practices of governance and practices of freedom in Iran. This philosophical wariness is not joined to any kind of dream of totally rearranging the Iranian society. The intervention here is not only a reflection upon the pluralistic mechanisms of politics in Iran, but also upon the Iranian political self. This issue of pluralism also raises the question of modernity and the West as the "other." In Iran, the process of democratization has always been related to the process of modernization. In other words, democratic theory and struggle for democracy among Iranian intellectuals has been part of the "modernization package." For more than a hundred years Iranian intellectuals and technocrats functioned as "carriers" of modern rationality and modern bureaucracy. Despite their engagement as individuals advocating freedom, tolerance, and transparency these men and women of the pen were not able to create an endurable democratic process in Iran. Yet, for the past decade there has been a rise of a democratic intellectual discourse in the Iranian civil society. There are three main reasons for such a rise. First, it has to do with the fact that for the first time in Iranian history the paradigm of "individualistic subject" is replacing that of "obedient subject" subservient to the autocratic monarch or the ruling theologian. Second, it is related to the philosophical crisis of the ideological traditionalist discourse in the Iranian society. And last but not least, it is directly influenced by the decline of revolutionary romanticism among the Iranian youth.

Today, the new generation of Iranian intellectuals is well aware of the fact that as an antidote to the "monolithic" and "one-view" formulas of the previous generations the political and intellectual urgency of Iran's encounter with the globalized modernity acquires a "dialogical exchange." This dialogue is an exposure of the "Iranian self" to the "otherness" of the modern West. It requires from the Iranian self a willingness to risk its political and cultural values and intellectual attitudes and to plunge headlong into a transformative process instead of being in a full position of imitation or rejection of modernity. In this cross-cultural, "exotopic" dialogue, modernity is no more reduced to the status of a simple instrumental object or rejected as a dangerous enemy of the Iranian identity. Today, a democratic notion of identity, emphasizing the formation of a pluralistic civil society in Iran, is more welcomed among the new generation of Iranian elites than romantic or traditionalist notions of Iranian identity. Perhaps for the first time since Iran's encounter with the West, modernity is being considered as a process that could provide us with lessons for the affirmation and development of our own identity without having fears of recognizing the heritage of modern times as ours. In helping to maintain this dialogical exchange with modernity from within the Iranian identity, Iranians could finally free themselves once and forever from the intellectual blackmail of "being for or against the West" or "having to choose between tradition and modernity." At a closer look, things become more complex; therefore, neither modernity nor tradition could be considered as simple recipes for a utopian life, but as "pictures of the future with dim spots" as Tocqueville describes it. If this book has one principal aim, it is to diminish the dim spots surrounding the history of the encounter of Iran with modernity and its political, social, and cultural consequences by overcoming the fallacious dichotomy of tradition/modernity and the related evolutionist view on unilinear progress of cultures. If there is one thing that modernity teaches us, it is that values are mutable, that is, subject to change. In this respect, dialogue between tradition and modernity is an urgent task in Iranian society in order to ensure that we will not continue to be tormented by monsters of our own creation.

Ramin Jahanbegloo
Washington, D.C.
August 26, 2002

Notes

1. Fereydoun Adamiyat, *The Idea of Freedom and the Making of the Constitutional Movement* (Tehran: Sukhan Publisher, 1961), p. 114, quoted by Ali Mirsepassi, *Intellectual Discourse and Politics of Modernization* (Cambridge: Cambridge University Press, 2000), p. 63.

2. Mehrzad Boroujerdi, *Iranian Intellectuals and the West* (Syracuse, N.Y.: Syracuse University Press, 1996), p. 111.

3. Masoud Razavi, *Afagh-e-Falsafeh* (Tehran: Farzan Publishers, 2000), p. 73.

4. Nikki R. Keddie and Rudi Matthee, eds., *Iran and the Surrounding World* (Seattle: University of Washington Press, 2002), p. 10.

I

THINKING MODERNITY

1

Iranian Society, Modernity, and Globalization

Jamshid Behnam

Translated by Alireza Rahbar Shamskar

THE HISTORY OF THE PAST 150 YEARS of Iran and the Middle East has been in-fused with the temptations of the West, modernity, and nationalism; this will continue to be the case for many years to come. Therefore, perhaps it is time to assess, even in a cursory manner, to what extent Iran has moved to-ward modernity over these years. Can Western modernity be the future goal, or should Iran seek a different path of modernity? If the latter, is it feasible?

The 150-Year Experience

In the mid-nineteenth century, Europe was enjoying a golden era. Signifi-cant achievements in the areas of science and technology, capitalism, and positivism were among the main reasons for this advancement. Nations all over the world were under colonialism, and a few major Western countries ruled the globe. Civilization was equated with Western civilization, and other nations had no option but to imitate that. Under such circumstances, and particularly during the war with Russia, Iran came face-to-face with that Western civilization. Iranians recognized the need for "awakening" and "reform" that, using the example of the Ottomans, were first initiated by Abbas Mirza and later followed by Grand Viziers Amir Kabir and Sepah-salar.

For a long time, Eastern societies, including Iran, lived with pride in their material and spiritual accomplishments. They believed they were among the greatest powers in terms of military might and civilization. But time gradually changed these beliefs. First they were forced to accept the West as an "equal" power, and then the West appeared as a dangerously competitive and dominant force.

During this period, there existed no structured philosophy to confront the expansion of the West. All Iranians wanted was a military power by which they could compensate for their past defeats. To create an efficient military, they needed to establish some military industries and a reformed bureaucracy. Hence began the period of sending students to Europe to study Western science and administration. The first group returned. But now we can say that they had not grasped the depth of the importance of Western civilization.

The consequences of the long history of encounters between Islamic, or Near Eastern, and Western civilizations became more pronounced in the nineteenth century. On the one hand, in the domain of religion, the results manifested themselves in movements like Mahdevism in North Africa and Babism and reformist Islamic thought in Iran, Egypt, Lebanon, and India. On the other hand, they also appeared in nonreligious, modernist reform movements that over time expanded and reached their peak by the formation of new constitutional and national governments. The political component of this latter movement aimed at autocratic or despotic rulers, and the sociocultural component aimed at social engineering and bringing about new ways of thinking and living.

In the final decades of the nineteenth century, the environment changed. Between the years 1880 and 1900 in Tehran, Istanbul, Cairo, Tiflis, and Calcutta a new generation of works, which had originated during the years of 1820–1840, were released. They were produced by authors, diplomats, and even enlightened merchants who through writing articles, manifestos, and books would propagate new ideas and advocate the fight against dictatorship and backwardness. Their attempt was to establish intellectual and ideological foundations necessary for change and reform and to compensate for past stagnation.

Two features characterized the members of this group of intellectuals. First, many of them lived in or frequently traveled outside the country. Second, the majority of them, based on their works, could be categorized both as constitutionalists and as modernist sociocultural reformers. For instance, even Seyyed Jamal-al-Din, who mainly focused on an Islamic renaissance, shared many of the ideas and goals of the modernists.

The next stage was spreading the ideas of the philosophers of this renaissance and attending the notion of development, the mythical foundation of modernity that denotes gradual transformation toward an ideal human society. Encouraged by the political dimension of modernity—ideas of freedom, equity, rule of law—Iranians turned to these ideas in order to challenge the social underdevelopment and despotic monarchy. The challenge in turn led to the Constitutional Revolution with the participation of the merchant bourgeoisie, intellectuals, and segments of the clergy. The roots of the Constitutional Revolution should be sought, externally, among overseas Iranian communities—including those in the Caucasus, Istanbul, Cairo, and Calcutta—and internally, in the Tobacco Movement.

Yet in this period, most Iranian intellectuals did not fully apprehend the complexity of the Western modernity and assumed that tradition and modernity could easily be fused. Many intellectuals and politicians of the time, though patriotic and seeking an independent Iran, did not oppose Western civilization. In contrast to the later intellectuals, they did not view the West only in terms of the colonialist policies of a few European countries. In the chaotic years during and immediately after World War I, many Iranian intellectuals, disillusioned with the unsuccessful Constitutional Revolution and its aftermath, gathered in Berlin and Paris and published periodicals like *Kaveh*, *Iranshahr*, *Farangestan*, and *Elm-o-Honar* and discussed modernity. Inside Iran, too, a small number of writers, in periodicals like *Daneshkadeh*, echoed a similar voice.

The ascendance of Reza [Pahlavi] Shah to power—ensued by the establishment of the national unity government, the centralized bureaucracy, and the pursuit of industrialization and of cultural Westernization—was accompanied by a neglect of the political components of modernity. This heralded the beginning of a development superimposed from above. Iran rejected the Turkish Kemalism, based on the acceptance of Western civilization and on the separation of politics and religion, and was content with a slower pace of change. However, like Turkey, Iran would emphasize nationalism and past glory while pursuing modernization.

In the years following World War II, intellectuals like those of *Sokhan* magazine would speak intelligently and informatively about the West. Yet the struggle for the nationalization of the Iranian petroleum industries brought about anti-Western sentiments and forestalled that logical path to the West. During the 1960s and 1970s, Iranian academia for the first time attempted through research and academic studies to educate themselves about the encounter between Iran and the West. It was in the 1960s, however, that under the impact of some social and political events the tide reversed and new ideas emerged in this area. Jalal Al-e Ahmad attacked "Westernization" or "Westoxication" and advocated a return to the encompassing Islam. Ali Shariati wrote about a "return to 'self.'"

Accordingly, forward-looking ideas dominating the era before and after the Constitutional Revolution gave way to inclinations toward tradition and antimodernity. Concerns about lost identity pushed some intellectuals toward a return to tradition and religion and even to nostalgia for the simple village life. As one author put it, everyone was searching for the "paternal home." Some intellectuals had socialist–nationalist tendencies. Some advocated the "Third World" and eventually became either Heideggerians or Islamists. All prescribed solutions ranging from a return to the past, to self, to an encompassing Islam, even to the village life and nature. However, from the 1960s onward, the era of "return" was combined with a kind of political culture and value system that opposed the West and modernization. In short, it was a cultural Romanticism, which brought to mind the memories of Germans escaping cities and returning to villages.

To confront Westernization, intellectuals resorted to reviving village-life traditions. All aspects of village and village life were idealized. In his works, Al-e Ahmad utilized the full force of the Romantic language to highlight the wrongs of industrialization and urbanization, the symbols of Western invasion. It became fashionable to write monographs about the villagers and villages that had not lost their roots and ways of life. In the words of one author, these monographs were a kind of "village discoveries." As a result of romanticizing and idealizing the past, and discovering or renewing traditional concepts and relations, religion gained strength.

Given the speedy process of development in the 1960s and 1970s, Iranian society reached significant social and economic achievements. However, because of the concentration of political power and curtailed political freedom, government's legitimacy, goals, and policies were questioned. Consequently, modernization, which enjoyed a particular priority in government goals and policies, became interchangeable with Westernization in the public eye. Islamic-Iranian and Western civilizations confronted one another, and being antigovernment was equated with being antimodernity. Islamic tendencies gained special position in social discourse, and some authors, tapping into society's antimodernization sentiments, paved the way for the advancement of a kind of Islamic sociology, where solutions for social anomalies would be grounded in Islamic teachings.

In these years, the Third World school of thought was popular, and works by Frantz Fanon, Aime Cesaire, and Albert Memmi were translated into Persian. Further, some intellectuals turned to Heidegger. But, because they did not grasp the depth of his thoughts, they became antimachine and antitechnology. In other words, "technophobia" resulted in resistance against the "evils" of machines and industrialization, when Iran was at the threshold of its economic modernization and the society yet was not hurt by modern technology.

Concurrent with the foregoing arguments about "return to" or "freedom from" "self" by Iranian intellectuals, a group of technocrat economists were busy planning and implementing five-year plans for the economic development of the country. In the years following World War II, the theory of "modernization" became very popular and provided a model for social, economic, and cultural development. At the time, most economists concurred on a few broad premises that this theory subscribed to. They included, firstly, a linear notion of history. The assumption was that all societies had to pass through the same stages that developed countries had. Secondly, in the process of passing through the stages, the characteristics of these societies would transform into something similar to those of the developed countries. That is, creativity, innovation, profiteering, self-interest, accepting democracy, and believing in the separation of religion and politics. And, thirdly, proper and correct usage of economic tools would inevitably direct undeveloped societies to their destination.

Modernization theory has a dual notion of the world, where traditional and modern societies are situated in opposing poles. The theory, nonetheless, does not provide any comprehensive, precise definitions of either tradition or modernity. It simply submits Western societies as modern, and Third World countries as traditional. According to the theory, there exist barriers in Third World countries that make development difficult to achieve. They include traditional, outdated institutions and systems of values; accelerating population growth; lack of public participation in running the society; and some particular beliefs. In short, modernization theory seeks "internal causes" in explaining underdevelopment.

In the same period, dependency theory was advanced in reaction and as an alternative to modernization theory. Dependency theory has a dual notion of the world, too. Industrialized and nonindustrialized countries comprise the "core" and the "periphery" of the world system, respectively. The core exploits the periphery, and as long as it maintains its dominance, periphery countries can hardly achieve independent development. In this theory, in contrast to modernization theory, internal characteristics, like traditional institutions or educational systems, are not obstacles to development. Rather, it is the exploitative relations between the core and the periphery that constitute the barrier. Hence, the theory searches for "external obstacles" in explaining the phenomenon of underdevelopment.

At the time, most developing countries modeled their development plans after modernization theory, though without pronouncing it explicitly. Economic growth, that is, quantitative growth in gross national product, became the goal. The hope was that such growth would ensure qualitative social changes. Yet they did not occur, and economic growth widened the income gulf in these societies.

Iran, too, more or less followed the path laid by modernization theory. The Islamic Revolution in 1978–1979, however, disrupted the trend. The first postrevolution decade was spent on returning to the Islamic past, rejecting the West, and confronting whatever had any indication of modernity. First, "monotheistic economy" and "the Islamic path to development" were put forward. Nationalization of banks, insurance companies, and big industries followed. Then, opposition to foreign investments along with "self sufficiency" emerged as the mottos of the revolutionaries. Yet in the 1980s, the tide reversed once again. Government pursued privatization of industry and expansion of trade and encouraged foreign investments. Religion, which had turned into an ideology in the early years of the revolution, gradually returned to its fundamentalist form and became an instrument for governing. By then, however, significant segments of the Iranian population had turned to the political values of modernity, including respect for democracy, civil society, and women's rights. Iranians welcomed a kind of reconciliation and coexistence with Western civilization.

As previously stated, from the nineteenth century onward, Iranian intellectuals responded variably to the issue of facing the West. Based on their ideological and philosophical stances, their responses ranged from idealizing to demonizing the West. The stages of "captivation," "emulation," "criticism," and even "rejection" emerged one after another and at times concurrently. The contradictory feelings of "fascination" and "hatred" toward the West made it difficult to find a proper position to deal with it. Whereas Malkum Khan advocated unequivocal acceptance of Western civilization and culture, Seyyed Hassan Taghizadeh wanted the same, with the condition that the Persian language be preserved. Ali Akbar Dehkhoda spoke of acquiring selective components of modernity. Mohammad Ali Jamalzadeh preferred a kind of "engagement" with Western civilization, and Mohammad Ali Furughi preferred the "contemporary civilization."

In the years between 1915 and 1930, too, there were intellectuals who advocated change, not a mere imitation of the West. Some of them believed that Iran must be "revitalized" [modernized], and some spoke of a kind of Iranian philosophy that would be the basis for the conditional adoption of modern civilization. In this period, Rashid Yassemi wrote, "modernizing means cutting and removing the old parts and replacing them with new ones."

In the first period, modernity is aimed more at confronting dictatorship and at struggling against economic dependence and scientific lapse, while in the second period (the era of Reza Shah) this limited modernization takes larger dimensions and becomes more authoritarian. Iran slowly enters its capitalist stage, and the Iranian economy turns into a government-directed economy. The third period is the era of planned economy, characterized by government's hasty policies, boosted by the surge in oil revenues, and a social current that does not accept the changes and fights against this modernization.

Modernity Criticized

In the second half of the twentieth century, a new debate regarding modernity began, and Western intellectuals themselves started to criticize it. In Iran, however, the debate over the West and Westernization continues. Injudicious, unfounded appraisals of the implications of modernity increasingly add to the existing uncertainties in this debate. Concepts like "modern," "modernity," "modernization," and "modernism" are muddled and, at times, treated as synonymous.

During the nineteenth and the first half of the twentieth century, colonizing countries transferred parts and pieces of Western modernity to their colonies. That transfer was deficient. After independence, the new leaders of colonized countries decided to import modernity via economic and political developments. This was called modernization. Yet these developments failed to bring about modernity as a particular culture to the newly independent nations. Consequently, they faced cultural dualism, and pro- and anti-Westernization forces quarreled. At the same time, some thinkers in Japan and the Middle East, who examined the encounter of Western and national cultures in a more logical way, determined modernization to be the most suitable blend of national culture with modernity. The latter was no longer regarded as merely Western, rather as the outcome of the aggregated knowledge and scientific advances of all cultures.

From the nineteenth century onward, Iranian and Turk authors and intellectuals used the term "modernization" (*tajaddod*) to mean "renewal." That is different from the meaning of the term in the West, where modernity is a sociological concept and a philosophical idea conceived in a different cultural context. Iranian intellectuals' desire for *tajaddod* was derived from Iran's lagging behind and Western civilization's advancement, and *tajaddod* was intended to create the best incorporation of national culture with modern values and beliefs. In other words, one should define modernization in Iran as the desire for change and innovation, shaped by temporal conditions and national identity.

The Issue of Modernity in Contemporary Iran

From the foregoing discussion, perhaps one can conclude that postmodernism, second modernity, the question of cultural disparities, new theories of economic development, fresh discourses regarding history, and the future of civilizations have all expanded the ground for discussions about modernity in a world that is exceedingly moving toward homogeneity. Yet in Iran, in spite of all the political and economic developments in the world, and in spite of the Islamic Revolution, squabbles over the acceptance or rejection of Western civilization continue with the same reasons as in the past. One difference, nevertheless, is that the establishment of the Islamic Republic and its policies have contributed to the emergence of two relatively new phenomena.

First, contrary to prerevolution governments, which were modernist, postrevolution governments have aimed at rejecting modernity in its conventional meaning in general and at preventing "Western cultural invasion" in particular, though the nature of the invasion and the identity of invaders are yet to be clearly described. Secondly, the notion of democracy—including establishment of civil society, gaining rights of citizenship, and separation of religion and state—is among topics that have engaged large segments of the Iranian people in recent years. The ensuing paradox between these two new phenomena has caused persistent confrontation among different intellectual and political tendencies, which can be identified as follows:

1. The conservatives, who are against Western modernity. They view it as anti-Islamic, and the West as *dar al-harb* (the land of conflict) and the land of infidels. In their encounter with the modern world, they resort to the Islamic past, and in this return recognize the Holy Scripture, the Quran, without the medium of any new interpretation, as their sole foundation of faith. Their intended homecoming is the early years of Islam and the tradition of the revered ancestors. In all, their outlook is fundamentalist and anti-Western, though it appears that some in this group now doubt their ideas and goals.

2. Religious modernists, who wish to reconcile Islam and modernity. Surely, this is not a new story; it goes back to the time of the Constitutional Revolution. In the years preceding the Islamic Revolution, religious modernists attempted to mend the break between Islam and modern science. Yet in the second decade after the revolution, many of them began to criticize the regime and its attempts to utilize religion as a political ideology. They also spoke about the relations between state and religion, society's right to self-governance and democracy, and the issue of "rights and duties" of the citizen. Their goal is clearly set on a new path that, as they claim, is paved by means of a reexamination of religion and a dialogue of civilizations.

3. The consequences of the Islamic Revolution in Iran prompted a number of Muslim intellectuals to reexamine their past understanding and positions. These reformers are not antagonistic toward the West and accept some underpinnings of Western civilization, such as freedom, democracy, women's rights, and civil society. They reject isolationism and at times regard themselves as postmodernist, though their readings of postmodernism can be rather ambivalent. For instance, there are those who propagate "Islamic feminism." Taking advantage of cultural relativism, acknowledged by postmodernism, Islamic feminists argue that there are differences between Western and Eastern women and conclude that the achievements of Western feminism would not be useful in Iran. There are similar arguments regarding human rights in Iran, too.

4. Modernists and secular intellectuals attempt to join the modern world and learn new ideas and introduce them to others. In the past two decades, a number of authors, particularly young philosophers, have been working to gain a proper understanding of the philosophy of modernity by referring to the original works of Western scholars and by igniting new debates over modernity in Iran.

If one puts ordinary events aside and takes a wider perspective of the situation of modernity in Iran, one can conclude that over the past eighty to one hundred years, there existed two main movements in Iran. First is a surface movement, which manifested as the consequence of modernization. This movement has more or less been affected by domestic and international events such as war, revolution, and changes in government policies. This movement has resulted in new economic and social structures and institutions. Reza Shah's plans for progress for the country, the five-year economic plans during his son's reign, and postrevolution efforts—necessitated by revolutionaries' desire to govern—have resulted in a somewhat steady trend toward establishing different aspects of modernization in Iran.

A second movement toward modernity is one that has been occurring slowly but surely at the depth of the Iranian society, and surfacing occasionally. This trend can be described as a one-directional, measured progress toward modernity, with no indication of reversing. French historian Fernand Braudel divides historical time into a few layers: first, a short time of events and political developments (a few decades); second, a mid time of cycles of economic changes and political revolutions (over a half-century); third, a long time of sluggish changes in civilizations and in collective mind-sets; and, finally, the nearly static time of geography, which represents the time frame of human relation with nature. Perhaps one could state that modernization occurs in the short time, while modernity materializes in the long time. Based on such a categorization, one can assume that Iran's in-depth passage toward modernity began at the time of the Iranian–Russian wars, and still continues.

The Future of Modernity in Iran

When exploring the future of modernity in Iran, one should remember that not only are new realities confronting Iran, but also ideas and theories of modernity have evolved. With regard to the former, it should be noted that as a result of Iranians' experience with the revolution and its aftereffects, people have been attracted to the political components of modernity. Further, advances in the means of communications and dissemination of information have brought Iranians into direct contact with Western and other societies in the world. More importantly, more than one million Iranians live outside the country and have come to experience and learn about non-Iranian civilizations and cultures, especially Western. Through contacts with their relatives and friends and via travel, the expatriate Iranians increasingly familiarize those inside the country with the foundations and manifestations of Western modernity.

Many thinkers of our present time argue that modernity should be assessed based on its capacity to respond to the evolving needs of societies, and on its ability to administer complicated systems. Alain Touraine contends that contemporary modernity should be divorced from its European origin and be viewed only as a flexible model that adapts to diverse temporal and spatial conditions.

Accordingly, the era of a bipolar view of the world is over. For the past few decades, arguments were constructed upon the duality of East and West, old and new, us and them, and tradition and modernity. Consequently, solutions, too, were based on either Westernization or anti-Westernization. Few would consider the possibility of living with two cultures and utilizing the strength of each. Nowadays, dimensions of the debate have broadened. For example, there exist new definitions of tradition, including one that defines it as the simple recurrence of some behavior over time. The concept of "cultural authenticity," however, goes further and to the origin of cultures. That which is authentic should be kept, while traditions could be abandoned. Moreover, through adapting themselves to the necessities of time, cultures regenerate themselves and acquire their places in the collective, global heritage of humanity.

In fact, many social scientists have concluded that even tradition cannot impede modernity. Contrary to some views, the relation between tradition and modernity is not mutually exclusive. There are subtle overlaps between the two. Therefore, to position them in opposing camps is not proper. Even in a modern society, tradition has its own designated place. In other words, modernity does not mean that people have to forget their collective memories and abandon their ethical and religious beliefs. Indeed, if an externally prompted modernization is not assorted with these memories and beliefs, it will be unable to take roots and will falter.

The other side of the coin is that neither anti-Westernization, which disregards realities of the world, nor isolationism is the solution. One no longer can accept that some societies are static, drifting, and replicating their histories. Such assumptions also indicate an ignorance of the history of development of societies. Every society has its own dynamism, yet no society in today's world can pursue self-sufficiency and still expect development. Development and modernity are grounded in modern science and technology that today are found in the West—as at times in the past were located in China, India, or in Iran and other Islamic societies. In other words, the West is the current custodian of these heritages of humanity.

Iranians' attempts to acquire material expressions of Western civilization and achieve economic growth have not been entirely unsuccessful. But these changes are not yet pinned to a strong intellectual and philosophical foundation. The solution lies in remaining in touch with the world and in gaining a genuine appreciation of cultures. Unfortunately, in the past few decades, the discourse in Iran has stalled at the level of whether or not to be Westernized. The real question, however, concerns modernity and modernization. Accordingly, it is pivotal that Iranian intellectuals, especially social scientists, view questions regarding the modernization of the country in light of today's realities and of new theories. In this effort, they should discard the century-old quarrel with the West; act without bias; pay attention to what others have contributed to this debate; and, more specifically, consult cultural studies produced by Middle Eastern and Indian intellectuals.

Today, the issue of encountering Europe, the United States, or the West should be discussed differently. We have entered a new world with the globalization of economy and culture. We are now facing the whole globe, rather than any particular state or even Europe. We have no option but to update ourselves and enter the present world. This does not necessarily mean the loss of Iranian identity, collective memory, and way of life.

There are countries that have traversed the path to development and modernity with success. To that end, we need to know the West, on the one hand, and to learn about the experiences of countries like Japan and Korea, on the other. The Arabs and the Turks, among other peoples, are searching for solutions to the issue of encountering civilizations through new interpretations of their cultures and histories. A comparative study of works by Arab, Turkish, and Japanese authors with those of Iranians will be valuable. While others are reexamining their cultures and seeking resolutions, most Iranian intellectuals find it sufficient to remain nostalgic, and simply criticize and reject the West.

To be or not to be Westernized is not the question. At issue is modernization and modernity. Therefore, the parameters of the debate should be expanded. To portray modernity as an illness and call it Westernization will not resolve any problems of Iran. The goal is not to become Westernized. The aim is to become competent to live in the contemporary world, and live with contemporary peoples, while maintaining cultural identity.

2

Keywords in Islamic Critiques of Technoscience: Iranian Postrevolutionary Interpretations

Mazyar Lotfalian

IN RECENT TIMES, A CALL FOR THE ISLAMIZATION of knowledge and science has been echoed both globally and locally. Although the contemporary Islamization of knowledge has focused more on changing Western-based social sciences, on the one hand, and teaching revealed knowledges such as the Shari'a,[1] on the other, there is also a relevance of the Islamization of knowledge to natural sciences and technology. The relevance of Islam(ization) to science and technology stems from at least two directions. First, the hermeneutics of Islam, which I explain below, encounters the discourse of modernity for the possibility of an alternative foundation in the condition of late modernity/ postmodernity. Second, there is historical and metaphysical relevance of medieval Islamic sciences as precursors to modern European natural sciences.

Some scholars (Salvatore 1997; Schulze 1987) have argued that around the 1870s and 1880s the modalities in which Muslim local discourses configured themselves began to be restricted by colonial onslaught and the Orientalist essentialism of Islam. This change in modes of dialogical understanding of self in relation to the other constricted Muslims facing the West in particular ways. Could Muslims have formed "indigenous" discourses?

In this chapter, I argue that a set of identifiable keywords points to the presence of "indigenous" understanding of science and technology in the Muslim world. Notions such as *sahwa* (awakening) and *asala* (authenticity) have played deconstructive roles in the Muslim encounter with modernity. I will discuss the genealogy of these keywords and the effect of them on understanding how science and technology should be reinvented. I will then focus on the Iranian experience.

Framing the Hermeneutics of Islam

I use the notion of hermeneutics of Islam to explain Islam not in its transhistorical form but in terms of both the evolution of Islamic intellectual discursive formations and of the landscape in which these discourses emerge and
interact with one another. I am interested in the ways that works by Muslim
writers, as diverse as Egyptian authors such as Sayyid Qutb and Al-Qardawi
and Iranian authors such as Al-e Ahmad and Seyyed Hossein Nasr have become generative for Muslims at large. It is not only important that the notion
of "systems" in the work of Qutb, "authenticity" in Al-e Ahmad, "metaphysics"
in Nasr, and "awakening" in Al-Qardawi became tropes of hermeneutics of
Islam for other texts, but also the fact that each author, by virtue of being located in a different time and space, conveyed different Muslim experiences.
Furthermore, the shift that occurred between 1870 and 1880 has continued to
go through different mutations. These tropes and keywords now travel
through media technology and can be abstracted from the contexts in which
they arise; it is this decontextualization that comprises, in part, the condition
of the hermeneutics of Islam.

In the history and social studies of science, writers such as Kuhn (1979) and
Fox Keller (1992) have argued that the language of science and scientific discourse and practice is not separate from the language and discourse that are
practiced in society and its institutions. In addition, studies that critiqued development emerged in the early 1990s, marking the end of modernization
theories that disregarded the context, life world, and cultures they were aim-
ing at. Current scholarly works on development (Escobar 1995; Sachs 1988;
Gupta 1998), too, have paid attention to the construction of modernization
theories as an integral part of other social and cultural constructions. Whether
their subject be theoretical discourses, in the case of Escobar or Sachs, or the
interplay between these discourses and local appropriations, in the case of
Gupta, these writers are all sensitive to the shifts of language and turns in
worldview or perspective that rule both science and culture.

The notion of keywords as a heuristic that points to the interrelatedness of
meanings of words and the shifts in their meanings as it relates to social patterns through different historical moments is indebted to Raymond Williams
(1976). Additionally, writers such as Fox Keller and Lloyd (1992) have used the
notion of keywords to show how there has been a shift in meanings in scientific practice and what that shift means. In this chapter, I use the notion of
keywords to show how the language of Muslim encounters with modernity
have produced key meanings in the context of a transcultural dialogue with
the West, that in turn have affected the development of science and technology. I also follow this notion in a different genealogical direction than

Williams took. I use "keywords" to refer to an aftereffect of the hermeneutics of Islam that takes form in various intellectual circles and takes place in many localities. In this chapter, I discuss how some key understandings have emerged as Muslims have been trying to interpret Islamic traditions in the encounter with the discourse of modernity. I will show the genealogy of important keywords whose meanings have had a bearing upon the development and understanding of science during the last century: that is, to explore how the meaning and understanding of technoscience have changed through the formation of the secular state and the resurgence of Islam. In this transcultural space where Muslims' encounter with modernity becomes a communicative and dialogical act, there are several moments worthy of description. I will start with interpreting how the split between tradition and modernity is formed and how this discursive formation affects the hermeneutics of Islam.

An Aporetic Moment between Tradition and Knowledge

One of the earlier meanings of technoscience in the modern Islamic world emerged during an Islamic movement at the turn of the nineteenth century. In the late 1800s, the Islamic reform movement Salafia, facing the onslaught of Western scientific and institutional discursive practices, sought to prevent the perceived marginalization of Muslim tradition. Seyyed Jamal ad-Din Assadabadi, or Al-Afghani, (1839–1897) argued that science in the West was the continuation of medieval Islamic science and therefore Muslims could adopt it while remaining Muslims and following their own traditions. In this interpretation, science and the effect of European planning were understood as inherently and potentially Islamic. Science and planning, such as that explored by Timothy Mitchell (1988) in his account of the effects of European colonial power on the urban structures and life in Cairo, were understood not in the context of the modern epoch as a set of interrelated epistemes, but rather as a disjointed body of objects that might even bear Islamic roots. This moment was marked by intellectual debates on the relevance of Western science (such as Darwinian evolution or Galileo's astronomy) to Islam and the creation of new imaginaries through the work of cultural translation (e.g., theater and cinema, or the formation of the "new curious individual" as a knowledge seeker).

Those arguments that were antitradition were primarily against the religious authority over the production of knowledge. Among the elements of this discursive formation were two broad categories. One category was the emergence of forms of critique through the translations of Western theater and cinema, which involved techniques of reflexivity through engagement in the public sphere, a kind of self-mirroring of public culture. The second category involved the actual taking on of new techniques and tools through the adoption of language (especially the written form, ecriture) and scientific techniques, theories, and processes as modes of modernizing processes toward the creation of a "new curious individual," including new scientific subjectivities.

Examples of a kind of work that concerns the creation of new knowledge through cultural translation can be found in the Iranian activist and writer Abdul Rahim Talibuf's work. *The Book of Ahmad* (1893, 1894) concerns itself with a new way of knowing. This book is written in a conversational mode unlike the language of the learned literati. The parallel between *Ahmad* and Rousseau's *Emile* is evident, suggesting a kind of a cultural translation. Talibuf's book sets the scene by arguing for the importance of developing the natural curiosity of children by letting them explore nature and experience it for themselves. His argument was directed at traditional Islamic schooling, calling for a kind of education that was not under religious auspices. For a time it was taught in Dar al Fonun, in Tehran, one of the first technical schools in Asia.

In this earlier moment, the effort of cultural translation was to reconcile ties between modernity and tradition. This effort was to introduce instrumental rationality, in forms of cinema, theater, and disciplines of self, through the act of translation into the Islamic cultural context. As we shall see in this chapter, science and technology as forms of instrumental rationality differ from these earlier forms of rationality.

The latter might be explained in terms of the appropriation of modernity, but the former, I argue, must be situated in the larger context of institutional, corporate, societal, and cultural shifts.

Constricting Tradition for Modernization

In the period between the 1920s and 1970s, there was a significant hermeneutics of Islam being advanced that bears upon the shift from a utilitarian to instrumental appropriation of knowledge. Two meanings of *tasawwur* (imagination, or imaginative appropriation) and *nezam* (system) emerged in this moment. These (key)words emerged to explain *islah* (reform) in the context of the state's utilitarian project. These were attempts by Muslim thinkers to recast the connection between faith and knowledge differently from that which the secular state conceived as utilitarian.

For instance, Seyyed Qutb (1906–1966), a prominent Islamic thinker in Egypt, and Mehdi Bazargan[2] (1907–1994), an Iranian Muslim who was associated with the reform of Islam, tried to overcome the problems posed by a utilitarian approach to knowledge. Both Qutb and Bazargan focused on *din* (the meaning of which differs from the Western concept of religion) as a source of knowledge. Qutb and Bazargan centered *din* on the individual being as he or she goes through changes; thus the meaning of Islam depends on this movement. For Qutb, knowledge depends on *tasawwur* (Salvatore 1997), which is in turn rooted in both the Muslims' sacred text and the individual's social reality.

Although both authors put an emphasis on *nezam* or system, Bazargan's effort is more compelling since he was himself an engineer. Bazargan's usage of scientific language, such as the theory of thermodynamics, where he tries to reconcile tradition with modernity by creating continuity between the two, was precisely to put Islam in movement as a source of knowledge in the system of social reality. For example, in instances of his involvement with major civil engineering projects of the time—reorganizing the oil industry and the Tehran water project—he tried to recast the utilitarian approach by inserting faith.

The hermeneutics of Islam contributed to the critique of knowledge as the meanings of *tasawwur* and *nezam* played a deconstructive role. The constriction between modernity and tradition was challenged by *islah*, or reform. Now knowledge had something to do with *din*. This is similar to what the early reformers, such as Al-Afghani, held, because they reflected on faith and religion as sources of knowledge, though they tried to overcome the seeming opposition (or antinomies) that existed between them. The effort of overcoming the antinomies of modernity and tradition through faith, in the decades to come, would be amended by the existential critiques of the new generation.

Authenticity and Technoscience

By the 1970s technoscience was appropriated and expropriated as instrumental: abstract notions such as "progress" and "lifestyle" were contained in the models driving the development plans of modernization efforts, where programs based on these abstract notions were transplanted and superimposed onto other cultures. Moreover, by the 1970s, in the context of the resurgence of Islam, discourses of authenticity were critical of the idea that the appropriation of technoscience was value-free, seeing it as resulting in the alienation of culture. However these discourses did not provide a guideline for an alternative.

Sahwa and its root *asala* emerge in the context of the global resurgence of Islam. These meanings tend to ground the early meaning of Islam-in-movement in a hermeneutics that calls for a knowledge-to-come. It is highly debatable whether the hermeneutics of authenticity in Islam has any roots in Orientalist discourses. But what is important for the purpose of this chapter is at least to connect these keywords to debates that have been taking place concerning the question of science and technology, and the role of authenticity.

The main theme that authenticity addresses, as far as technoscience is concerned, is alienation. The denaturalization of language and culture is the object of the discourse of authenticity. As in the work of Martin Heidegger (1977), *techne* is understood by authenticity as both revealing and an obstacle. Modern technology for Heidegger is a mode of truth that passes from covered to uncovered. *Techne* for him is a denaturalization of language through *arraisonnment* of nature and being through calculation.

The discourse of authenticity has been influential among Iranian thinkers. "Westoxification" (Gharbzadegi), for instance, which became one of the main tropes of the Iranian revolution, is a search for authenticity. Authenticity or *asala* (or *asalat* in Persian) in Islam is about the uniqueness of being, bound by time and space. Iranian interpretations of Gharbzadegi, which is attributed to the Iranian author Al-e Ahmad, merged with understandings that are associated with the resurgence of Islam concerning the West. This is what I have previously called an epochal understanding of the West (Lotfalian 1999) that marks the recent resurgence of Islam. This epochal understanding of the West sees technoscience as metaphysical, a set of interrelated epistemes that are connected to religion, culture, and language. In the Iranian context, early traces of the epochal understanding of the West can be seen in the earlier work of Shayegan (1979) and Seyyed Hossein Nasr (1968).

The intellectual merging of authenticity and this epochal understanding has had two direct effects on understanding technoscience: first, science and technology can no longer be seen as tools without any culturally embedded values. Second, development and progress can no longer be separated from the eschatological structure of change in its religious and cultural sense. The Islamic argument against value-free science is not an argument against positivism in science. Twentieth-century Western debates on positivism were different in that there was a particular view of science at stake. The hermeneutics of Islam on authenticity aims at the secularization process and its affect on knowledge production. It may resonate with what is called "the science wars" in the West, but I argue that conflating the two is not productive. In what follows, I will offer the example of the Iranian revolution as an illustration of this complexity.

Postrevolution Discourse

There are several authors who have been both writing about science and technology in Iran and have been active decision makers in the development of science and technology. Among them there are the physicists Reza Mansouri (1999) and Mehdi Golsahni (1998), and the philosophers Reza Davari Ardakani (1998) and Abdolkarim Soroosh (2000); the latter two have both been at different points members of the High Commission of Cultural Revolution. In the context of this chapter, I will be considering the discourse of Davari Ardakani, since he is the only member of this group who discusses the question of authenticity and science and technology.

The emergent discourse of authenticity was an important turn in the appropriation of technoscientific identity prior to the Iranian Revolution and affected the intellectual understanding of science and technology. However, during the Cultural Revolution in Iran, there was a turning point in the understanding of what constituted authenticity. A new understanding had emerged. Davari Ardakani (1995) explained this differentiation in meaning by reflecting on how Gharbzadegi assumes an immunity from cultural invasion, especially technological invasion: "In the case of cultural invasion, you might have heard about reference to immunity. This is not bad. They say that one should establish immunity. We cannot stave off everything. If we prevent the spread of one thing, another will appear. Technology is such that we cannot prevent its spread."

Davari Ardakani (1995) characterizes Al-e Ahmad's Westoxification as a call for immunity. He continues, "if infatuation with the West is analogized to microbes and an infectious disease, immunity is a good idea. But have we diagnosed this disease?" He asserts that in order to get rid of the disease we should be able to vaccinate, but we cannot do that if we don't understand what the disease is about. He suggests that this disease is rather a phenomenon that can only be rejected by stopping the dependence on it, a way of overcoming rather than moving away from it. He criticizes Al-e Ahmad's Westoxification as a rejection without understanding the element of its critique.

The Cultural Revolution directly effected Iranian institutions. Although technical institutions were less affected, the attempts by the Cultural Revolution to narrow or close the gap between *hoze* (seminary) and *daneshgah* (university) did tacitly impact their functioning. This narrowing of the gap was supposed to happen through an Islamization process, a process in which Islamic thought, or *tafakor-e islami*, would replace the discursive practice of Western science. It has nearly been the undoing of the secularization of the institutions. In Iran the discourse of authenticity has treated the development of science and technology as only an intellectual problem. It has tended to generate a critique from outside the field of science, regardless of how science is practiced.

The discourses of authenticity and epochal understanding have shifted from rejection as immunization to the realization that Western technoscience must be overcome. This overcoming implies that there are other competing discourses and their condition of possibility must be understood rather than wished away.

Conclusion

The debates on knowledge and society around the late nineteenth and early twentieth centuries could be conceived as an attempt to link science and technology or any knowledge system to modernity, as social constructive projects—human mastery over nature, human autonomy, or technological control and efficiency. It has been the aim of this chapter to ask whether such a linkage to modernity is adequate to provide a critique of such discourses of knowledge.

A genealogy of keywords in the hermeneutics of Islam shows how these keywords have emerged as a result of transcultural debates between Muslim intellectual discourses and the discourses of modernity throughout the last century. It is appropriate to ask whether there is a new context in which knowledge systems are developed, and whether there is a need for a new frame in which cultural critique should be anchored.

Davari's (1998a) argument is compelling in that he points to a complex set of questions that have emerged in Iran since the beginning of the Iranian revolution. His questions concern the nature of science and technology: Is there a new condition for science in the West? Does science have a solid foundation, or are its foundations constructed and dependent on particular conditions of possibility? Davari argues that if the foundation of science is not on solid ground, as the postmodernists have argued, we then need to ask if this condition has anything to offer to us for the development of science and technology. This is a double bind that means that science is not dependent on the West as a place but as particular construct, rooted in the Western modern epoch. In this context the predicament of a non-Western culture is that it needs to come up with a new science that overcomes this science, while it needs this very science.

In postrevolution Iran, the epochal understanding of the West continues to be a dominant discourse. However, the new argument that Davari advances is an attempt to rework the epochal understanding in dialogical relationship to the West. Davari argues (1998b) that the critique of the West as having reached a dead end as a technological society should not be conceived as a sign of the impossibility of new thoughts. Rather, he argues that there will be an increase in the possibility of new thoughts to overcome this impasse. He attributes the former understanding to Alameh Tabatabai, who influenced the prerevolution generation of Islamic thinkers. The latter, though, should be the new attitude toward the West, which encourages us to learn about the West in order to overcome it.

What keywords show is the change in the texture of the landscape where Muslims try to articulate new understandings. The texture of this landscape has changed since the last turn of the century, where earlier reformers did not articulate any existential concerns. *Islah* only meant appropriation of knowledge without a loss of Islamic identity. In contrast, during the 1970s, *sahwa* and *asala* began to mark the landscape differently; life and the knowledge that defines it had to become Islamic. These keywords have been mobilizing forces in the development of science and technology, but what remains an ongoing problem for Muslims is to find a frame in which competing discourses can be accounted for socially and culturally.

Notes

A related version of this chapter was published in 2001. Reprinted by permission of Sage Publications Ltd. from Mazyar Lotfalian, "Knowledge Systems and Islamic Discourses," *Cultural Dynamics* 13, 2: 213–43, copyright © Sage Publications Ltd., 2001.

1. In this chapter, I use Arabic transliterations for the Islamic keywords unless it is indicated otherwise in the text.

2. The example at hand can be shown in the life history of Mehdi Bazargan. Bazargan was a member of intellectual circles, in Iran, from the very beginning. His association with the group, with a range of Islamic thinkers such as Allameh Tabatabai and Ayatollah Taleghani, is evident in the discussion over the predicament of Shi'ism after the death of Ayatollah Borujerdi in 1962 and the eventual rise of the shah's "White Revolution." In this group Bazargan and Taleghani were interested in praxis, wanting to appropriate Western technology without importing its "ideology." What interests me here is what marks Bazargan's effort with respect to the rest of the group. His appropriation of technoscience indicates an effect on his discourse both similar and different from the reformers of the turn of the century.

References

Al-Faruqi, Isma'il Raji. 1986. *Toward Islamic English*. Ann Arbor, Mich.: New Era Publications.

Al-Qaradawi, Yusuf. 1982. *Islamic Awakening between Rejection and Extremism*. Herndon, Va.: International Institute of Islamic Thought.

Davari Ardakani, Reza. 1995. *Religious Call and Cultural Inroad*. Mashreq, *Artistic & Cultural Monthly* Vols. 2–3 (February and March): 13–18, translated by www.netiran.com.

———. 1998a. *On Science* (Dar-bareh ilm). Tehran: Hermes Press.

———. 1998b. *On the West* (Dar-bareh ghrab). Tehran: Hermes Press.

Escobar, Arturo. 1995. *Encountering Development: The Making and Unmaking of the Third World*. Princeton, N.J.: Princeton University Press.

Fox Keller, Evelyn, and Elisabeth A. Lloyd, eds. 1992. *Keywords in Evolutionary Biology*. Cambridge, Mass: Harvard University Press.

Golshani, Mehdi. 1998. *From Secular Science to Religious Science* (Az elm e secular ta elm e dini). Tehran: Institute for Humanities and Cultural Studies.

Gupta, Akhil. 1998. *Postcolonial Developments: Agriculture in the Making of Modern India*. Durham, N.C.: Duke University Press.

Heidegger, Martin. 1977. *The Question Concerning Technology and Other Essays*. New York: Harper Torchbooks.

Kuhn, Thomas S. 1979. "Metaphor in Science." In *Metaphor and Thought*, ed. Andrew Ortony. Cambridge: Cambridge University Press.

Lotfalian, Mazyar. 1999. "Understanding Muslim Technoscientific Identities through a Metalinguistic Landscape." *International Institute for the Study of Islam in the Modern World (ISIM) Newsletter number 4*: isim.leidenuniv.nl/newsletter/4/index.html.

Mansouri, Reza. 1999. *Iran 1427: National Determination for Scientific and Cultural Development* (Iran 1427: azm e melli baraye tose'e elmi va farhangi). Tehran: Motalea't e Farhangi.

Mitchell, Timothy. 1988. *Colonising Egypt*. Cambridge: Cambridge University Press.

Nasr, Seyyed Hossein. 1968. *Science and Civilization in Islam*. Cambridge, Mass.: Harvard University Press.

Sachs, Wolfgang. 1988. *The Gospel of Global Efficiency: On Worldwatch and Other Reports on the State of the World*. IFDA Dossier, no. 68 (November/December): 33–39.

Salvatore, Armando. 1997. *Islam and the Political Discourse of Modernity*. Reading, U.K.: Ithaca Press.

Schulze, Reinhard. 1987. "Mass Culture and Islamic Cultural Production in the Nineteenth-Century Middle East." In *Mass Culture, Popular Culture, and Social Life in the Middle East*, ed. Georg Stauth and Sami Zubaida. Frankfurt: Campus.

Shayegan, Daryush. 1979. *Asia dar barabar-e gharb* (L'Asie Face A L'Occident). Tehran: AmirKabir.

Soroosh, Abdolkarim. 2000. *Reason, Freedom, and Democracy in Islam*. Translated and edited and with a critical introduction by Mahmoud Sadri and Ahmad Sadri. Oxford: Oxford University Press.

Talibuf, Abdul Rahim. 1894. *Ketab-e Ahmad Jild 2* (The Book of Ahmad Vol. 2). Istanbul: Akhter.

———. 1893. *etab-e Ahmad Jild 1* (The Book of Ahmad Vol.1). Istanbul: Akhter.

Williams, Raymond. 1976. *Keywords*. Oxford: Oxford University Press.

3

The Relevance of John Locke to Social Change in the Muslim World: A Comparison with Iran

Nader Hashemi

SPEAKING AT A SYMPOSIUM on political change and democracy in the Muslim world, Richard Bulliet, an eminent historian at Columbia University, offered the following note of caution.

> Notions like human rights, equality and civil liberties did not come from documents. They came from struggles. Anyone who is aware of the feminist movement in this country can see such a struggle taking place; a struggle that has yet to succeed but that probably will in time. Struggles cannot be fought from the outside; they must occur internally. What struggles will take place within the community of Muslims I would not hazard to say. Nor would I venture an opinion as to whether the Muslims of the twenty-first century will follow the direction of the West in their controversies over political and social norms, or whether they will find unique solutions to unavoidable contradictions. Either way, conflict, diversity, and evolutionary change seem inevitable despite the powerful appeal of a traditional core of norms and values.[1]

Bulliet's observation is significant because it serves to remind us that the modernization of the West did not begin with democracy, human rights, and free markets—as usually represented in the euphoria about Western values. Rather the origins lay in struggle, controversy, and debate. Today parts of the Islamic world—the Islamic Republic of Iran in particular—are consumed by a contestation of ideas similar to that which took place in Europe during the Reformation, Counter-Reformation, and Enlightenment periods. This chapter is an attempt to explore what the Muslim world can learn from Western political theory in terms of its own process of political modernization. The focus will be on the writings of John Locke and the relevance of his ideas to understanding political change in Muslim societies. Locke's classic work the *Two Treatises of Government* will be scrutinized with special attention to his dispute with Sir Robert Filmer on the question of property rights and the definition of legitimate authority. The second half of this chapter will make some cursory observations on the Locke–Filmer debate in the context of contemporary politics in Iran. The thesis that will be advanced is that a fundamental prerequisite of meaningful political change in societies, where the dominant political idiom is theological, is the gradual reformation of religious thought. The examples of seventeenth-century English Christianity and twentieth-century Iranian Islam are cases in point.[2] Furthermore, it will be argued that religious reformers are better equipped than secular thinkers to lead such a transformative process. In other words, the most desired avenue for social change is through a reformation of religious ideas, which may eventually open doors for the promotion of democracy, pluralism, and tolerance.[3] The example of John Locke—a founding father of the liberal democratic project—is a perfect illustration of this thesis.

Relevant Notes on the Political Philosophy of John Locke

John Locke is widely viewed as a founding father of modern democratic and liberal thought.[4] By the standards of his time he was as intellectually advanced as he was politically progressive. His liberal–democratic demeanor, however, developed gradually. It is largely forgotten that in his early years, Locke opposed religious pluralism and was a proponent of an authoritarian state.[5]

In 1660, John Locke wrote his first major political treatise, the *Two Tracts on Government*.[6] He was at Oxford University at the time, where he set out to answer the following questions: first, "whether the civil magistrate [could] lawfully impose and determine the use of indifferent things in reference to religious worship?" and second, "[could] the civil magistrate specify indifferent things to be included within the order of divine worship, and impose them upon the people?" After considerable reflection, his answer to both questions was an unequivocal "yes." A recounting of the argument in the *Two Tracts* is beyond the scope of this chapter. Suffice it to say that the dispute revolved around the question of religious freedom: in particular, to what extent a diversity of worship should be allowed in society and who the final arbiter in making these decisions should be, the state or the individual.[7]

Locke's position was to favor "order" over freedom of religion. His views were undoubtedly a product of his time, dating to the English Civil War and the ensuing chaos that enveloped England. He lamented "all those tragical revolutions which [had] exercised Christendom these many years [had] turned upon this hinge, that there hath been no design so wicked which hath not been so kind to itself as to assume the specious name of reformation . . . none ever went about to ruin the state but with pretence to build the temple." It was the confusion of "ambition and revenge" with "the cause of God" that had devastated England, and Locke's remedy was to defend the cause of political order over claims of religious authenticity.[8] In short, Locke was criticizing the politicization of religion in the service of personal gain.

What is interesting about Locke's worldview at this stage of his life, observes John Dunn, is his belief in the "firm subordination of religious sentiment to the demands of politics. Whatever its origins, political authority, to be adequate to its tasks, must be total."[9]

Seven years later, while serving as a confidante and assistant to Lord Anthony Ashley Cooper, a prominent figure in English politics, Locke was to revisit the questions that he had debated during his Oxford years, albeit from a different angle. The conclusions he reached this time were markedly different. In his posthumously published *Essay Concerning Toleration* (1667), in a reversal of his earlier authoritarian views, he would affirm that civil peace and social harmony could be advanced by "making the terms of Church communion as large as may be."[10] Locke was responding to religious debates in England where the Anglican Church was attempting to stifle pluralism by insisting on religious uniformity. Quakers, Catholics, Baptists, Presbyterians, and other minority groups who refused to conform to Anglican forms of worship were subjected to imprisonment, exile, and persecution. John Locke's 1667 essay, addressed to King Charles II, was motivated by this pressing social concern. He argued that individuals possessed moral autonomy in matters of indifferent religious beliefs and practice and under no circumstances should they be violated.

Locke also introduced the idea "that the kind of sincere belief necessary for salvation cannot be acquired by force and compulsion but only by argument and persuasion. The use of coercion thus creates either enemies (as with the non-conforming Dissenters) or hypocrites (as with those who outwardly complied)."[11] Locke's argument in favor of the moral sovereignty of individuals in matters of religion was a significant development in the evolution of Western liberalism and modern notions of human rights. Implicit in Locke's argument was the idea that coercion and compulsion on matters of sincere belief would only be resisted if enforced by the state. This could only lead to greater unrest and instability, hence his newfound conclusion that political order could best be preserved by "making the terms of Church communion as large as may be." The themes of individual agency, popular sovereignty, and natural rights were to be taken up in greater detail in his influential *Two Treatises of Government*.

Before turning to an analysis of this work, it bears mentioning that Locke's political theory was rooted within a Christian epistemological framework. The salience of this point will manifest itself in the second part of this chapter with respect to political change in the Muslim world. At this stage of the discussion, it is significant to point out, as John Gray has done, that Locke's liberalism was "firmly embedded in the context of Christian theism."[12] The largest group of books in Locke's private library (870 titles, nearly a quarter of his entire collection), for example, are in the category of theology, and his last two books, *The Reasonableness of Christianity* (1695) and *Paraphrases of St. Paul's Epistles* (1707), dealt explicitly with religion.

The pivotal transformation of Locke's political ideas from the *Two Tracts on Government* (authoritarianism) to the *Two Treatises of Government* (liberalism) resulted from a reconsideration of how social order and harmony could best be preserved. As seen earlier, his *Essay Concerning Toleration* indicates that his political thought was moving in a new direction.

Locke's primary methodology in making this paradigm shift—often forgotten in contemporary scholarship—was via a dissenting religious exegesis, the details of which are discussed below.

The Locke–Filmer Debate

John Locke's *Two Treatises of Government* were intended in large part to be a refutation of the views of Sir Robert Filmer, a royalist ideologue and writer of considerable intellectual aptitude. As the title of his most famous tract indicates, *Patriarcha or The Natural Power of Kings* (1680),[13] Filmer was a traditionalist who believed in the divine right of kings. He was the leading defender of the principle of absolute hereditary monarchy in England at the time. Filmer maintained that the power of a monarch is analogous to the natural power a father exercises over his offspring. Such power is not only absolute but is a form of personal property that the monarch owns and is entitled to pass on to his heirs.

In Locke's riposte to Filmer, one can detect the outline of the modern liberal democratic argument of individual rights and the theory of the negative state. This becomes evident in Locke's *Second Treatise of Government*, where he discusses the question of property and legitimate authority.

The Problem of the Right of Property

The problem of the right of property in the context of the Locke–Filmer debate begins with the great natural law writer Hugo Grotius. Filmer attacked

Grotius's notion that over the course of history a set of understandings emerged among men whereby they agreed to voluntarily divide up ownership over all that they collectively possessed.[14] Filmer questioned the notion of whether the unanimous consent of human beings, at a point in time, would be binding on any subsequent set of human beings that were either not a party to the original agreement or had changed their mind about its merits. Filmer argued that "property could only be . . . secure and legally valid, if, like political authority itself, it were the direct expression of the will of God."[15]

Locke's intervention in the debate is extremely subtle but builds in intensity as he develops his argument. At the outset of the *Second Treatise* he is in agreement with Filmer that according to both reason and revelation, the earth and its inhabitants derive their existence from God. Locke affirms that "men being all the workmanship of one omnipotent, and infinitely wise maker; all the servants of one sovereign master, sent into the world by his order, and about his business; they are his property, whose workmanship they are . . . sharing all in one community of nature" (§ 6).[16] Furthermore, "God gave to mankind in common" the earth (§ 25) and "God has given us all things [for men] . . . to enjoy" (§ 31).

How do men come to acquire a private right to property, according to John Locke? Labor is what distinguishes what is privately owned from what is held in common. "The *labour* of his body, and the *work* of his hands . . . are properly his," Locke states. "Whatsoever then he removes out of the state that nature hath provided, and left it in, he hath mixed his *labour* with, and joined to it something that is his own, and thereby makes it his *property*" (§ 27). Labor is thus a natural power of man that derives from God. Furthermore, a rational understanding of man's place in nature commands its exercise. Its usage is wholly beneficial and part of the natural order of things. In short, by affirming that through labor first begins "*a title of property* in the common things of nature" he has answered Filmer's criticism of Grotius on how men might acquire a right to private property without common consent. Filmer's views on the nature of political authority would be the next area of challenge.

The Nature of Political Authority

Locke's commentary on the nature of political authority invoked a much more elaborate response than his comments on the right to private property. Perhaps because it had direct bearing on a central thesis of his political philosophy—the right to rebellion—he addressed it at greater length and with more rhetorical energy.

Recall that, according to Robert Filmer, all humans owed their obedience to their rulers because God had given the earth to them, in particular the land in which they lived, to this ruler. "Divine appointment had ordained it to be monarchical," wrote Locke, paraphrasing Filmer.[17] The relationship between ruler and commoner was essentially a master–slave relationship and one for which, in his earlier writings, Locke had demonstrated some sympathy.

In specific terms, Locke charged that Filmer was guilty of misinterpreting the scriptures. While this thread of reasoning runs throughout Locke's critique of Filmer, with regard to the nature of political power, Filmer's mistake is assuming that paternal power is synonymous with political power. They are quite different, insists Locke.

> These two *powers, political* and *paternal,* are so perfectly distinct and separate; are built upon so different foundations, and given to so different ends, that every subject that is a father, has as much a paternal power over his children, as the prince has over his: and every prince, that has parents, owes them as much filial duty and obedience, as the meanest of his subjects do to their's; and can therefore contain not any part or degree of that kind of dominion, which a prince or magistrate has over his subject. (§ 71)

Paternal power, according to Locke, is only legitimate when the subject is not capable of reasoning. The father's power over his children is proof of such. Quoting from the Anglican theologian Robert Hooker, Locke asserted that adulthood is attained and paternal power suspended "when a man may be said to have attained so far forth the use of reason, as sufficeth to make him capable of those laws whereby he is then bound to guide his actions" (§ 61).

When the subject is a rational adult, power must be exercised in accordance with the consent of the subject. According to Locke, "all peaceful beginnings of *government* have been *laid in the consent of the people*" (§ 112). Furthermore, the nature of political authority is rooted in the notion of reciprocity. When discussing paternal power, Locke refers to the "duty which is incumbent on" parents toward their children (§ 58). He develops this idea further to assert that legitimate authority is obtained by virtue of the services rendered by the ruler to his subjects. Thus, far from being the owner of his subjects, the ruler was actually their servant. From the twin notions of consent and obligation emerges the outline of John Locke's social contract that was to be developed further by other political philosophers.

For the purposes of this chapter, what is significant is not the actual content of Locke's political theory, but the methodology he used in arriving at his conclusions. Note the numerous references to the Bible, to theologians such as Robert Hooker rather than Thomas Hobbes as sources of legitimacy, and finally note the constant reference to God. In fact, the thrust of Locke's critique of Filmer is that Filmer is in error because he has engaged in a false religious analogy (i.e., assuming paternal power is the same as political power). Locke proceeds from this point, through his dissenting religious exegesis, to shape the outlines of his political theories—limited government, right to private property, social contract, popular sovereignty, and the right to rebellion. What does the above discussion have to do with understanding social change in the Muslim world? In short, everything.

The Relevance of John Locke to the Contemporary Middle East

The political philosopher Norman G. Finkelstein has observed that "to compare phenomena is not to equate them." In the case under consideration, it should be stated clearly that the political turmoil afflicting seventeenth-century Europe is not equivalent to the problems confronting the twentieth-century Middle East. Referencing the historian Marc Bloch, Finkelstein adds that "a primary purpose of historical comparison is the identification of differences. Yet, there is no point in studying history if one cannot draw upon crucial common features; otherwise one's findings risk being dismissed, justly, as trivial."[18]

In studying the political philosophy of John Locke at the end of the twentieth century, in light of the political and religious debates in the Muslim world, one is struck by the similarity of the two cases. This similarity is most pronounced in the Islamic Republic of Iran, where, as a result of the 1997 presidential election, an open and vibrant political climate emerged that has significantly transformed the political culture. The proliferation of independent newspapers, journals, and magazines is the best measure of this change.[19] These publications were devoted to exploring and debating fundamental philosophical and political questions vital to the long-term viability of Iranian society. Notwithstanding the repeated efforts of the conservative establishment to censor and stifle this debate, civil society continues to explore important questions related to democracy in a Muslim context, with a particular focus on the normative relationship between religion and politics in Iranian society.[20]

Rather than a mere struggle between moderates and extremists, as often represented in journalistic coverage of Iran, the current tension is better described as a public clash among Islamists groups vis-à-vis the future of Iran's Islamic Revolution. On one side of the debate are the conservative clerics who control all of the major levers of power. A weltanschauung that grants political authority to the clerics informs their ideology. The details as to how they arrived at this position are beyond the scope of this chapter. What is important is that their theory of government is backed not only by the constitution but also critically by the religious sentiments of a significant portion of the population.[21] Much of the Islamic world, Iran included, continues to be a very religious society where questions of theology resonate in the hearts and minds of the masses. A manipulation of this sentiment is a critical battleground among rival political forces. A statement by Ayatollah Jannati, a leading clerical hawk, concisely captures the perspective of the conservative elite: "The people of Iran are considered in [view of Islamic] law, as orphans and minors, and Islamic scholars and clerics as their guardians and parents, who have to see to all of their needs."[22]

On the other side of the political spectrum is a diverse reformist camp of religious thinkers and laypersons who have widespread support among intellectuals, women, and student groups.[23] In response to Ayatollah Jannati, the reformers responded with an editorial of their own.

> How can a society which has more than one million university students and 17 million high schoolers, and overall the people have adequate access to international media, be considered as orphans and in need of a guardian, especially from one class [of society]? If their understanding of Islam is really this, why are they being polite—put aside the constitution of the Islamic Republic once and for all! Why do you spend so much then on colorful elections? In this geometry of command, all of these are unnecessary extras.[24]

The important phrase to pay attention to in this riposte is: "If their understanding of Islam is really this." Much of the political debate in Iran today takes place within a religious framework and idiom. The quarrel is essentially an internecine war among the Islamists aptly described in the subtitle of an article by Eric Rouleau as "Islam Confronts Islam in Iran."[25] The references and debates, therefore, are fundamentally about what type of Islam should be followed, who the interpreters of Islam should be, and, critically, where does sovereignty lie—with the people or the clerics?

The enveloping context in which this debate is taking place is both unique to Iran and the rest of the Muslim world. As far as Iran is concerned, the historical antecedents of the emergence of a religious discourse on Islam and democracy can be traced back to the early twentieth century in the debates between Ayatollah Mirza Mohammed-Hossein Na'ini and Sheikh Fazlollah Nuri following the 1906 Constitutional Revolution. For the next seventy-five years, the primary concern was the curtailing of secular political despotism that the Pahlavi regime embodied. When the clerics consolidated their power in the early 1980s, the focus shifted to the question of religious despotism and prospects for democracy. The fact that the state was now controlled by a religious class, who were ruling and justifying their politics in the name if (Shi'a) Islam, posed a series of new challenges that Islamist activists and religious reformers had to face.[26] The parallels with Locke's England are worth noting here, particularly as they relate to the state's use of religion to justify authoritarianism and to the themes of toleration, popular sovereignty, and freedom of expression—all justified within a religious idiom—that Islamic reformers invoked on their side of the debate.

In scrutinizing the speeches of reformers, one comes across statements criticizing those Iranians who "suppose [that] the more retarded a society is, the better protected its religion will be" (President Khatami) and "why does the Koran carry the harshest criticisms of the prophet? [Because] it was not in the nature of the prophet to stifle discussion of opposing points of view" (former minister of culture, Atoallah Mohajerani).[27] The conservative clerics on the other hand fire back that the "threat coming from nationalists and liberals is serious. We must be aware. They are weakening the beliefs and convictions of our people" (former speaker of the Majles, Ali Akbar Nateq Nouri)[28] and "it will be great danger to the national security and people's faith if the enemies of the Islamic revolution control or infiltrate the press" (Ayatollah Khomenei).[29]

The parallels between the principle of the divine right of kings and the divine rights of clerics, the Bible and Quran, Christianity and Islam, and the era of John Locke and Muhammad Khatami are evident. In both cases the debate about the future direction of English/Iranian society has occurred and is occurring by a reinterpretation of religious thought and a subtle movement—in the realm of ideas—in the direction of pluralism, tolerance, and democracy. It is not a coincidence, for example, that the magnum opus of Iran's leading philosopher, Abdolkarim Soroosh, is on the theme of a reinterpretation of religious knowledge, *Qabz va Bast-i Tiorik-i Shari'at* (The Theoretical Contraction and Expansion of the Shari'a).[30]

Furthermore, the incarceration and banning of the writings of Ayatollah Ali Hossien Montazeri, one of the most learned and senior clerical figures in Iran, speaks to the Iranian regime's legitimacy problem. It is religious personalities such as this who pose a grave risk to the conservatives, primarily because their liberal interpretation of Islam is popular and undermines the religious authenticity of the clerical establishment. Secular political figures can be easily dismissed as lacking revolutionary or Islamic credentials; theologians such as Montazeri and Mohsen Kadivar pose a more serious challenge precisely because of their solid religious credentials and their competing interpretation of the relationship between Islam and politics.[31]

Conclusion

When studying political philosophy in the twentieth century, the religious roots of modern liberalism often escape our attention. A critical reading of the

John Locke–Robert Filmer debate reminds us of the theological origins of modern politics. Locke is credited with writing the outline of liberal democracy. His ideas were to be taken up and expanded further by other theorists, such as Voltaire, Thomas Paine, and John Stuart Mill. The methodology used by Locke in articulating his political philosophy should not be forgotten. In his critique of Filmer's defense of royal absolutism, the core thrust of Locke's argument was that Filmer had engaged in a false religious analogy. "The Scripture says not a word of it," was Locke's common refrain as he proceeded to break new ground in Western political philosophy.[32]

In the Muslim world today, a similar rethinking of religious ideas has emerged with parallels to seventeenth-century England. The day after his election to a second term in office, President Khatami commented that the "[p]eople showed their commitment to *the real meaning of religion* and demands for freedom and justice. . . . The need of the moment and the future is to stabilize and deepen democracy and realize the rights of the people alongside religion."[33]

We are all observers of this Muslim political drama as it plays out. As Eqbal Ahmad once observed, a primary lesson to be learned from the European experience of political modernization that is relevant to a Muslim context is that "no significant political change occurs unless the new form is congruent with the old. It is only when a transplant is congenial to a soil that it works."[34] This truism about social change applies as much to Locke's England as it does to Khatami's Iran where a reinterpretation of religious thought is a critical variable influencing the process of political development.

Notes

I would like to thank Ausma Khan and Shabbir Akhtar for their useful feedback on this chapter.

1. Richard Bulliet, "Rhetoric, Discourse and the Future of Hope," in Richard Bulliet, ed., *Under Siege: Islam and Democracy* (New York: Middle East Institute of Columbia University, 1993), pp. 10–11.

2. Having said this I do not foreclose the option of revolutionary change as an acceptable mode of political transformation.

3. For a recent manifestation of this thesis in the most populous Muslim country see Robert Hefner, *Civil Islam: Muslims and Democratization in Indonesia* (Princeton, N.J.: Princeton University Press, 2000). On the question of Islam, secularism, and social change in the Muslim world, I have always taken to heart Abdullahi An-Na'im's recommendation that "[t]o seek secular answers [to the Muslim condition] is simply to abandon the field to the fundamentalists, who will succeed in carrying the vast ma-

jority of the population with them by citing religious authority for their policies and theories. Intelligent and enlightened Muslims are therefore best advised to remain within the religious framework and endeavour to achieve the reforms that would make Islam a viable modern ideology" (*Toward an Islamic Reformation: Civil Liberties, Human Rights and International Law* [Syracuse, N.Y.: Syracuse University Press, 1990], p. xii).

4. See Quentin Skinner, *The Foundations of Modern Political Thought* (Cambridge: Cambridge University Press, 1978) and Brian R. Nelson, *Western Political Thought: From Socrates to the Age of Ideology* (Englewood Cliffs, N.J.: Prentice Hall, 1982), 160.

5. On Locke's early years and his support for authoritarianism and opposition to religious pluralism, see John Dunn, *Locke* (Oxford: Oxford University Press, 1984), pp. 22–59.

6. John Locke, *Two Tracts on Government,* ed. Philip Abrams (Cambridge: Cambridge University Press, 1967).

7. For a succinct summary, see Dunn, pp. 22–25.

8. John Locke, *Two Tracts on Government,* pp. 160–61, cited by Dunn, p. 23.

9. Dunn, p. 24.

10. David Wootton, ed., *Political Writings of John Locke* (New York: Mentor Books, 1993), p. 210.

11. James Tully, *An Approach to Political Philosophy: Locke in Contexts* (Cambridge: Cambridge University Press, 1993), p. 53.

12. John Gray, *Liberalism* (Minneapolis: University of Minnesota Press, 1995), p. 13.

13. Sir Robert Filmer, *Patriarcha or The Natural Power of Kings,* ed. Johann Sommerville (Cambridge: Cambridge University Press, 1991).

14. Dunn, p. 36.

15. Dunn, p. 37.

16. John Locke, *Second Treatise of Government,* ed. C. B. Macpherson (Indianapolis, Ind.: Hackett Publishing, 1980), p. 9.

17. From chapter 9 of *First Treatise of Government,* "Of Monarchy by Inheritance from Adam," in Wootton, p. 247.

18. Norman G. Finkelstein, *Image and Reality of the Israel–Palestine Conflict* (New York: Verso, 1995), p. 89.

19. For an excellent overview of the rise and fall of the liberal press in Iran see Adam Tarock, "The Muzzling of the Liberal Press in Iran," *Third World Quarterly* 22 (August 2001): 585–602.

20. The remarks in this section are based on a recent visit to Iran in March 1999. While there, I had the opportunity to meet with a wide cross-section of Iranians, including student leaders, human rights activists, women, religious leaders, and members of the opposition. For an excellent sampling of the current state of Iranian politics see the special issue of the *Middle East Report* 29 (Fall 1999), "Pushing the Limits: Iran's Islamic Revolution at 20."

21. Absent a free and fair referendum, there is no accurate way of knowing the political and religious preferences of the Iranian people. According to this author, notwithstanding all that has happened in Iran over the past two decades, large segments

of the population continue to be moved by religious arguments and sentiment. The religious positions advanced by the mainstream clerics have a deep resonance in the hearts and minds of their constituency, albeit less so among the growing numbers of Iranian youth.

22. *Neshat* (Persian daily), January 30, 1999.

23. For a sampling of the debate in Iran, see Christopher de Ballaigue, "The Struggle for Iran," *New York Review of Books,* December 16, 1999.

24. Editorial, *Jahan-e-Islam* (Persian daily), February 1, 1999.

25. For an excellent overview of the internal Iranian debate, see Eric Rouleau, "A Model for the Muslim World? Islam Confronts Islam in Iran," *Le Monde Diplomatique* (June 1999).

26. Forough Jahanbakhsh, *Islam, Democracy and Religious Modernism in Iran (1953–2000)* (Leiden: Brill, 2001), p. 141.

27. Cited by de Ballaigue, "The Struggle for Iran."

28. Ali Raiss-Tousi, "Iran Demonstrators Denounce Israel, Khatami Allies," *Reuters,* December 31, 1999.

29. Nazila Fathi, "Iranian Leader Bars Press Bill of Reform Bloc," *New York Times,* August 7, 2000.

30. Abdolkarim Soroosh, *Qabz va Bast-i Tiorik-i Shari'at* (Theory on the Contraction and Expansion of the Shari'a) (Tehran: Mu'assassah-yi Farhangi-yi Sirat, 1990). In English the standard reference is *Reason, Freedom, and Democracy in Islam* (Oxford: Oxford University Press, 1999).

31. Geneive Abdo, "Rethinking the Islamic Republic: A 'Conversation' with Ayatollah Hossein 'Ali Montazeri," *Middle East Journal* 55 (Winter 2001).

32. Wootton, "Of Monarchy by Inheritance from Adam," p. 246.

33. Emphasis added. *Associated Press,* "Re-elected Iran Leader Vows 'Freedom, Justice,'" June 11, 2001.

34. Eqbal Ahmad, Interview with Emran Qureshi, December 21, 1994.

II

THEOLOGY AND MODERNITY

4

Negotiating Modernity:
Ulama and the Discourse of
Modernity in Nineteeth-Century Iran

Monica M. Ringer

THE ULAMA HAVE LONG FASCINATED HISTORIANS OF Middle Eastern history. In the modern Middle East and Iran more specifically, no group has so successfully defeated attempts at categorization, simplification, and, on the political scene, marginalization. It is not simply the oft-cited failure to anticipate the Iranian Revolution of 1979 that has thrown social scientists for a loop. More importantly, the ongoing attempt in Iran to reify a modern Islamic state has seriously debilitated modernization theories predicated on the necessity of secularization of the educational and legal institutions, if not the political system as well. The "great experiment" unfolding in Iran today has demonstrated the urgency of reconsidering what modernization entails, what modernity is or could be, and whether or not binary categories such as "traditional" and "modern" don't in fact contribute to confusion and prejudice rather than clarity and innovative synthesis. Despite profound constitutional, intellectual, political, and social problems associated with the development of an Islamic "democracy" in Iran, the Islamic government, the ulama, and Iranian society at large have demonstrated enormous resilience as they negotiate the construction of an Islamically based democratic government. Of primary importance are issues concerning the relationship between political and religious authority; the reconciliation of pluralism with the shari'a, human agency with divine will; and the nature and future shape of the ulama as an institution. For many reasons, the ulama themselves are at the center of much of the debate, both as actors and as religious authorities able to dominate interpretation of sacred texts.

These questions, in one form or another, are not new. They originated in the nineteenth-century debates surrounding modernization as it was formulated and reformulated over the course of the century, finally erupting into armed conflict in the Constitutional Revolution of 1906–1911. Contemporary Iranian conceptions of modernity consciously respond to the legacy of the nineteenth-century experience. Whether accepted, rejected, or transcended, the nineteenth-century resolutions to modernization established much of the reform agenda, as well as the paradigms of modernity, tradition, and progress that continue to inform the contemporary debates.[1]

The nineteenth century is something of an enigma. It was a period of political reform, increased contact with the outside world, and intellectual ferment. It was also a time of political conservatism, economic weakness, and intellectual censorship. The century was dominated by attempts at modernization and reform, and the ensuing political and intellectual struggles. A by-product of modernization was the emergence of the "modernization dilemma." From the very outset of the century, individuals reflecting on Iran's weakened position vis-à-vis the European powers were conscious of a radical break with the past. In both the travel literature of this period, as well as in personal memoirs and essays urging reform, there is a clear sense that times had changed, and that the world had entered a new epoch, or *"asr-e jadid."* It is significant that this break with the past was at the same time a clear sensation, yet neither fully understood, nor fully articulated. Those individuals who grappled with the ramifications of a new epoch and sought to bring Iran into a new phase and modernize thus came to the conclusion that something must be done, before having conceived of what that something ought to entail. Nineteenth-century reform literature is itself a quest for understanding what this new epoch meant, and what modernization should consist of and what modernity ought to look like.

The conceptualization of a future modernity was part and parcel of the modernization process. This imagining of modernity in nineteenth-century Iran constituted the evaluation and choice of possible pathways of change. In the broadest sense, society must determine the causal prerequisites of change, impediments to change, and the form that such a change should take. This necessarily involved an assessment of the continued viability of existing administrative, legal, and educational institutions. It also necessarily involved an assessment of existing cultural and religious traditions from a similar standpoint—which traditions could and should be maintained, which ones should be dispensed with, which ones should be reshaped, and which new traditions should be constructed.

From the very outset, modernization was conceived of in relation to Europe as a result of the obvious power disparity of Europe vis-à-vis Iran. Like their counterparts in Russia, Prussia, Egypt, Central Asia, and the Ottoman Empire, the initial impetus behind the modernization movement in Iran was the defeat of Iranian forces by European armies. A defensive military reform program gradually led to a full-fledged modernization movement. Throughout the nineteenth century, reformers (and their opponents) were acutely aware of the very real danger of European imperialist policy in the region. Europe thus served as an important initial catalyst in considering the need to reform, a model of modernization, and at the same time, the specter of loss of territory and political autonomy that failure to reform would enable. This inevitably led to the emergence of the "modernization dilemma"—a paradigm that would shape all subsequent conceptions of Iranian modernity. Simply put, the modernization dilemma is the attempt to use European institutions as models for Iranian modernization, and to adopt European technology and know-how, while at the same time guarding against a loss of cultural agency and authenticity.

At first glance, modernization made great strides. Crown Prince Abbas Mirza's military reform program (Nezam-e Jadid) initiated at the outset of the century evolved into a call for substantive political reform by the turn of the century. The cornerstone of the reform agenda was the call for constitutional government (or at the very least, some sort of parliamentary check on the authority and arbitrariness of the shah).[2] At second glance, however, the reform movement in the nineteenth century seems illusory. Despite the efforts of a number of prime ministers and individual activists, very little institutional change had been effected. Indeed, one might deem nineteenth-century attempts at modernization an abject failure. However, the import of the modernization movement in the nineteenth century is not due to its successes and achievements. Rather, its significance lies in the debates themselves, and in the intellectual, political, and social fault lines that emerged from these debates.

The ulama played a unique role in these debates, both as actors (reformers and opponents of reform) and as the direct or indirect targets of many reform programs. On the one hand, many of the most active reformers (particularly in the educational reform arena) were members of the ulama. On the other hand, many of the staunchest opponents of reform (particularly in the educational arena) were members of the ulama. The ulama, as the repository of religious authority because they enjoyed high social status and controlled both the educational and legal establishments, dominated intellectual and cultural discourse—and in so doing effectively shaped a cultural and moral weltanschauung articulated in the language of Islam. Modernization challenged all of these roles and prerogatives. The ulama were besieged on all fronts: institutional, social, cultural, and intellectual.

The Threat to the Ulama of Educational Reforms

In the most general sense, upper-level ulama, like other political and land-owning elites, stood to lose from various attempts at governmental centralization and rationalization of the administration, tax collection, office tenure, and appointments. This facet of resistance to reform measures is well within the age-old boundaries of central–local and center–periphery tensions. The reform agenda intensified its drive in these areas over the course of the century, engendering much opposition from all who stood to lose, and leading to the downfall of many a reform-minded prime minister.[3] However, to the extent that modernization entailed attempts to secularize the educational and judicial systems, the ulama were confronted with a very new sort of threat—a threat that if realized, would sever their control over these two key systems, and thus their institutional independence, financial remuneration, employment opportunities, political leverage, social status, and dominance of cultural and moral discourse.

The establishment of the first state-sponsored, European-style secondary school—the Dar al Fonun—in 1851 constituted the first frontal attack on the ulama's educational monopoly. Although some students had been officially dispatched to Europe for study prior to this time, these students did not challenge existing Iranian educational institutions.[4] Founded with the intention of creating a new elite administrative and military cadre, the Dar al Fonun offered an alternative body of knowledge from that of the traditional mosque school/seminary: the *madraseh.* Modern sciences, medicine, and European languages taught at the Dar al Fonun were all subjects outside the purview of the traditional educational system. The institutionalization of the adoption of European sciences into Iran threatened the very foundations of the ulama. The ulama were neither the creators, interpreters, or mediators of the new information, knowledge, or ideas expressed in the curriculum. As a channel to prestigious government employment, the Dar al Fonun presented an alternative means of acquiring status on the basis of European education and texts. The Dar al Fonun thus emerged as a purveyor of cultural and intellectual capital—formerly the sole prerogative of the *madraseh* system. For the first time there emerged a symptomatic distinction between "useful" European-style education and the traditional body of scholastic knowledge transmitted in the *madraseh,* which in contrast connoted nonuseful and purely religious knowledge.

The teaching of European sciences at the Dar al Fonun was condemned by some ulama. Alarmed at what they considered the propagation of anti-religious ideas, some ulama opposed the instruction of "new" sciences. Religious scholars were concerned that modern science would lead to materialism and atheism. In particular, European heliocentric astronomical theory became the focus of many attempts at refutation. Religious scholars were determined to preserve the geocentric vision of the universe that they believed was attested to in the Quran and Hadith.[5] The perceived threat to religious traditions was exacerbated by the growing influence of European science and its reinforcement of social prestige (and avenue for government appointments) associated with the Dar al Fonun. This led members of the ulama to feel a loss of social preeminence and intellectual standing.[6] It also led directly to the channeling of academic talent away from the *madraseh* into a European-style institution. Indeed, the absence of adequate terminology for new scientific (and medical) discoveries and the recourse to the use of French terminology contributed to a "communication breakdown" between scholars trained in modern versus those in traditional sciences.[7]

The ulama response to the dangers of the Dar al Fonun were varied. Some religious scholars denounced the school and equated growing European scientific hegemony with alien cultural intrusions and the loss of political autonomy to European governmental maneuvering.[8] Others, however, opted for intellectual dialogue with new scientific and medical theories. In many cases this was limited to polemical attacks. For example, the practice of autopsy was decried as Islamically unclean. Other scholars, however, did engage in serious dialogue with new ideas and theories. By the end of the nineteenth century, for example, as a result of decades of periodic wrangling with mathematic proofs of heliocentrism, religious scholars were able to reconcile this new and radically different cosmological theory with Islamic traditions.[9] In 1860, some ten years after the establishment of the Dar al Fonun, the head of the school and Minister of Education E'tezad al Saltaneh added a faculty appointment in traditional medicine to the school. In his announcement to this effect, it is not stated whether this was done as a result of lobbying from within the traditionally trained medical profession, or whether the decision was made in order to allay misgivings expressed by parents of medical students at the school concerning European-style medicine.[10]

By the turn of the century, with the establishment of some two dozen European-style primary schools (the New schools) that taught European sciences and languages, the ulama came face-to-face with the threat of institutional marginalization. The establishment of primary schools—as deliberate models for a universal system of education—were not supplementary in nature (as had been the elite Dar al Fonun preparatory school and other similar institutions), but rather constituted a bid to completely replace the existing traditional education system. Moreover, these New schools contested the ulama's role in forming, defining, and transmitting morals and values. Apart

from very basic religious instruction, they imparted a radically different curriculum than the traditional schools. They consciously promoted the secularization of morality and responsibility—deliberately orienting the children toward service to the nation and urging them to take responsibility for changing
the country. As articulated by Yayha Dowlatabadi, a leading educational activist (and himself a member of the anti-orthodox religious establishment),
primary education would create the literate citizenry necessary for the establishment of a constitutional government and for the formation of a new leadership. The products of the New schools were primed to become the future
leaders and creators of an Iranian modernity.[11]

One of the characteristics of the New schools was in fact the synthesis of traditional and European curricular matter. This was arguably one of their greatest achievements as they went beyond simplistic imitation and adoption of European institutions, instead offering a selectively chosen hybrid curriculum
designed to meet Iran's modernizing needs.[12] At the same time, the educational
reformers' creativity and determination to create a uniquely Iranian modernity
proved more dangerous to the traditional educational establishment than the
establishment of an entirely European parallel system would have been. Indeed,
it was the appropriation of elements from both curriculums that made the New
schools real alternatives to the traditional system. The New schools were thus
able to claim indigenous roots and objectives and to some extent avoid accusations of "aping" the West. They were able to attract students whose parents
might have been hesitant to send them to schools that did not teach basic religious practice and Arabic. Yet at the same time their clear emphasis on European languages and social and hard sciences reinforced the marginalization of
traditional subjects as supplementary or preliminary. In another example, the
School of [Law and] Political Science (Madraseh-ye Olum-e Siyasi) taught international law as well as traditional *fiqh*. This was correctly understood by the
religious establishment as an attempt to appropriate and thus undermine *fiqh*,
and the school had much difficulty finding a qualified jurist (*faqih*) to instruct
the students. It was only when the school director claimed to be preparing the
students to fend off un-Islamic ideas and cultural influences of the dominantly
European legal curriculum (which included international relations) that they
were able find an *alim* willing to offer it.[13] However, despite all protestations to
the contrary, the teaching of *fiqh* was transparently a means of moving beyond
the shari'a and/or nominally "reconciling" secular laws to the "intent" of the
shari'a and privileging European legal systems.

It is impossible to generalize about an "ulama response" to the New schools.
First, because unlike the secondary and largely supplementary schools like the
Dar al Fonuns that were established by high government officials (Amir Kabir
and Mirza Hosayn Khan, for example) for the advanced training of government

and military cadres, the New schools were established by educational activists. Some of these activists were prime ministers and prominent social elites. Others, however, hailed from the merchant classes, lower-ranking government officials, and the ulama itself. Many of the most active educationalists were themselves ulama, and almost always from the lower echelons of the hierarchy and/or exponents of anti-orthodox (Baha'i, Azali) religious views. For example, Mirza Hassan Roshdiyeh's new teaching methods and schools were used as models for many similar "Roshdiyyeh" schools in Tabriz, as well as the two dozen or so New schools established by the Society for Education (Anjoman-e Ma'aref) in Tehran. Yahya Dowlatabadi and Malek al-Mottekalemin established many New schools in Tehran and Isfahan, respectively, and were themselves Azali Babis.

Opposition to the New schools was dependent on specific local conditions and was rarely coordinated. The New schools were opposed on a variety of fronts. First, they were accused of perverting the Arabic alphabet due to their phonetic instructional methods. Second, they were repeatedly attacked and destroyed by mobs of irate seminary students (*tollab*) who jealously viewed them as institutional competitors and who suffered pecuniary losses from a decrease in the availability of tutoring positions. The destruction of New schools was not prevalent in Tehran, but was a clear and present danger in Tabriz depending on the level of official protection offered. A number of New schools were destroyed in Tabriz at the instigation of an leading cleric, Hajj Mohammd Yazdi Taleb al-Haqq, who used his sermons to incite angry crowds that he then directed to demolish the New schools, as well as Armenian coffeehouses and taverns. On several occasions, scholars issued fatwas denouncing the teaching of European languages in the New schools. By and large these were ignored. On another occasion, a fatwa was issued insisting on the teaching of religious subjects in the New school—seemingly more an attempt at synthesis and inclusion than an outright condemnation of the New schools as such. In Tehran, there is less evidence of outright opposition to the New schools, and this likely has much to do with the concentration in the capital city of political and social clout behind educational reforms. However, such reformers as Dowlatabadi made a point of establishing a school for *sayyeds* (the Sadat school) and the Islam school (founded by Mohammad Kermani Nazem al-Islam) sought to attract sons of ulama by exempting them from the uniform dress code—an exception noted in the school's constitution.

The Threat to the Ulama of Judicial Reforms

Many of the dangers that educational reform posed to the ulama were also present in the threat of judicial reform. The distinction between new and traditional, secular and religious knowledge was echoed in the realm of law. Modernization was conceived of as entailing secularization of both the educational and judicial systems. Reformers thus emphasized the importance of reducing the judicial prerogatives of the ulama in order for centralization and rationalization to proceed. Reformers who advocated the establishment of a European-inspired constitution, in order to resolve the "modernization dilemma," were forced into a position of insisting that Islamic law (the shari'a) would in fact inspire constitutional law and that the principles underlying these two systems were inherently reconcilable. However, this debate clearly called into question the very basis of religious law (not to mention the sincerity of attempts at superficial reconciliation!). Was, as Sheikh Fazlollah Nuri would argue during the course of the Constitutional Revolution, the very idea of man-made law a direct challenge of the prophetic mission and an explicit denial of the sufficiency of God's provisions for mankind—as embodied in the shari'a?[14] However, this attempted reconciliation was only the tip of the proverbial iceberg. The more fundamental challenge to the ulama lay in the fact that the shari'a was subject to this debate at all. That government officials, ambassadors, essayists, and other reform-minded individuals in their essays and journal articles presumed to discuss these matters, and moreover, to subject them to public opinion directly challenged the monopoly of the ulama (or the *fuqaha,* more specifically) on religious authority.

Indeed, no challenge was more painfully felt than the very fact that reformers debated at all on issues of knowledge, culture, law, and education that were formerly the preserve of the ulama—a debate that in essence constituted a bid by the reformers to replace the ulama in their role as social leaders—the beginnings of the modern gage intelligentsia. Particularly alarming were reformers' reinterpretations of religious texts and traditions and their attempts to identity irrevocable principles of Islam that could then be reconciled to modernization and the importation of a European-style constitution. Moreover, by proposing to synthesize tradition with modernity, Islam with secular constitutions, and religious instruction with European sciences and foreign languages, but orienting Iranians' loyalty toward the nation rather than the monarch or a religious-based value system by rebuking the ulama for having failed to lead the country in the direction of progress (overwhelmingly defined in a Eurocentric manner), and by publishing journals that sought to reach directly to the public, reformers usurped the moral and cultural authority of the traditional elites and effectively attacked the foundations of the ulama's authority in Iran.

Conclusion

While the ulama suffered many defeats in the nineteenth century, they were not definitively dislodged from their positions of cultural and social prominence. The modernization debates themselves threatened the ulama's hegemony in many areas of social, political, intellectual, and even religious life. Yet as a consequence of the ulama's centrality in these areas, the debates themselves were shaped by ulama resistance, reformulation, and reaction. The debates are thus characterized by the enduring intellectual centrality of the language of Islam. Islamic traditions served as legitimation (symbolic or real) for all positions, as all positions necessarily grappled with the issue of reconciliation with the sacred texts. It was imperative in presenting any vision of the future, and any project of modernization, to portray this as protecting Islam and Iran's cultural traditions. Since modernization projects were modeled on European institutions, reformers were forced into the awkward and ultimately defensive position of fending off accusations of selling the country to foreigners and of hastening the dissolution of Iran's traditions. In this regard, the ulama were in a very strong position of projecting themselves as the guardians of the national interest, and the bastion of Iran's religious and cultural traditions—a position that they protected into the next century and beyond.

Because the ulama found themselves threatened by reform projects as a group, they are often portrayed as opponents of modernization and reform. Ulama are often depicted as backward, ignorant, and hopelessly tied to outdated religious traditions. In contrast, "reformers" are assumed to be progressive, secular-minded, and overall well-intentioned in their attempts to improve Iran. This is clearly not only an oversimplification, but an obscuring of the real motivations and considerations of both reformers and ulama. More dangerous even is the tendency of the terms themselves ("progressive," "conservative," etc.) to become laden with implicit connotations that further contribute to the solidification of the bipolar understanding of modernity and its conceptions. This inhibits any clear understanding of the issues and motivations of nineteenth-century actors and debilitates attempts to breakdown and move beyond the distortions that this bipolarity creates. For example, there is much more consensus between reformers and their ulama opponents than there would be in the twentieth century, with the development of the cultural chasm—or cultural schizophrenia.[15] The ulama were not alone in expressing cultural antipathy toward blatant Westernization. Secular-minded reformers, too, were concerned about the cultural baggage that accompanied the adoption of European-style institutions. The majority of reformers decried blind imitation of the West and found the manifestation of European culture on the part of some of their more enthusiastic Europhiles objectionable. One especially poignant example of this is when E'tezad al-Saltaneh, the first minister of education and director of the first European-style secondary school (the Dar al Fonun), and himself an advocate of Newtonian physics, had one student physically punished for his insistence on speaking a pretentious admixture of French and Persian. Indeed, the crux of the modernization dilemma was itself an attempt to delimit the cultural impact of modeling new institutions after European ones. All participants in the debate over modernization (and by extension over culture and traditions) were forced to attempt resolutions of the modernization dilemma. By the end of the century, many reformers recognized that the success of the reform movement depended on recognizing and resolving the issue of importing foreign institutions—and not simply for tactical reasons or posturing.

It is thus imperative that we cease to discuss "the ulama response" and instead recognize the complexities of the ulama in the process of modernization and the debate on modernity. The ulama must be treated individually in terms of their positional relationship to the following fields: relationship to the state, the religious hierarchy, social and economic status, intellectual stance toward modernization, and Shiite intellectual traditions. Their individual and collective responses, however, have not yet been fully teased out of the history of modernization. The reasons for this are not simply ideological. Another obstacle has been the nature of the sources.

Most of the material on the debates surrounding modernization and the construction of an Iranian modernity take the form of essays, memoirs, travel accounts,[16] journals, and newspapers written by reform-minded individuals. The majority of this written material was authored by government elites and secularizing-oriented intellectuals. The readership is amongst themselves and also begins to be directed toward an educated, literate public audience by the last quarter of the nineteenth century. There are occasional references to opposition on the part of the ulama to reform measures, but very little detail as to the reasons behind this opposition. Reformers frustrated by ulama resistance neither provide their opponents' rationale, nor any specifics about the individual religious figure indicated. This in and of itself contributed to a simplistic and dismissive approach to the ulama—an approach that was exacerbated by a strong vein of anticlericalism. The religious establishment or even various *madrasehs* did not at this time have journals or other written forums that discussed questions of modernization. The ulama audience largely remained themselves—and opponents of modernization did not engage in direct confrontation in literary space. This was due to the conjunction of several circumstances. First, the lack of serious monarchical commitment and accompanying censorship that prevented the emergence of an open, public forum for much of the century. Second, there were relatively few reformers involved in the debate. Third, at no time in the nineteenth century did reformers have the luxury of time—the perception of a constant and imminent danger of European incursion led reformers to engage in polemics. In contrast to the Ottoman discourse of modernization and modernity, the Iranian discourse was more limited in scope, as well as in depth of analysis. As a result, urgent questions concerning national identity, the future shape of the shari'a, and the role of religion (and the associated problem of morality) in a secular society, had neither been fully digested nor even seriously broached in the Iranian discourse.

The dearth of sources should not lead us to presume, however, that the ulama in general were unaware of the long-term implications of reform, or uninterested in the larger questions of negotiating an Iranian modernity. The very fact that advocates of change felt the need to justify their ideas vis-à-vis religious and cultural traditions is evidence enough of the involvement of many members of the religious establishment in these questions. However, the sources themselves, particularly as they are addressed to larger public audiences, witness a creation of a new public space that was dominated by reform advocates in an attempt to mobilize mass opinion. As such, this new space wrested away some of the edge that the ulama hierarchy enjoyed in accessing and shaping popular opinion.

Notes

1. For a discussion of the educational debates in nineteenth-century Iran, see my book *Education, Religion and the Discourse of Cultural Reform in Qajar Iran* (Costa Mesa, Calif.: Mazda, 2001).

2. On the reform movement in Qajar Iran, see Shaul Bakhash, *Iran: Monarchy, Bureaucracy and Reform under the Qajars 1858–96* (London: Ithaca Press, 1978) and Guity Nashat, *The Origins of Modern Reform in Iran, 1870–80* (Urbana: University of Illinois Press, 1982).

3. The most notable examples are the reform-minded prime ministers Amir Kabir (in office 1848–1851) and Mirza Hosayn Khan Sepahsalar (in office 1870–1873) who served under Naser al-Din Shah (r. 1848–1896) and Mirza Ali Khan Amin al-Dowleh (in office 1897–1898) who served under Mozafar al-Din Shah.

4. Students dispatched to Europe on official missions were not perceived to be a threat since their numbers were limited, and their situation considered exceptional. That they would later play an important role in championing European-style modernization was not immediately appreciated by opponents of modernization.

5. See Kamran Arjomand, "The Emergence of Scientific Modernity in Iran: Controversies Surrounding Astrology and Modern Astronomy in the Mid-Nineteenth Century," *Iranian Studies* 30, 1–2 (1997): 5–24.

6. See Arjomand, "The Emergence of Scientific Modernity."

7. See Arjomand, "The Emergence of Scientific Modernity." This is also attested to by the need for the first generation of instructors at the Dar al Fonun to write many of their own textbooks, and to generate new Persian terms or employ French terms already in use.

8. See, for example, medical instructor Jakob Polak's complaints about the ban on autopsy, and the directives given to all teachers not to become political actors while in Iran. Jakob Polak, *Persien, Das Land und seine Bewohner* (Hildesheim: Olms, 1976).

9. See Arjomand, "The Emergence of Scientific Modernity."

10. See my discussion of the 1860 "education manifesto" in *Education, Religion and the Discourse of Cultural Reform*, pp. 84–87. A complete translation of the text of the manifesto, published in *Vaqaye'-e Ettefaqiyeh*, is in progress.

11. Yahya Dowlatabadi, *Tarikh-e Mo'aser ya Hayat-e Yahya Dowlatabadi*, 4 vols. (Tehran: Ferdowsi, 1362), vol. I, p. 193.

12. For a discussion of the new schools as institutional manifestations of an emerging "indigenous solution," see my article (in Persian) "Madares-e Novvin dar Iran-e Qarn-e Nuzdahom" ("New Schools in Nineteenth-Century Iran: The Indigenous Approach"), *Irannameh* vol. XVIII, (2 Spring 2000).

13. Hosayn Mahbubi-Ardakani, *Tarikh-e Mo'assesat-e Tamaddoni-ye Jadid dar Iran* (Tehran: Tehran University Press, 1975) vol. I, pp. 402–3; and Chengiz Pahlavan, "Madraseh-ye 'Olum-e Siyasi," in *Hoquq-e Asasi: Yani Adab-e Mashrutiyat-e Dowal* (Tehran: 1368), pp. 337–38.

14. See Sheikh Fazlollah Nuri, "The Book of Admonition to the Heedless and Guidance for the Ignorant," translated and edited by Hamid Dabashi, "Two Clerical Tracts on Constitutionalism," in Said Amir Arjomand, ed., *Authority and Political Culture in Shiism* (Albany: SUNY Press, 1988), pp. 334–70.

15. I am borrowing this term from Daryush Shayegan, *Cultural Schizophrenia: Islamic Societies Confronting the West* (Syracuse, N.Y.: Syracuse University Press, 1992).

16. On travel literature as a window into the modernization debate, see my article, "The Quest for the Secret of Strength in Iranian Nineteenth-Century Travel: Rethinking Tradition in the Safarnameh," in Nikki R. Keddie and Rudi Matthee, eds., *Iran and the Surrounding World: Interactions in Culture and Cultural Politics* (Seattle: University of Washington Press, 2002). I was particularly struck by the difficulty of advocates of reform in addressing the question of the danger of affecting Iran with a European-style morality that was inextricably associated in the mind of its detractors with concepts of political freedoms.

5

Mehdi Haeri Yazdi
and the Discourse of Modernity

Farzin Vahdat

THE THOUGHT OF MEHDI HAERI YAZDI CAN potentially occupy a very significant place in the current debates on modernity and Islam in Iran. His ex-
pertise in Islamic philosophy and other Islamic fields of learning as well as his
formal training in modern Western philosophical traditions enabled Haeri to
explore the fundamental issues of modernity and Islam to an extent and depth
that is unrivaled, at least in Iran, if not in other Islamic societies.

What characterizes Haeri's discourse is the relative paucity of ideological
and polemic approaches toward the questions involved in modernity and
Islam. In fact, in addition to the recondite nature of philosophical issues with
which he engaged, this approach disposed him toward an elitist attitude in his
writing, which seems to have caused him to deliberately shy away from writing
for a larger public, in contrast to other contemporary Islamic thinkers in Iran.
For this reason, his thought, the promulgation of which spanned some three
decades, may seem inaccessible even to experts and as a result has not received
the attention that it deserves. In this chapter I intend to present his work to a
wider audience and hopefully bring out the significance of his thought for the
issues of modernity and Islam in Iran and possibly other Islamic societies.

For this reason, I would like to suggest that the best way to analyze Haeri's
thought on modernity is to view his discourse along three different dimensions or levels of analysis. The first dimension and the deepest level is his discussion of ontology or, more accurately, theontology. At this level, which is the
most abstract and comprises a large portion of his discourse, Haeri deals with
questions such as existence, God, and humans' location in this vast and esoteric expanse. The second level is what may be called his philosophy of ethics

or practical reason in which he discusses the philosophical principles of human action and ethics. The third dimension and the least abstract is his discussion of political and social issues that are derived from the two previous dimensions.

The main thesis of this chapter suggests that at the first level, his theontological dimension, Haeri posits the notion of subjectivity primarily for the Being and the Divine, and human subjectivity assumes a secondary and derivative status. Yet, even at this level human subjectivity is not totally denied, even though it is given an epiphenomenal position. Thus in his theontology Haeri leaves a space for the development of the human subject and its sociological and political ramifications. Secondly, it is in the two other dimensions, his discussions of the ethical/practical sphere and the political realm, that this space for human subjectivity is expanded, and he builds an ethical/practical discourse and sociopolitical vision based on a rather developed notion of human subjectivity. As a result, in Haeri's discourse as a whole we can observe a reconciliation between Islam and modernity in that both Divine subjectivity and human subjectivity exist side by side, albeit in different dimensions and at different levels, and the notion of human subjectivity garners elaboration and expansion to give rise to the idea of modern universal citizenship in the sociopolitical realm without damaging or interfering with the notion of Divine sovereignty and subjectivity.

Haeri articulated the last aspect of his thought, his more direct sociopolitical views, in a relatively accessible book entitled *Philosophy and Government* (Hekmat va Hukumat), which he wrote in the last years of his life and published outside Iran. This book has never been published in Iran, but has been used by some scholars in the country, notably religious thinkers, to deconstruct the notion of the Guardianship of the Jurist (Velayat-e Faqih) and envision an Islamic polity more compatible with modernity and democracy.[1]

Mehdi Haeri Yazdi was born in 1923 in Qom. His father was the renowned Ayatollah Abdul Karim Haeri Yazdi, who made Qom the major center of Shi'a studies inside Iran. Mehdi studied Islamic jurisprudence, theology, and most significantly Islamic philosophy with his father and other prominent Shi'a scholars in Qom and other places in Iran and received his ordination as an ayatollah. He also earned a doctorate from the University of Tehran in the field of theology. During this period Haeri developed an intense interest in Western philosophy and spent many years in the United States and Canada, which led to a doctorate in analytical philosophy from the University of Toronto in 1979. After that he returned to Iran to teach Islamic philosophy at the University of Tehran. He died in the summer of 1999 at the age of 76.[2]

Early in his career, Haeri embarked upon a notion of human subjectivity that was grounded in his philosophical inquires. Philosophy for him was a vehicle to learn the truth and the secrets of creation, insofar as human capacity allows, and thereby achieve a likeness of the Divine (*Elm-e Kolli*, p. 1). In fact, like many other Islamic thinkers in Iran, Haeri attributed divine qualities to the Logos-possessing human. Thus, in one of his earlier books called *Universal Knowledge* [*Elm-e Kolli*], published in late 1950s, Haeri wrote:

> The sacred self of man, just like a heavenly being, is clear from any abomination and pollution of matter in its origins. Man's power, knowledge, volition, life, vision, and auditory ability are the manifestations of the holy essence of the Divine. The powerful God has created for this celestial being a dominion like His own in which man can be a willful agent and an absolute ruler. Man is in likeness to the transcendent God . . . and like God, man in his [own] dominion is in the position of command and creativity (*Elm-e Kolli*, p. 23).

In Haeri's early thought, the ability to act, which in humans is combined with consciousness and volition, is the source of agency that leads to power (*Elm-e Kolli*, 91). This agency in humans, according to Haeri, is mediated through our faculty of representation whereby we create pictures of the external objects in our minds which in turn become the ground for our action and the power of agency. Moreover, these representations are under our willful control, because they are formed by the creative capacity of our mind (*Elm-e Kolli*, pp. 95–96).

Following Ibn Sina, Haeri believed that the "perfection" of the self is possible most directly via the study of philosophy. Paraphrasing Ibn Sina, Haeri asserted that "speculative" philosophy is the active agency through which the self, insofar as *intellectus in actu* ('*aql bil fi'l*) is realized, achieves perfection (*kavosh ha-ye aql-e nazari*, p. 32). The transformation of humans from the realm of materiality to the sphere of intellect is achieved as a result of philosophical development. This transformative power of philosophy, in Haeri's reading of Mulla Sadra, is the goal of and the ultimate desire of humans seeking perfection and release from entanglement in matter (*aql-e nazari*, pp. 32–33). The high status that Haeri attributed to philosophy led him to view philosophy as constitutive of human authenticity, a far cry from a conservative Islamic notion of authenticity.

> Inasmuch as the truth of philosophy in general is but the knowledge of existence and beings and understanding of reality, it is clear and necessary that this particular form of human knowledge is directly related to the reality and essence of man himself. This is because understanding reality is either necessary or alternatively it is the distinguishing feature [differentia, *fasl*] of humans from other animals. Accordingly, we must admit that philosophy is not only the human mode of thinking, it is also what constitutes our essence and our real boundary [separating us from other beings]. . . . The question of, what is philosophy?, is

identical to the question of what is man? . . . Because man possesses a distinguishing feature such as Logos . . . his [essence] is the same as philosophy (*aql-e
nazari*, pp. 35–36).[3]

Philosophy and Being

In spite of the central role that Haeri gave philosophy in human affairs and
the pivotal place of human existence for philosophy, he believed that the essential question that lies at the core of philosophical inquiry is that of Being.
The philosophical tradition, especially metaphysics and ontology, he maintained, was primarily concerned with Being, and this Being has constituted
the predicate in philosophical propositions such as "God exists," "reason exists," "self exists," and "matter exists" (*aql-e nazari*, p. 28). Haeri, following
Sadra, also believed that Being and God are not different and that modern
European philosophers are at fault for denying the Being and God as predicates in logical judgments. Haeri criticized Immanuel Kant in particular for
arguing that Being is not a real predicate and simply a copula, merely connecting the subject and the predicate in a proposition (*aql-e nazari*, pp.
107–15).[4] Based on these premises, Haeri argued that primacy and authenticity should be given to the Being. Invoking Ibn Sina and, more importantly,
Sadra, Haeri argued that since the knowledge of all essences is dependent
upon Being, and the knowledge of Being depends upon itself, the realization
of everything is possible only through Being, and realization of Being is not
possible except through itself. Since Being does not need anything else to be
realized it is in the position of primacy and authenticity. Just as an object is
white because of its whiteness and whiteness is not white because of anything
else, in the same way the Being is self-realizing and "in its authenticity [*isalat*]
and existence is self-made and needs no agent for its realization and has not
acquired this authenticity from elsewhere" (*aql-e nazari*, p. 77). The corollary
of this argument is, obviously, the primacy of Existence over essence, which
Haeri considered the truth of philosophical existentialism.[5] The upshot of
this argument was that only the Being, and in fact the Supreme Being, is a
self-subsistence reality, and all other beings derive their existence and their
status from it (*aql-e nazari*, p. 99).

In this scheme one can easily ascertain the secondary and derivative position that human beings are allotted. In this regard Haeri chastised the Western existentialist philosophers, naming Jean-Paul Sartre in particular, because
while they profess the precedence of Existence in relation to essence, they ultimately give authenticity [*isalat*] to essence and the related notions of human
mind and subjectivity over Existence (*aql-e nazari*, pp. 90–91).

These formulations constituted Haeri's early views on theontology according to which, while the primacy belongs to the Being, human subjectivity is not totally denied as I tried to demonstrate above. However, Haeri's more mature metaphysical theontological views were framed in a grander scheme to which he devoted much time and energy.

Mapping the Universe: The Pyramid of Existence

The discussion of the notion of the "Pyramid of Existence" constituted a part of Haeri's doctoral dissertation that he completed at the University of Toronto in 1979. Haeri analogized the entire system of existence to a pyramid, at the apex of which is the Supreme Being, and other beings receive their existence from this Supreme Being. The point of analogy between the vast expanse of Existence and the pyramid, Haeri argued, is that while the apex of the pyramid is indivisible and, from the point of the lower echelons, invisible, it is also encompassing toward all other points of the pyramid; in a similar manner the Concealed Divinity is the only One fully in possession of self-subsistence and independence and yet other beings receive their existence and subsistence from that Being (*heram-e hasti*, p. 175). God, at the apex of the pyramid, Haeri posited, is pure existence and self-subsistence [*wujud bil dhat*], and in no other point of the pyramid are beings self-subsistence and self-supporting. However, other points in the pyramid, that is other beings except the Supreme Being, do receive the substance that Haeri calls "existence" and that makes there being possible as a blessing issuing from the apex (*heram-e hasti*, p. 195).[6]

Haeri borrowed a set of conceptual terms from Mulla Sadra to articulate the same idea, which illuminates the core of his theontological and cosmological views. According to Mulla Sadra's thesis, in Haeri's rendition, the Supreme or Necessary Being is pure existence, but humans, animals, and other celestial and terrestrial beings all share the same substance of existence, but to varying degrees in correspondence to the position that they occupy on the pyramid. As we reach the bottom of the pyramid we encounter matter that contains the least degree of that substance, namely, existence. Haeri called this phenomenon, after Mulla Sadra, the Unicity of Being in Differentiation (*wahdat wujud tashkiki*), or just the principle of *tashkik*, which can be translated as "existential variance."[7] He elaborately discussed these theontological issues in the *Pyramid of Existence*.

> I want to explain the category of [existential] differentiation [*tashkik*] and propose the notion of Unicity of Being in Differentiation for the reality of existence: an existence which the universe, God, humans and all beings, have in common.

This means that all [beings] are the [different] stages [*marateb*] and determinations of this Undivided Being. All beings are the manifestations and stations [*marahel*] of this Undivided Being; God in this Existence, the universe, and humans in the universe all share the sameness of One Being. There is nothing more than one determined Undivided Being and we call that the Unicity of Being. . . . [However] based on the principle of Differentiation, this Being, while a determined real Unicity, contains the very plurality of stages and [different] manifestations. This type of plurality which is predominant in the reality of Being harbors no contradiction toward the Unicity of Being (*heram-e hasti*, pp. 134–35).

What Haeri is suggesting in this highly abstract passage, it seems, is that all beings in the universe are but from one source, and yet there are differences in the intensity of the substance of existence that these beings possess, which counts for plurality of beings, and yet there is no contradiction in all this. He provided the example of a weak and a strong light. What is common between, as well as what differentiates, strong and weak light is the light itself. The reality of the light is the same; what differs is the weakness and the strength in the light (*heram-e hasti*, p. 134). This brings Haeri to the closely related notion of "unity in difference and difference in unity," which he also adopted from Mulla Sadra. In accordance with the tenor of this concept, Haeri maintained, in ordinary logic wherever we think of plurality, then there is no unity, but in the logic of *tashkik*, what is the basis of differentiation is also the basis of unity (*heram-e hasti*, p. 134). This is the same as Mulla Sadra's solution to the same problem in which the notion of "unity in multiplicity and multiplicity in unity" constitutes a major achievement, in contrast to the non-philosophical and unsophisticated approach of Muhi al-Din Ibn 'Arabi (the idea of unicity of being, *heram-e hasti*, p. 101).

From this grand scheme, Haeri deduced the status of humans in terms of contingence, in contrast to the necessity of Being. He argued that possibility or contingence (*imkan*), as opposed to the necessity of Being, characterizes the imperfection and weakness of humans' existence. Human existence is marred by existential weakness, essential dependence, and lack of self-sufficiency and self-subsistence (*aql-e amali*, p. 92). In this context, Haeri used another Sadraian concept to describe the relation of all contingent beings, including that of humans, to the Being—an idea of that may be translated as "[existential] poverty" (*faqr*) of all contingent beings. In the last pages of the *Pyramid of Being* Haeri wrote

The entire truth of the phenomenal world, is nothing save a "from" [*az*]. However, since this "from" has an existence, its [existence] is nothing but a shadowy and dependent being. It is not authentic. . . . The truth of entire phenomenal world, whatever is [except the Being itself], is nothing but dependence. . . .

Therefore when you say "I," this "I" is false. . . . There is no "I" or "you," because you cannot know your own essence independently. You may achieve this [i.e., self-knowledge] if you assume your absolute dependence on the Origin. In that case you do not exist anymore, whatever that exists is Him or is "from" Him. The attribution of being can only be applied to the Origin and this is the [meaning of] the "existential poverty" of contingent entities as opposed to the Substantial Necessity [of the Being] (*heram-e hasti*, pp. 299–302).

In a related vein, Haeri argued that human status is that of (epi)phenomenon in relation to the Being. Accordingly, he argued, in Islamic philosophy one cannot speak of human subjectivity—one cannot say "I." When one says, "I" did this or that, or "'I' went," this is a falsity, because we are not in possession of an "independent personality." We might entertain the idea of having an independent personality, but we are an absolute epi-phenomenon, "a very weak manifestation of an infinite source of being" (*Metaphysic*, p. 36).

In sum, Haeri's theontological formulations can be thought of in terms of a pyramid, at the vertex of which is the Supreme Being, and other beings receive their existence from this Supreme Being. As we descend from the peak to the base of this pyramid the intensity of the substance that he calls "existence" is reduced at the lower levels and rungs but the substance itself is not totally lost. Thus humans and animals and other celestial and terrestrial beings all share the same substance of existence, but to varying degrees, and as we reach the bottom of the pyramid we encounter matter that contains the least degree of that substance. As we saw, in this scheme, the Being or Existence is primordial and human status is secondary and derivative, and epiphenomenal with significant implications for negation of human subjectivity. Yet, in this formulation, it is wrong to assume that human subjectivity is totally denied, and in a dialectical fashion human status is, as we will see below, to a significant degree redeemed.

Philosophy of Ethics

Haeri's discourse on philosophy of ethics and what he called "normative ethics," while closely related to his theontological reflections, gave considerably more free rein to human subjectivity with significant implications in the sociopolitical sphere. In this endeavor Haeri stayed away from the theomorphic approach to human subjectivity and utilized his training in Anglo-American analytical philosophy to adopt what may be called an epistemological approach. In other words, instead of addressing human subjectivity in terms of approximation to God and appropriation of his attributes, Haeri broached human subjectivity in terms of the knowing subject and in the context of the process of achieving knowledge. In this regard, Haeri consistently considered knowledge, that is, human knowledge, to be made of the same material as, and qualify to belong to, the order of Being. He therefore deemed a lofty status for knowledge.[9] In a related vein, as we saw before, Haeri believed that philosophy and philosophical inquiry, defining human intellectual and moral action, constituted the authentic essence of being human. In order to give substance to these views, Haeri, in his discussions of ethical philosophy, posited a dual scheme of subjectivity, one belonging to the Divine and the other belonging to humans.

Dual Structure of Subjectivity

Haeri argued that the creative capacity of the human mind is closely associated with free will, and by the virtue of this free will humans are capable of producing their own norms and values, free from any external interference, even from God. In fact, based on these premises, Haeri constructed a dual structure of sovereignty and subjectivity, one for God and one for humans. In his book on practical reason, titled *Investigations of Practical Reason* (Kavosh ha-ye 'aql-e 'amali), Haeri argued that as God is the creator of nature and universe, in the realm of norms and values humans are the sovereign. He wrote

> [On] the meaning of God's successor. In virtue of his [free] will and [sense of] responsibility, man is the lord and creator of deeds and actions that take place in the realm of norms and values. And like the Creator of Existence who created the entire universe and the "azure dome" of Being from nothingness, man also is the maker and creator of his various deeds and actions and [responsible for] the transformations of his own world. If we accept the principle of man's sovereignty over his internal and external worlds, [then] the deeds and the consequences of his free will can be considered as equally real as the objective realities of the natural world and the universe that have come into being as a result of God's will (*aql-e amali*, p. 54).

In this passage we can see that in Haeri's view, as God is the creator of nature and the material universe, in a similar fashion humans enjoy sovereignty and subjectivity in the realm of ethical norms and values. The term that he often used to convey this approach to the construction of norms and values was the Perso-Arabic term "*maqdurat.*" This term may be translated as the objects over which one has power. Since Haeri believed that norms and practical/moral values are created by humans, he often referred to them as *maqdurat.* He argued that as humans possess, at a very microlevel, a will similar to that of the God of creation, their will is manifested in their own creation of *maqdurat* as principally moral, practical norms and values. As humans, Haeri believed, we are also "the lord of the 'created world' of our actions. . . . That means that we possess a volition similar to that of God and if we want we can give order to our *madurat* or make them disorderly. The difference is that our will is not applicable to the entire universe and is confined to our *maqdurat* within the parameter of our power" (*aql-e amali*, p. 85).[10]

This view, on Haeri's part, was in turn grounded in his approach to the fields of, on the one hand, pure or speculative reason and, on the other hand, practical reason. While he posited that with regard to pure reason, human subjectivity is limited, in the sphere of practical reason we are very much the sovereign. He wrote

> Because in principle the realities of the world are of two kinds, this type of duality has permeated the human mode of thought also, dividing the acquiring of knowledge into two categories. [On the one hand], speculative philosophy [qua knowledge] is applied to those objective realities that are beyond [the domain of] our will and [sphere of] freedom. . . . Practical philosophy [on the other hand], applies to other realities in life that are under our control. To be sure, al-Farabi and Ibn Sina as well as other Islamic thinkers . . . defined the [notion] of practical philosophy in such a way that the [domain of practical philosophy and] ethics applies to *maqdurat*, while our knowledge in speculative philosophy is confined to non-*maqdurat* [i.e., material objects in universe]. However, we should add here . . . that there is no difference between practical philosophy and speculative philosophy with regard to acquiring knowledge and thinking about the realities of existence. Both types of philosophy explore the objective realities and real entities. . . . [T]he only difference is that some of these realities are under the power and control [that is, they are in the domain of practical philosophy] of humans and some of them are without their control. . . . Otherwise, there is no substantial difference in our mode of acquiring knowledge and manner of thought (*aql-e amali*, pp. 85–86).

This attempt to bring together the two domains of practical and speculative philosophy, as we will see below, had its roots in Haeri's attempt to resolve one of the most profound gaps that has been the crucial division in the history of modernity in the West, namely the schism between speculative reason and practical reason, or between science and moral–practical spheres, or between *is* and *ought*.

Is and Ought: Hume and Kant

At many points in his discourse, but especially in his book *Discoveries of Practical Reason*, Haeri referred to, and attempted to overcome, the chasm that

David Hume (1711–1776) applied to the spheres of *is* and *ought* or facts and norms.[11] Taking Hume to task for his hemming-in of the issues, Haeri broached the idea of the relationship between moral propositions and factual judgments in the broader context of human mental capacity and modes of acquiring knowledge.

Haeri's stratagem in addressing these issues was to appeal to the creativity of the human mind in forging moral values and norms and its manifestation in free will, a phenomenon that is also closely related to our capacity to acquire knowledge about nature. Haeri argued that the same mental capacity of humans that makes possible the acquiring of knowledge is also at work in the creation of practical norms and values. As a result he insisted that the separation of the *is* and *ought* and in fact the gulf that some Western positivistic approaches, since Hume, have presumed between, on the one hand, speculative reason that has to do with the acquisition of knowledge about nature and practical reason that deals moral/practical issues, on the other hand, was unwarranted. In this respect he wrote

> The meaning of practical philosophy is that one gains knowledge over one's acts; one is the "efficient cause" [*'illat fa'ili*] over one's actions, because one is created to possess knowledge and freedom over one's actions. . . . [T]he more you have knowledge over things and the more you comprehend your relations to the [world] of being and the source of being through speculative philosophy, the better and more wisely you can act and reconstruct the world around you. As a result, the practical philosophy is in reality a branch of speculative philosophy, except that it is the type of knowledge that its object is the acts and the *maqdurat* of the subject of knowing (*aql-e amali*, p. 9).

Haeri argued that what lies at the core of being human is the closely related faculties of free will and the capacity to know, and that the two are inseparable (*aql-e amali*, p. 51). As a result, Haeri paid much attention to the role of free will in human affairs. It is thanks to free will that humans can bring about changes in the world of facts and transform the realm of *is*. Because "humans possess freedom," Haeri wrote, "and have free volition, they can change the being of things or create them from nothingness. Man has the complete freedom to create things or make changes in their being" (*aql-e amali*, p. 168). Based on these premises, Haeri concluded that "the gist of our argument and the source of the troubles in [pitting] the facts against [moral] injunctions, [lies in ignoring the] question of [free] will. In our opinion, all the intellectual disorder and incongruous discourses that have created a gap between facts and [moral] imperatives [*bayasti-ha*] . . . stems from the reality that the questions of necessity [*jabr*] and free will have not been properly analyzed and discerned" (*aql-e amali*, p. 170). In fact, Haeri believed that there is an undisrupted concatenation that connects metaphysics, concerned with issues of the Being, to the realm of science, dealing with facts of nature, and continues to the practical/moral sphere. In other words, according to Haeri, in Islamic philosophy there is a concatenation starting from the Being leading to the *is* and from there connecting to "what ought to be," and there are no breaks in links within this chain. In this respect, he wrote, "[it is] due to the fact that both 'is' and 'ought' derive from the core of Absolute Being, that philosophy is divided into speculative and practical philosophy or rationality. However, both branches of philosophy revolve around the realities of Being and there are no difference between these two branches of philosophy. The baffling gap that Hume promulgates between 'is' and 'ought' is entirely invalid and unacceptable in Islamic philosophy" (*aql-e amali*, p. 94).[12]

Even though Haeri believed that these questions were elaborately discussed and answered in Islamic philosophy, he sought further answers to these questions in Kant's analytical philosophy.[13] He thought that in the Kantian system we can also see the connection between the evaluative judgments and the realm of being, or the *is*. Haeri thought of freedom in the Kantian sense as a category belonging to the realm of being, with deep metaphysical roots, and that freedom was the most important link that connects the *is* and the *ought*. Using his own philosophical language that considered the *is* as a category belonging to the realm of *being*, Haeri wrote:

> In our opinion Kant wishes to retort to Hume that we can deduce the evaluative propositions such as "ought" and "ought not," from our [categories] of "being" [i.e., the "is"]. One of these [categories] of being is freedom, that is free will [*ikhtiar*]; and [by that we] mean the noumenon of freedom. This is the being-in-itself [*wujud fi dhatih*] of freedom, not the phenomenon of freedom. . . . These are the [categories] of being that can deliver to us the evaluative propositions, since if we do not have freedom, these moral propositions have no meaning at all (*Metaphysic*, p. 91).

In this passage we can recognize the pivotal role that the notion of human free will and freedom in general play at this level of analysis in Haeri's discourse. As such, Haeri considered free human volition as the foundation of ethical norms. Without free human will, the notion of human responsibility and commitment would be impossible. It is free volition, Haeri argued, that creates responsibility (*aql-e amali*, pp. 50–51). In this sense, it is human reason alone that determines what is good and what is evil. The determination of good and evil by reason (*aql*), itself grounded in free human volition, is therefore even outside the sphere of religion. The determination of good and evil by religion, Haeri thought, runs into logical contradiction, because perception of good and evil has an a priori character in humans and in this sense outside the sphere of religious ordinances (*aql-e amali*, pp. 215–20).

The most important corollary that Haeri derived from his discussion of human free will was the idea that free volition lies at the very the foundation of the edifice of society and politics. As he put it

> In all the three branches of ethics [*ilm al-akhlaq*], i.e., the cultivation of morals [*tahdhib akhlaq*], household management [*tadbir manzil*] and politics [*siyasat mudun*], the foundation is the human will. If there were no volition, you could not regenerate and cultivate your self and your character. If you did not possess volition, you could not organize your household management or economy on the basis of natural or mathematical order. If you did not have a will, you could not harmonize your relations with your city, your household, the country [you live in], or with other countries in the world. [This is] because the foundation of all these three branches [of ethics] is the will, the autonomy of the will, and in fact the decisiveness of the will (*aql-e amali*, p. 112).

Haeri's crucial emphasis on the role of free human volition in his views on the philosophy of ethics should be viewed as his nurturing of human subjectivity. It is in the last stage of his discourse, his thought on the social and political spheres, that this development yields very concrete results in establishing universal human subjectivity and its materialization in rights of citizenship.

Politics

The third dimension of Haeri's discourse is comprised of his political and social visions, which were based on the conceptualization of human subjectivity in the ethical sphere discussed above. Haeri's most explicit and concrete views on politics and social issues were articulated in his last book, *Philosophy and Government,* which was published in 1995 outside Iran because of the censor. However, even before this book, Haeri had laid some of the groundwork in his earlier works. One important fundamental idea was the notion of the individual as the carrier of human subjectivity. Consistently throughout his intellectual career, Haeri recognized the significance of the individual in modern society. Haeri criticized the political philosophies of Jean Jacques Rousseau and Marxism for short shrifting the individual and giving the priority to the collectivity.[14] In his view, Marxism and the communist and even socialist regimes treat the individual as a mere instrument bereft of any rights of individual membership in society. "Ontologically," individuals in these societies, Haeri contended, "enjoy no [rights of] membership, but are reduced to instrumentality. As such, they have no human rights. An instrument is an instrument. It is not a end in itself. . . . The rights that belong to society does not apply to it. . . . It has no rights; right to life, dignity. . . . Its blood and life has no sanctity unless it is an instrument for the benefit of the collectivity" (*Metaphysik*, pp. 42–43). Haeri also criticized Western democracies for reducing individuals to numbers and statistical facts (*heram-e hasti*, p. 219).

This view of the individual and the collectivity was also based on some of Haeri's philosophical reflections. The individual as a microcosm of the universal, Haeri maintained, is a "complete" and autonomous entity and therefore shares all the rights and privileges that belong to the universal. As the individual human being carries all the privileges of the human species, so does the individual member in society have all *the rights and the autonomy that one can consider for the collectivity (hekmat va hukumat*, pp. 88–89). Based on these views, Haeri firmly believed in individual and social freedoms such as the freedom of thought and even of religion in a politically pluralist system for both the Muslims and non-Muslims in an ideal state (*hekmat va hukumat*, p. 117).

Despite his persistent emphasis on the individual and the sanctity of her or his rights, since individuals live in societies and among collectivities, Haeri thought, there should be some type of equilibrium between the individual and the collectivity. Moreover, even though he firmly believed that responsibility requires freedom and the individual, Haeri was critical of the arbitrariness and whimsicality that the individual may bring about (*aql-e amali*, pp. 80–81).[15] For these reasons, he believed that the truth of the individual is only realizable in the society and the collectivity, and conversely, the reality of the collectivity can only materialize in that of each member of the society (*aql-e amali*, p. 174). In his *Philosophy and Government*, Haeri developed a theoretical framework that, based on a view of natural rights, he attempted to ground the reconciling of the individual and the collectivity. In fact, this scheme, as we will see later, is in close parallel to the notion of intersubjectivity, or more accurately universalization of subjectivity, as opposed to mere subjectivity.

Natural Anthropology of Proprietorship

In *Philosophy and Government* Haeri introduced a form of natural anthropology that laid the theoretical foundations of his political views in this last major work before his death. Based on the Islamic endorsement of private property, Haeri accorded the individual sovereignty and subjectivity over her or his property, which as an act of appropriation of nature is indispensable for one's subsistence. He called this private proprietorship [*malekiyat-e khususi*] (*Philosophy and Government*, pp. 96–97). Since we live in a social space, this private proprietorship, Haeri maintained, must be disseminated and universalized. He used a *fiqhi* notion and the corresponding terminology, *malekiyat khususi mosha'*, to convey this concept, which can be translated as "universal individual proprietorship," or, for short, universal proprietorship (*Philosophy and Government*, pp. 97–98). What he emphasized very often in this book was that the notion of universal proprietorship must not be conflated with a collective notion of proprietorship where the individuality of proprietors is obliterated in the amorphous totality of the collectivity (*Philosophy and Government*, pp. 104–5, 109).[16]

In fact what Haeri has in mind here seems to be a notion of human subjectivity based on natural rights and its universalization, which is very close to the idea of intersubjectivity, the promise of the modern world, and the foundation of a just polity. In a significant passage Haeri wrote

> Government in [our tradition, (i.e., Islam)] is based on the idea of proprietorship. It is not a proprietorship based on [positive] law or conceptual [constructs]; rather it is an ownership grounded in nature. The right to property in general is derived from the exclusive ownership of on object by another entity [i.e., subject] that totally dominates the object. The right to property by humans in their environment is one of the natural and original rights that is not subject to legislation or construction. This exclusive relation is called "private proprietorship" [*malekiyat-e khususi*]. Private proprietorship is realized in two ways: one is particular and the other *mosha'*. . . . What is meant by *mosha'* is the universalization and "inter-penetration" of private proprietorships and not a collective ownership. This type of *mosha'* property is the [foundation] of a free and open [social] space in which the multitude of humans have of necessity picked to live inter-subjectively as in a city or a nation-state. This is the meaning of the Islamic and human principle, "people are dominant over their properties."

In positing the notion of human subjectivity in these terms, Haeri rightly invested the individual as the primary carrier of subjectivity. In contrast to someone like Ali Shariati, who considered human subjectivity as the privilege of the collectivity, Haeri has repeatedly endowed the individual as the beneficiary of modern subjectivity. In *Philosophy and Government*, Haeri wrote

> In the most glorious Koran as well as in the religious rules and requirements and in Islamic ethics, whenever humans in general, or as Muslims, or the faithful, are addressed, whether [they are called upon] as individuals or as collectivities, the real addressee is the individual. Because in the same way that individuals are autonomous due to essence of being human, so are they absolutely independent in their ethical responsibilities and religious duties. Even if such terms as tribe and community (*ommat*) and the like have been used [in the Koran and other religious sources], the reference is to the individual in the community, not their sum total. A collective unit is nothing but an imaginary and abstract phenomenon and it is not reasonable to charge an unreal entity [i.e., the collectivity] with responsibility. It is only the real and autonomous individual who must accept the

burden of human responsibilities and discharge them (*Philosophy and Government*, p. 159).

This type of privilege and responsibility that Haeri attributed to the individual, to be disseminated and universalized among the citizenry, constituted the foundation of the nation in the modern sense for him (*Philosophy and Government*, p. 119). In this sense, the construction of national identity and sovereignty that is often based on religion, race, or even language, is implicitly rejected. This autonomy and independence of the individual subject, and its dissemination and universalization, constitutes for Haeri the foundation of a democratic state.

Once he established the autonomy of the individual as the basis of citizenship in the community, Haeri pointed out the absurdity of the notion of the Guardianship of the Jurist, which has been the ideological mainstay of the Islamic Republic. Guardianship, according to Haeri, is only for minors and the invalid, not for autonomous individuals who can claim the rights of citizenship. Elaborating on this theme in the last parts of *Philosophy and Government*, Haeri delivered devastating blows to the notion of the Guardianship of the Jurist and pointed out the central contradiction that this notion and institution has contained ever since its conceptualization and implementation (*Philosophy and Government*, pps. 177, 216–17, 219).

Haeri proposed the principle of representation, or *vekalat*, as the principle of organization in a democratic society that should replace the notion and institution of Guardianship of the Jurist. And of course, this entails a full parliamentary system and the election of public officials who are unconditionally accountable to their constituencies.

Notes

1. See, for example, writings by Mohsen Kadivar.

2. Most of the biographical information presented here is taken from Masoud Razavi, ed. *Afaq-e Faslafeh: Az Aql-e Nab ta Hekmat-e Ahkam* [Horizons of Philosophy: from Pure Reason to Philosophy of Law] (Tehran: Farzan Ruz, 2000).

3. Haeri makes no bones about the fact that he considered only a few elite individuals capable of pursuing philosophy. He forbade (*haram*) the teaching of philosophy to the "majority of people" because, he thought, they do not possess the vision and the discerning required for the intricate issues involved in philosophy. See *aql-e nazari*, p. 34.

4. In his argument against Being as a real predicate and thereby negation of the primacy of Existence, Kant wrote:

"Being" is obviously not a real predicate; that is it is not a concept of something which could be added to the concept of a thing. It is merely the positing of a thing, or of certain determinations, as existing in themselves. Logically, it is merely the copula of a judgment. The proposition, "God is omnipotent," contains two concepts, each of which has its object—God and omnipotence. The small word "is" adds no new predicate, but only serves to posit the predicate in its relation to the subject. If, now, we take the subject (God) with all its predicates (among which is omnipotence), and say "God is" or "There is a God," we attach no new predicate to the concept of God, but only posit the subject in itself with all its predicates, and indeed posit it as being an object that stands in relation to my concept. The content of both must be one and the same; nothing can have been added to the concept, which expresses merely what is possible, by my thinking its object (through the statement "it is") as given absolutely" (*Critique of Pure Reason* [New York: St. Martin's, 1965], pp. 506–7).

In this very important passage, Kant criticizes the traditional ontological assumption that the predicate in a logical proposition constitutes the proof of Being. As a result, Kant argues, the notion of predication cannot be attributed to the Most Perfect Being. Haeri took issue with these arguments and tried to counter them. Haeri's most significant counterargument claimed that Kant attempted to reduce all existential propositions to synthetic ones and as a result ignored the analytic type of judgments in regard to the questions of Being and reduce the Being to mere copula. This approach, Haeri insisted, is very much opposed to the Islamic philosophical tradition that regards existential propositions as belonging to the analytic type, therefore holding the Being as predicate. See *aql-e nazari*, pp. 107–15.

5. Viewed in prosaic terms, the paradoxical and elusive notions of existence and essence can be thought of as the objective external reality and its rendition by the mind, respectively. For a lucid discussion of the pair notions of existence and essence in Islamic philosophy and in the philosophy of Mulla Sadra—as well as Mulla Sadra's philosophy in general—see Fazlur Rahman, *The Philosophy of Mulla Sadra* (Albany: SUNY Press, 1975). For Mulla Sadra's philosophy, see also James Morris, *The Wisdom of the Throne: An Introduction to the Philosophy of Mulla Sadra* (Princeton, N.J.: Princeton University Press, 1981) and Hossein Nasr, *Islamic Life and Thought* (London: George Allen and Unwin, 1981).

6. While in Persian or Arabic there cannot be any distinction between "Existence" and "existence," Haeri uses the term *wujud* in slightly different senses. By rendering *wujud* as "Existence," I intend to convey his understanding of the entire system of Being. In other contexts, Haeri uses *wujud* slightly differently, that is as the "substance" that constitutes the being of all beings no matter at what level of hierarchy.

7. In his book on Mulla Sadra's philosophy, Fazlur Rahman has translated *tashkik* as "ambiguity." However, in order to avoid any misunderstanding about the connotations that ambiguity may carry, Haeri has insisted that *tashkik* should be understood as differentiation and variance in regard to existence. For this reason I have translated *tashkik* in this context as differentiation or variance.

8. In addition to the theontological system presented here, Haeri developed a parallel scheme in his book, written in English, *The Principles of Epistemology in Islamic Philosophy: Knowledge by Presence* (Albany: SUNY Press, 1992). In this book, which may be thought of as an application of epistemological approach to his

theontological views, Haeri delineated the dialectical relation between human knowledge, and therefore subjectivity, and "presence," an epistemological code for the "order" of Being. In the light of the analysis presented here, the following passage, worth quoting at length, may shed light on what otherwise might seem an esoteric book by Haeri.

> This inquiry will begin with an examination of knowledge by presence. On the basis of this knowledge, we will also try to establish the truth of the performative self-identity [subject of knowledge] in the human being. Then we will turn to its most important implication, which is the philosophical solution the paradox of mystical unity of the self with the One, and the One with the self. The analysis of the nature of knowledge by presence will then be extended: first, to specify the connotation of the concept of knowledge by presence as identical with the concept of unqualified meaning of the being of the self-identity of human nature; and second, to bring to light its radical implication, which is the rational explanation of mystical experience. Hence, mystical unity taken as anther form of knowledge by presence is expressed through the notion of the annihilation (*fana*), and the annihilation of annihilation (*fana al-fana*), which results in unity with the absolute truth of Being. However, heuristic exigencies, as well as the attempt to related mysticism to philosophy, has led this study to view the mystical annihilation and absorption as forms of knowledge by presence, yet depicted as two separate notions, interrelated in a unitary simplex, where God and the self [subject] are existentially united. While this unitary consciousness signifies an absolute oneness in truth, intellectual reflection on it yields a material equivalence between God and the self. In that case it can be inferred that the formal equation of mysticism is: "God-in-self = self-in-God"(p. 3).

In this epistemological equivalent to his theontological inquiries, Haeri articulated the secondary and epiphenomenal status of humans in the notion of "knowledge by presence," whereby humans qua "knowledge" is fused in the Being qua "presence": "In this prime example of presence-knowledge [i.e., the case of immediate self-knowledge that is not based on representation], the meaning of knowledge becomes absolutely equivalent with the very "being" of the self, such that within the territory of "I-ness," to know is to exist and to exist is to know. This is the meaning of self-objectivity of knowledge by presence" (p. 81). This view is the opposite of what Suhrawardi, according to Haeri's interpretation, seems to have posited with regard to human subjectivity.

> Basing himself on the grounds that whatever one knows of oneself by virtue of presence must count as the sole reality of one's self, he [Suhrawardi] believes that it follows that the existence of the performative "I-ness" [i.e., the subject] is absolutely pure, and that the purity of the "I-ness" in existence is nothing but its "independence" from being in another. Since in the scope of this knowledge nothing can be found in an act other than the "I-ness" of the self, the objective reality of the self must be in conformity with a mode of being that does not exist in another. This kind of existential independence counts for substantiality [i.e., the self-sufficiency of the human subject]" (p. 91).

This type of pure human subjectivity, Haeri suggested, is opposed to the notion of knowledge by presence, where the "dualism between the subject and the object, or

'I-ness' and 'It-ness'" is eliminated. However, just like his theontological views, Haeri postulated redemptive escape for the subject. In a chapter on "Mystical Unity" in *The Principle of Epistemology in Islamic Philosophy,* he wrote

> we can legitimately say that the self, as a substitute instance of emanation, enjoys knowledge of God by the presence of absorption. We can legitimately say that the self is known by God through knowledge by presence of illumination. Because of the identity of these two senses of presence in reality [emanation and absorption], they are also identical in their proportionate degrees of presence. That is to say, to the same degree that God has presence by illumination in the reality of the self, the self also, to same degree, enjoys its presence in God in the sense of absorption. Thus, in that particular stage of being, God and the self are identical (p. 146).

The precise mechanism that Haeri proposed for this redemption was the notion of the "annihilation of annihilation" [*fana al-fana*].

> The ultimate degree of annihilation is a "double" annihilation which in Sufi language is called "fana al-fana" meaning "annihilation of annihilation." In correspondence with the logical double negation, double annihilation implies the completely positive state of unitary consciousness, called in Sufi terminology baqa', meaning the unity of continuity with the One. Just as double negation logically implies affirmation, so also double annihilation arrives existentially at the complete unity with the reality of the Principle. This is what the self is in itself, which is its ever-presence in God and God's ever-presence in the self. This is the meaning of unitary consciousness (p. 158).

9. On the lofty status, that of belonging to the order of Being, that Haeri attributed to knowledge, see, for example, *aql-e nazari,* pp. 120–48.

10. The more humans have control and subjectivity over the sphere of norms and values that they have created, Haeri believed, the more they can act with decisiveness and determination. And this is desirable from the viewpoint of practical ethics, since indecisiveness and "moderation" is not of value here (*aql-e amali,* p. 11).

11. In a well-known passage on the impossibility of deriving moral injunctions and *oughts* from descriptive statements, Hume wrote

> In every system of morality, which I have hitherto met with, I have always remark'd, that the author proceeds for some time in the ordinary way of reasoning, and establishes the being of a God, or makes observations concerning human affairs; when all of a sudden I am surprised to find, that instead of the usual copulations of propositions, is and is not, I meet with no proposition that is not connected with an ought, or an ought not. This change is imperceptible; but is, however, of the last consequence. For as this ought, or ought not, expresses some new relation or affirmation, 'tis necessary that it should be observed and explained; and at the same time that a reason should be given, for what seems altogether inconceivable, how this new relation can be a deduction from others, which are entirely different from it (David Hume, *A Treatise of Human Nature,* ed. David Fate Norton and Mary J. Norton [Oxford: Oxford University Press, 2000], p. 302).

Haeri transcribed this passage in *Discoveries of Practical Reason* in English and provided a translation for it that became the basis of his discussion of Hume. See Haeri,

Discoveries of Practical Reason, pp. 14–16. For contemporary Western analysis of Hume's position on these issues, see, for example, Lewis White Beck, *Essays on Kant and Hume* (New Haven, Conn.: Yale University Press, 1978) and David Fate Norton, ed., *The Cambridge Companion to Hume* (New York: Cambridge University Press, 1993). On one of the latest important attempts to fill the gap between facts and norms from a critical theory perspective, see Jürgen Habermas, *Between Facts and Norms: Contributions to a Discourse Theory of Law and Democracy* (Cambridge, Mass.: MIT Press, 1996).

12. See also *aql-e amali*, p. 65.

13. A significant part of Kant's system was in response to Hume's type of skepticism about human intellectual capacity. And it is in Kant's discussion of predications and specially the notion of "synthetic a priori" that Haeri finds the space to posit human subjectivity qua capacity to know and act. Kant's discussions on predications and synthetic a priori in the analytic part of his philosophy was in response these types of questions. Kant demonstrated that we can achieve new knowledge with certainty, and he called this synthetic a priori. In Kant's philosophical system it is implied that this synthetic a priori knowledge or judgment is possible only because of the creative faculty of the human mind and its capacity to think novel phenomena. In this regard, Haeri elaborately discussed the issues involved in predications (*mahmulat*) and different forms of judgments in Ibn Sina and Mulla Sadra. He found similarity between Sadra's discussions of predications and those of Kant. But he acknowledged Kant's innovative understanding of synthetic a priori judgments. However, Haeri finds fault with Kant's rejection of the notion of God in the existential argument for God's existence. For Haeri's discussions on different types of predications in Kant and Islamic philosophers see, for example, *aql-e amali*, 145ff. See also Haeri's discussion of Kant in *Metaphysic*, pp. 75–100. On Hume and Kant and the notion of synthetic a priori in relation to human mental creativity, see, for example, James B. Wilber and Harold J. Allen, *The Worlds of Hume and Kant* (Buffalo, N.Y.: Prometheus Books, 1982), pp. 105–6.

14. For Haeri's critique of Rousseau's prioritizing the collectivity over the individual, see, for example, *hekmat va hukumat*, pp. 85–87 and pp. 90–95.

15. In this context, it must be noted that Haeri, like many contemporary Islamic theorists in Iran, was very much in favor of suppressing the "inner" nature and the domination of the spirit over the "instincts." The domination of nature, whether it is the outer nature or the inner nature, has characterized the Western journey toward subjectivity, with certain dire consequences that appear in full-fledged modern period in the West. Here we can see a very close parallel between the Islamic and Western paths to modernity. In *Philosophy and Government*, Haeri, describing the stage of rationality and humanism, wrote

all the acts of volition that issue from the human individuals, must naturally be accompanied by rationality and responsibility. For this reason, the deeds and acts of the individual must be under the supervision of his practical reason that has separated him from other being in creation. . . . It is in this respect that the meaning of human freedom, which is a rational and intellectual freedom, is differentiated from the absolute freedom that is synonymous with barbarity. The point is that even the natural animal inclinations and impulses that exist in the natural being and life of humans . . . must come under the command and rule of his superior nature which is his faculty of thought and intellect. . . . Therefore, all the inclinations and impulses in the natural and animal existence of man must be guided by his superior power and conquered by his human faculty and reason (*Philosophy and Government*, p. 115).

16. In this respect, in a rather sweeping generalization, Haeri wrote

[T]he difference, between, on the one hand, the society that Rousseau and all other Western sociologists have envisioned, and the society that we are now designing based upon the universal individual proprietorship, on the other hand, will be clear. The society of Rousseau and the sociologists . . . is derived from social contract and establishment of an all-inclusive union coinciding totally to the collectivity. . . . [However, in the society based upon the natural universal individual proprietorship], every single one of the citizens consistently enjoys an autonomous individual identity in all aspects of her or his natural or rational existence and nothing except death can encroach upon her or his individuality and autonomy (*Philosophy and Government*, p. 111).

6

Utopia of Assassins: Navvab Safavi and the Fada'ian-e Eslam in Prerevolutionary Iran

Sohrab Behdad

THE HISTORICAL-ISLAMIC BACKGROUND OF THE 1979 revolution in Iran and the populist character of the Islamic Republic have received careful scrutiny in the literature.[1] However, the impact of Navvab Safavi and the Fada'ian-e Eslam on shaping a distinctly populist–utopian dimension in the Islamic revivalist movement in the 1979 Iranian Revolution has received little attention.[2]

Mojtaba Navvab Safavi (1924–1956) was the founder of Fada'ian-e Eslam, a militant fundamentalist organization in Iran. This organization was active from the early 1940s to the mid-1950s, when Iran enjoyed a brief period of democratic freedom. In January 1956 Navvab Safavi and the other leaders of the Fada'ian-e Eslam were executed. Fada'ian-e Islam's principal objective was establishing an Islamic social order. Navvab Safavi, in his *Barnameh-ye Enqelqbi-ye Fada'ian-Eslam* (1950) and in a series of articles in his weekly newspaper, *Manshor-e Baradari*, draws the outline of an ideal Islamic social system.

The historical significance of Navvab Safavi's thought is in the impact that he and his organization had on the development of the Islamic character of the Iranian Revolution. Ayatollah Khomeini himself had a close affinity with Navvab Safavi, whose political career begins with the assassination of Ahmad Kasravi in the spring of 1945 in response to Khomeini's condemnation of his call for an Islamic reformation. A number of influential personalities in the Islamic Republic and some important Islamic political organizations (Hey'at-ha-ye Mo'talefeh Eslami) had some background in the Fada'ian-e Eslam. But more importantly, Navvab Safavi and his organization, by formulating the detailed plan of an Islamic utopia, established the vision, discourse, and cultural tone for a popular social movement that led to the Islamization of the Iranian Revolution. This chapter is a study of Navvab Safavi and Fada'ian-e Eslam's utopia.

Seyyed Mojtaba

Seyyed Mojtaba Navvab Safavi was born in Tehran in 1924, about the same time that Reza Khan was establishing the reign of the Pahlavi monarchy. Navvab Safavi's father, Seyyed Javad Mir-Lohi, was a cleric who, according to Navvab Safavi's biographer, put the clerical robe aside under Reza Shah's anticlerical campaign and practiced law, "defending the oppressed."[3] Seyyed Javad was arrested in 1935 or 1936 for the "slapping in the face" of Ali Akbar Davar, Reza Shah's minister of justice. Seyyed Javad was imprisoned for three years, and Seyyed Mojtaba was raised by his maternal uncle, Seyyed Mahmood Navvab Safavi, whose family name he adopted.[4] Seyyed Mahmood was a judge with an apparent secular orientation. He provided secular schooling for Seyyed Mojtaba, who went to Hakim Nezami public elementary school and continued on in the German Technical High School, both in Tehran.[5]

These years coincided with Reza Shah's secularization campaign. He established secular public education and judiciary systems, promoted secular national ceremonies, discouraged religious public practices, outlawed the widespread use of clerical garb ('aba *va ammameh*), and in 1936 forcefully promoted the unveiling of women.[6]

Navvab Safavi in his youthful years acquired a religious tendency and reportedly took part in, or possibly even organized, some anti-Reza Shah demonstrations. In 1942, when Iran was occupied by the Allied forces and Reza Shah had abdicated power, Navvab Safavi completed high school. He found a job as a metalworker an oil company and went to Abadan in May/June of 1943.[7] He worked in Abadan for six months until he became involved in a workers' protest against a British manager and fled to Najaf in Iraq in order to avoid arrest.[8] In Najaf he worked as a carpenter for half the day and studied as a seminary student the other half. We do not know who his mentors were, but it has been reported that he studied to the level of *kifaya*.[9] His biographer, who praises him and attributes to him many outstanding intellectual and human characteristics, reviews this period of Navvab Safavi's life without any specific details except that he took a room in the Madreseh-ye Bozorg Akhond and for "about three years and a half learned so much that, like the companions of Ali and the friends of Hosein in that mid-day of Ashora in Karbala, no shield was left between him and the truth to prevent his rebellion."[10] But, according to the account of one of Navvab Safavi's followers, his stay in Najaf could not have been much longer than a year since he could have not arrived in Najaf sooner than in the fall of 1943 and returned to Tehran in the fall of 1944 or winter of 1944–1945. Therefore, his theological studies in Najaf were very brief.[11]

Kasravi and Kashf al Asrar

Seyyed Mojtaba returned to Tehran to "take care of" Ahmad Kasravi, who had begun promoting Islamic reformation, or what he called *pakdini,* in a monthly journal named *Mahnameh-ye Peyman* (established in 1933) and in numerous books and pamphlets. Kasravi had received theological training and in his youth was a cleric, but later he became a secular judge. Even his orthodox opponents admit that Kasravi was an able theologian and regard his *Shari'ate Ahmadi* as the best book on the fundamentals of Islam and Shi'ism of his time.[12] Later, however, Kasravi began condemning fanaticism and advocating reform to introduce rationalism in Islam. In *Piramoun-e Eslam* he claims "there are two Islams."

> [O]ne is the religion that that honorable Arab man brought one thousand, three hundred and fifty years ago and was established for centuries. The other is the Islam that there is today and has turned into many colors from Sunnism, Shi'ism, Esmaili, Aliollahi, Sheikhi, and Karimkhani, and the like. They call both Islam, but they are not one. They are completely different and are opposite of one another. . . . Nothing is left of that Islam. . . . This establishment that the mullas are running not only does not have any benefits but it also causes many harms and results in wretchedness.[13]

More than thirty years later, Ali Shariati, another Muslim reformist, presented Islam in a way similar to that of Kasravi and succeeded in mobilizing Muslim intellectuals in a social movement that led to the 1979 revolution, while facing harsh criticisms from the clerical establishment.[14] The call for an Islamic renaissance and for Islamic rationalism had begun in Iran at least as early as the end of the nineteenth century and the Constitutional Revolution (1905–1911) when "progressive ideology" (*andisheh-ye tarraqikhahi*) was gaining ground in the intellectual and political discourse.[15] Among the early proponents of Islamic reformation were modernist intellectuals such as Mirza Malkum Khan and Mirza Fathalikhan Akhundzadeh. Kasravi's contemporary, Reza Qoli Shariati-e Sangelaji, was also another Muslim reformist. As a respected theologian, he advocated a reform (*eslah-e din*) in Islam to reflect modern realities.[16] Although from a theological perspective Shariat-e Sangelaji was a more serious challenge to the clerical establishment than Kasravi,[17] in the popular and intellectual arenas Kasravi, as a prolific author and an able

historian with some strong views about modernization of Iranian culture, received wide public attention in the early 1940s. Kasravi's attack on the fanaticism of Islam angered the clerical establishment. His *Shi'igari* (1942) was immediately banned and a new printing appeared with the title of *Bekhananad
va Davari Konand* (They Read and Judge). In *Bekhanid va be Kar be Bandid*
(Read and Act) Ayatollah Khomeini attacked Kasravi for his condemnation of
Islam and the holy Imams of Shi'is. Khomeini criticizes the Muslims and the
Muslim establishment for not taking any action against Kasravi.[18]

Starting in 1934, a monthly magazine named *Homayoun* began publication
in Qom.[19] Many articles in this magazine advocated Islamic reformation and
criticized Islamic fanaticism, superstition, and traditionalism in a condescend-
ing language appealing to the lay readers. The publisher and editor of this magazine was Ali Akbar Hakamizadeh Qomi, the author of *Asrare Hezar Saleh* (The
Secrets of a Thousand Years), published in 1943. This book, which is "full of
ridicule and insult to the holy religious ceremonies and the Shi'i clergy,"[20] was
brought to the attention of Khomeini by a group of angry *bazaaris*.[21] At that
time, Khomeini was instructor of philosophy at the Qom seminary.[22]

In 1944 Ayatollah Khomeini published *Kashf al-Asrar* (The Unveiling of Secrets) in condemnation of Islamic reformism, in general, and Shariat-e Sangelaji, Kasravi, and Hakamizadeh Qomi, in particular.[23] Although the last two
are not mentioned in the book by name, the targets of Khomeini's attacks are
quite clear. He referred to Kasravi as "that addlebrain who claims to be a
prophet"[24] (it was alleged that Kasravi claimed being a prophet), and condemned him and his followers for "burning religious books, which have come
to [us] at the sacrifice of the blood of martyrs"[25] (it was known that Kasravi
had book-burning ceremonies). Khomeini addressed all believers and asked
how it is that "you have not risen against this shameful book with its igno-
minious title[26] which appears to have been written with the words of jinn."[27]

> Our faithful believers, our honorable brothers, our Persian-speaking friends, our
> courageous youth! Read these manifestations of crime, these shameful publica-
> tions, these kernels of division and animosity, these invitations to Zoroastrian-
> ism . . . these condemnations of our sacred religion, and try to do something;
> with a national uprising, with a religious uprising . . . with a strong will, with an
> iron fist, rid the earth of the seeds of these dishonorable, shameless beings. . . .
> We are condemned in the court of our religion, we are disgraced in the view of
> the prophet of Islam. Yes! Rise up courageously and honorably, so that the arro-
> gant do not make you surrender.[28]

Khomeini calls those who make such attacks on Islam "corrupt on earth"
(*mofsed fi al-arz*) and expects "the scholars . . . who see themselves as
guardians of the faith, the Quran and the religious sacred beliefs, to shatter the
teeth of these jerks with their iron fists and to crush their heads under their

courageous feet." He expects that an Islamic government would "execute these offenders in front of the supporters of the faith."[29]

It is reported that Navvab Safavi in Najaf became angered reading one of Kasravi's books,[30] or about Kasravi.[31] He approached the *mojtaheds* and received a fatwa from Allameh Sheikh Abdolhosein Ahmad Amini[32] and (or) Ayatollah Seyyed Muhammad Taqi Khonsari to kill Kasravi.[33] For his travel to Tehran Navvab Safavi received financial support from Seyyed Asadollah Madani (who thirty-five years later served in the Assembly of Experts to draft the constitution of the Islamic Republic, was appointed as the Imam Jomeh Tabriz by Khomeini, and was assassinated in 1981[34]), Allameh Ahmad Amini (the author of the widely respected encyclopedia of Shi'ism, *Alqadir*), and Ayatollah Abolqasem Mosavi Kho'i (the Grand Source of Imitation of Shi'is in 1970s and 1980s, who died in August 1992).

It is not known if there was a direct connection between Khomeini and Navvab Safavi. One account suggests that there could have been a connection because at the time of publication of *Kashaf al-Asrar* Khomeini was an instructor at the Qom seminary and Navvab Safavi was a student there.[35] Other accounts have expressed doubt about the existence of such a connection.[36] There were only a few months from the time that Navvab Safavi left Najaf until the assassination attempt against Kasravi. There is no report that Navvab Safavi was ever a student at the Qom seminary, although it is reported that he attended the Faculty of Theology of Tehran University for a few weeks in the fall of 1944.[37] It is quite likely, however, that Navvab Safavi had read *Kashf al-Asrar.*

Upon arrival in Tehran, and with the encouragement of Seyyed Mahmood Taleqani, Navvab Safavi decided to engage in public debate with Kasravi.[38] Kasravi agreed, but after several days of debate, Navvab Safavi reached the conclusion that Kasravi must be annihilated. He bought a gun for 450 *toman* with the money that A(qa) Sheikh Hasan Taleqani, the father of the imam of the mosque in Ekbatan Avenue, acquired from two shopkeepers in his neighborhood.[39] Navvab Safavi attacked Kasravi on April 28, 1945. The attack did not prove fatal, but on March 11, 1946, as Kasravi was entering the prosecutor's office in the central building of the Ministry of Justice to respond to the blasphemy charges made against him, followers of Navvab Safavi, Seyyed Hosein Emami and Seyyed Ali Muhammad Emami, bazaari shopkeepers, attacked and killed Kasravi.[40]

Formation of Fada'ian Islam

Navvab Safavi was imprisoned for two months after his unsuccessful attempt on Kasravi's life.[41] A merchant named Oskoo'i posted bond for his release.[42]

When Navvab Safavi was released from prison, he decided to establish an association. It is claimed that Navvab Safavi even contemplated becoming a
"rural guerrilla." But a brief visit to tribal people, whom he found strongly
dominated by their lords, dissuaded him from the idea.[43] He decided to organize a terrorist organization by recruiting young devotees from the old and
traditional neighborhoods of Tehran. Haj Mehdi Araqi states that, after the
victory of the 1979 revolution and in admiration for his leader and mentor,
Navvab Safavi thought that he should "make use of individuals who, up to
now, have disturbed the peace in neighborhoods, like hoodlums (*obash-ha*) in
the neighborhoods, roughnecks (*gardan-koloftha*), thugs (*lat-ha*), and the
neighborhood bullies ('*arbadehkes-ha*)."[44]

Navvab Safavi thought that by doing this he would accomplish two objectives. First, he would "reform some deviants" and, second, since these individuals are well recognized in their localities, people would wonder about the
cause of their metamorphosis. This demonstration effect would attract more
young people to the cause. According to this follower, at first, this was the
characteristic of the individuals who gathered around Navvab Safavi, while
later on he attracted "the young people who were relatively religious" and were
impressed by his devotion to the cause of Islam.[45] Of the twenty-nine followers of Navvab Safavi arrested in 1952, nine were unemployed, four were ped-
dlers, and the rest were craftsmen (shirt maker, weaver, carpenter) or students.
Their average age at the time of arrest was twenty-five.[46]

Thus, in 1945, Navvab Safavi declared the formation of Fada'ian-e Eslam
(Devotees of Islam). In his declaration he states

> We are alive and God, the revengeful, is alert. The blood of the destitute has long
> been dripping from the fingers of the selfish pleasure seekers, who are hiding,
> each with a different name and in a different color, behind the black curtains of
> oppression, thievery and crime. Once in a while the divine retribution puts them
> in their place, but the rest of them do not learn a lesson. . . . Damn you! You trai-
> tors, imposters, oppressors! You deceitful hypocrites! We are free, noble and
> alert. We are knowledgeable, believers in God and fearless.[47]

This declaration is an attack on those who damage

> the foundation of the faith and the Quranic knowledge in the name of religion
> . . . have no mercy on the privation of the poor, throw dirt on the blessed blood
> of Hosein (peace on him) . . . make deals with robber barons and know of the
> degenerated morality of the youth of today and of their disgust from religion
> when they sow the seeds [of ruin and division].[48]

This is a proclamation of revenge and retribution. It begins with *howal'aziz*,
a reference to God's attribute, appearing in the Quran repeatedly, as the "all

powerful."[49] In fact, *howal'aziz* became the trademark of Fada'ian-e Eslam and appeared invariably on their pamphlets, leaflets, and above the title of their newspapers. God's might, on the heading of the declaration, was followed with the Persian words *din va enteqam* (faith and retribution). Equating God's power with the Fada'ian-e Eslam's retaliation (*qesas*) and retribution (*enteqam*) was the central theme of the organization. The declaration cites many verses of the Quran, including the famous martyrdom verse: "Never think that those who were slain in the cause of God are dead. They are alive, and well provided for by their Lord" (3:169). It warns those who have accumulated wealth by exploiting people to prepare themselves for "the bloody trial" of the divine justice.

> You filthy criminals! . . . You know the details of your crimes better than anyone else. . . . We have no fear and no need for anyone's help. . . . You are the source of wretchedness, faithlessness, and oppressions. By God! Our blood is boiling, and the blood of the devotees of the faith is boiling and need more blood. Giving our lives away is a delight for us, but we will not give our lives before we get yours.[50]

In the declaration there is no reference to Iran, "country," or "nation," but instead to the faith and "Islamic nations." Similarly, the call is not to fellow citizens (*hamvatan* or *hamshahri*), but to the Muslims of the world.

> The chains of subjugation and serfdom on five hundred million Muslims of the world are shatterable. For years these dreadful chains have kept the nations of Islam apart. . . . These chains are made and set by those who have been living in ignorance and savagery years after the coming of the Islamic civilization and the call of the Quran. . . . Muslim people of the world, rise up! Come to life! So that we can win back our rights.[51]

Navvab Safavi and the Fada'ian-e Eslam entered the political arena in the turbulent years that led to the premiership of Muhammad Musaddeq and the nationalization of the Iranian oil industry in 1951, followed by the U.S. CIA coup d'état of August 1953.

Political Activism of Fada'ian-e Eslam

In 1946, having returned to Iran, Kashani took Navvab Safavi and his organization under his wing and utilized them as means of political agitation, mass mobilization, and even assassinations. A follower of Navvab Safavi reports that Kashani and Navvab Safavi pledged to establish an Islamic government.[52] This, however, is not close to the truth since Ayatollah Kashani avoided entangling himself in fundamentalist issues until the last days of the Musaddeq government. Kashani, unlike the traditional position of the fundamentalist clergy since the Constitutional Revolution (1905–1911), supported the constitution, for which he said "the blood of many of our courageous and patriotic people has been sacrificed."[53] When in the heat of the campaign for nationalization of the oil industry Fada'ian-e Eslam raised the issue of closing liquor stores, imposing Islamic dress codes for women (*hejab*), and expelling women from governmental jobs, Kashani declared those who say these are "British agents, have bad intentions, or are just fools."[54] Navvab Safavi and his followers repeatedly criticized Kashani for not including in his political campaign "the holy title of faith and Islam."[55]

The alliance of Kashani and Navvab Safavi, however, remained strong until spring of 1951, when Musaddeq formed his cabinet. In this period the Fada'ian Eslam assassinated Abdolhosein Hazhir, the court minister, in the heat of parliamentary campaigns for the Sixteenth Majles, on November 4, 1949. Hazhir had confronted Ayatollah Kashani's forceful opposition in his short tenure as prime minister in 1948. Seyyed Hosein Emami, who assassinated Hazhir, was arrested immediately and faced execution on November 9, 1949. Less than two years later, on March 7, 1951, Khalil Tahmasebi, another member of Fada'ian-e Eslam, a twenty-six-year-old carpenter, assassinated General Haji Ali Razmara, who had become the prime minister on June 26, 1950. Razmara opposed nationalization of the oil industry.

Following the assassination of Razmara, Ayatollah Kashani declared that Khalil Tahmasebi "must be freed since he had carried out the assassination to serve Iran and its Muslim people. Razmara was hated and condemned by the people and this young man had only carried out the order of the court of public consensus."[56] In March 1951, Navvab Safavi issued a declaration. It begins with *howal'aziz* and continues: "The son of Pahlavi and the other criminal leaders of this illegitimate regime must know that if in three days our courageous brother Khalil Tahmasebi (Abdollah Rastegar) is not freed with full respect, they will be approaching the fall to hell. . . . And we will take care of them one by one in revenge for their past and present crimes."[57]

In assassinating Razmara, who was considered by Ayatollah Kashani and his allies to be an agent of Britain, Fada'ian Eslam carried out a political action in the context of the existing political conflicts. However, in his declaration demanding Tahmasebi's release from prison, Navvab Safavi reiterated his own ideological commitment toward the formation of an Islamic society. "Now, you the son of Pahlavi, and you the deputies in the Majles and members of the Senate . . . you and your associates must know that if you do not follow all the precepts of Islam, one by one, according to the book of the Fada'ian-e Islam [a reference to the *Barnameh-ye Enqelabi*, discussed below] you would be approaching the fall into hell."[58]

The declaration has three addenda (*tabsereh*) warning all the opposition groups and their newspapers that "Iran is the country of the followers of Muhammad and his descendants, and whoever takes the smallest step in violation of Islamic law will be dealt with in accordance with the rules of Islam"; "that the journalist must be warned not to publish sexually provocative pictures of disrespectful women"; and "the small and mischievous political cliques, dependent on the decadent foreigners," must stop their propaganda if they do not wish to be subject the retribution of the people of this "land of followers of Muhammad."[59]

On March 20, 1951, the law for the nationalization of the Iranian oil industry was passed and the activity of Anglo-Iranian Oil Company ceased, and in April 1951 upon expression of inclination of the Majles and the Senate, the shah issued the royal decree for Musaddeq to become prime minister. As Musaddeq formed his cabinet with the support of Ayatollah Kashani, the relation between Kashani and Fada'ian-e Eslam became strained. On May 10, 1951, Navvab Safavi declared, "I invite Musaddeq, other members of the National Front and Ayatollah Kashani, to an ethical trial."[60] Fada'ian-e Eslam even contemplated assassinating Musaddeq in May 1951, and Musaddeq, who found their activities disrupting when he was maneuvering out of the post-oil nationalization crisis, ordered the arrest of Navvab Safavi on June 3. While Navvab Safavi was in the Qasr prison in Tehran, Mehdi Abdkhoda'i, a sixteen-year-old Fada'i-e Eslam, son of Sheikh Gholamhosein Mojtahed-e Tabrizi, made an unsuccessful assassination attempt against Hosein Fatemi. Fatemi was the editor of *Bakhtar-e Emroz* newspaper, a member of Musaddeq's cabinet, and a vocal secular, nationalist opponent of the Fada'ian Eslam's Islamic fundamentalism. Fada'ian-e Eslam alleged that Fatemi had secret dealings with the U.S. government. Abdkhoda'i was tried as a juvenile and was kept in prison for twenty months.[61]

When Navvab Safavi was released from prison in February 1953, Kashani and Musaddeq had already begun parting ways. Kashani's faction, in strong opposition to the Tudeh Party and Musaddeq's attempt in accommodating it, began to rely increasingly on Islamic issues and moved toward becoming an opposition force against Musaddeq. The Islamic-populist politicians, most notably Makki, Baqa'i, and Haerizadeh, as well as the royalists and the anti-royalist conservatives, joined forces to oppose Musaddeq. The Tudeh Party also remained in opposition to Musaddeq for his attempt to solicit the support of the United States. The CIA coup d'état of August 19, 1953 and the return of the shah to power ended Iran's brief experience with political democracy.

Post-Coup d'État Years

Kashani, Navvab Safavi, and the Fada'ian-e Eslam celebrated the coup d'état as a victory over the danger of Communist and Soviet domination of Iran. A few days after the coup, on August 25, 1953, Ayatollah Borujerdi, the Grand Source of Imitation of Shi'is, congratulated the shah on his return from his brief exile in Rome. On the same day, Navvab Safavi published a declaration rejoicing over the fall of Musaddeq and asking the shah to follow the rules of Islam.

> If Musaddeq's government had remained [in power] for another two days and the power plays of the foreign worshipers had continued, the anger of the Muslim people would have exploded with more force than it did and they would have pulled out with their hands and teeth the veins of everyone of the despicable lackeys of the Soviet Union. . . .
>
> The country was saved by Islam and with the power of the faith. . . . The Shah and prime minister and ministers have to be believers in, and promoters of, Shi'ism, and the laws that are in opposition to the divine laws of God . . . must be nullified. . . . The intoxicants, the shameful exposure and carelessness of women, and sexually provocative music . . . must be done away with and the superior teachings of Islam . . . must replace them. With the implementation of Islam's superior economic plan, the deprivation of the Muslim people of Iran, and the dangerous class difference would end. [In this way] the Shah and the legitimate government can live in peace and happiness. On this matter our revealing book (the program of the Fada'ian-e Eslam) has shown the way.[62]

In the years immediately following the coup d'état, Navvab Safavi enjoyed a close association with the court and the government of Prime Minister General Fazlollah Zahedi. Navvab Safavi's biographer even claims that he was offered the position of minister of education and the trusteeship of Imam Reza's endowment fund (Astan-e Qods-e Razavi) and the freedom to make use of its colossal revenues in the way of Islam, as he wished. It is very doubtful that he in fact received any such offers from the coup d'état government of General Zahedi, although it is quite probable that the regime made attempts to appease him for his support of the coup and its heavy-handed political oppression, including the mass arrest and execution of the members of the Tudeh Party. It is reported that Navvab Safavi entertained the possibility of running for a seat in the Majles from Qom.[63] His biographer points out to the post-revolutionary sympathizers of Navvab Safavi that he took advantage of his cozy relationship with the court and General Zahedi only to advance the cause of Islam.[64] In 1954 Navvab Safavi attended the Islamic Conference in Jordan, then traveled to Egypt and learned about Ikwan al-Muslemin and its leader, Hasan al-Banna (1906–1949).

By 1955 Navvab Safavi became disillusioned with the post-coup d'état government, which clearly had no intention of promoting the Islamization of society and was becoming more and more a part of the political, economic, and cultural orbit of the West. The formation of the Baghdad Pact between Iran, Iraq, and Turkey (later to include Pakistan and be known as CENTO), under the guidance of the United States, was the turning point of the shah's regime in becoming dependent on the American and British governments. On November 16, 1955, Mozaffar Zolqadr, of the Fada'ian-e Eslam, made an unsuccessful attempt to assassinate Hosein Ala as he entered the memorial service held for Ayatollah Kashani's son. A few days later, on November 22, Navvab Safavi and a number of his followers were arrested. On January 17, 1956, Navvab Safavi, Seyyed Muhammad Vahedi, Khalil Tahmasebi, and Mozaffar Zolqadr were executed, following a summary trial in the same military court that ordered the execution of many members of the Tudeh Party. The execution of the leaders of Fada'ian-e Eslam was carried out without any expression of opposition or attempt for intervention by the clerical establishment, especially by Ayatollah Borujerdi, who enjoyed the power of the Grand Source of Imitation.

State and the Structure of Government

Barnameh does not have a vision of the state that is any different from what existed in the Iran of 1940s. Most importantly, it does not advocate a theocratic state. In this respect *Barnameh*'s position is distinctly different from the views of Ayatollah Khomeini, who, twenty years later, advocated Islamic government by the rule of the just jurist (*velayat-e faqih*).[65] Navvab Safavi's main concern in terms of the clerical establishment was the presence of some undesirable elements in the rank of clergies, which *Barnameh* wants the Sources of Imitation to take care of. It also promotes some minor changes in the religious establishment such as changes in the curriculum of the *madrasa*, certification of preachers (*rowzehkhan*), overseeing of the public mourning processions for Imam Hosein, and better management of religious buildings and endowments.[66]

Above all, *Barnameh* accepts monarchy. The shah is viewed as the father of the family. He should be benevolent and fatherly in ruling the people. His faith and virtues should be such that people learn from him religious faith and virtues. He, as a father, should know how everyone is doing and that no one will go hungry or lack clothing. Then, "as long as there is anyone alive in the family no one would dare to be disrespectful toward him, not to mention wanting to expel him from his home and family. Yes! The Shah must be a father, to be a father and the Shah."[67] The second printing of *Barnameh* was in the days that the shah was spending time in exile in Rome awaiting the turn of events in Iran. The shah had on many occasions expressed his devotion to Islam, such as saying in a radio speech in 1951 that "The best way to alleviate [antagonisms] is to apply the laws of Islam. If we live as true Muslims class conflict will give way to class harmony and national unity."[68] Clearly, Navvab Safavi did not have any opposition to the institution of monarchy or even to the shah himself as long as he carried out his duties as a devout Muslim. *Barnameh*'s specific demands of the monarch are that the trustees of the religious endowments (such as those of Imam Reza and his sister Ma'soumeh Kobra) be faithful and pious Muslims. Furthermore, the green flag of Islam must be placed, in addition to the Iranian flag, at all offices of the court, big mosques must be built, and "good sounding mo'zenins make the sound of *Allaho Akbar* echo in the buildings of the royal court."[69]

Barnameh asks for a Majles constituted by free election of devoted Muslims. It also suggests, in agreement with the position of Sheikh Fazlollah Noori, who opposed the Constitutional Revolution by defending the rule of Shari'a (*mashro`eh*), that the Majles is not empowered to make laws, since the laws of society are those of the Shari'a. This Majles would nullify all the un-Islamic laws passed since the Constitutional Revolution, and it would be only a forum for consultation.[70]

In this context *Barnameh* reviews the general structure and programs of twelve ministries. These are the very same ministries in operation in the 1940s and 1950s, including ministries of education, justice, interior, finance, health, culture, agriculture, foreign affairs, war, post and telegraph, and roads. *Barnameh* also proposes its program for the ministry of court.

According to *Barnameh* each ministry will pursue the conduct of affairs assigned to it, in an Islamic spirit. The issues of concern are Islamic ceremonies, education, vices and women, and economic policies.

Islamic Ceremonies

Each ministry is expected to carry out appropriate religious ceremonies in its offices throughout the country. In all offices the green flag of Islam must be placed along with the flag of Iran, mosques must be built, and the sound of *azan* and *Allaho Akbar* must be heard from them. Clothes worn in public are viewed as slogans and flags that should reflect the religious allegiance of the nation. It is therefore a responsibility of the Ministry of Interior to make European hats and ties ("the harness of colonialism") illegal, and uniform clothes for men would possibly be made.

Education

Barnameh calls for compulsory elementary education for five years, and high school would train students in the areas of students' specialization. Only courses such as chemistry, physics, natural sciences, mathematics, and medicine, which are useful for society, would be taught, and "a large number of courses would be eliminated."[71] Half of the day would be for theoretical courses, and the other half for practical ones. In this way those students who do not make it to college would have learned a trade when they complete high school. This is a format very close to the technical school that Navvab Safavi attended. The other proposals of *Barnameh* are teaching of Islamic courses instead of "excessive" playing hours and a complete separation by sexes. Iranian public schools have always been separated by sex. In addition, *Barnameh* would prohibit men from teaching girls and women from teaching boys.

Barnameh's strong criticism is directed to university education. It asks

What has happened to Iranian students, who upon their graduation have learned nothing but idol worshipping, treason and wastefulness? . . . Yes! The criminal minded statesmen must die and virtuous and knowledgeable teachers of Islamic thought and of Iranian affairs must teach the basic elements of sciences in a simple way to the children of Islam so that . . . [we] will become immune to the political infusion that results in criminal activities, faithlessness, wretchedness and pursuit of lust instead of science and knowledge.[72]

Ayatollah Khomeini had a similar complaint about the university system, which he attempted to cure with his cultural revolution about thirty years later.[73]

Economic Policy

Barnameh spells out specific economic policies without addressing the general characteristics of the economic system. However, about a year after the publication of *Barnameh*, Navvab Safavi explained his view of an Islamic economic system in his column on Islamic economics in *Manshor-e Baradari*. He condemned both communism and capitalism. In communism the "workers and shopkeepers (*kaseb*) . . . have no control over their work and over their gains from it . . . and what they do is more like forced labor of prisoners than the work of free human beings."[74] On the other hand, capitalism provides "unlimited rights" and allows "anyone to accumulate as much as they can and in any way that they can, even if these people bring all the existing capital under their control."[75]

These lines of demarcation drawn by Navvab Safavi between Islam, capitalism, and communism have become the hallmark of the plan for the economic
system promoted by the Islamic revivalist movement and many "Islamic economists."[76] More than thirty years later, in order to settle the dispute among
various tendencies in the Islamic movement in Iran, Ayatollah Khomeini tried
to draw the same lines between Islam and other economic systems.[77] He stated
in his last will

> Islam does not approve of an oppressive and unbridled capitalism that deprives
> the oppressed masses who suffer under tyranny. On the contrary it firmly rejects
> it both in the *Quran* and in the Sunna. Some who . . . are ignorant . . . have pre-
> tended . . . that Islam is in favor of unconstrained capitalism and private prop-
> erty. . . . They have misinterpreted Islam and have covered its enlightened face
> [Neither] is Islam a regime that opposes private property, like communism,
> Marxism and Leninism. . . . Islam provides for a balanced regime. My advice . . .
> is . . . do not be influenced either by the empty propaganda of the pillaging and
> oppressor pole of capitalism or by the atheistic pole of communism.[78]

The details of *Barnameh,* however, reveal that Navvab Safavi's "third way"
is a Sismondian capitalism[79] of shopkeepers and artisans where altruism,
charity, and religious taxes (*zakat* and *khoms*) act as leveling devices in a society that would honor everyone equally and would provide for all their needs.

In this utopia, where usury is forbidden, the majority of the population
would work as shopkeepers and artisans while some would be employees of
the government. The peasants' fate would not be much different in this idealized Islamic society than it was in the 1940s. While *Barnameh* advocates improvements in the education of the rural population and in the irrigation system, and requires regular prayers in the offices of the Ministry of Agriculture,
it pays no attention to the system of rural land ownership and does not promote any form of a land reform.[80] It appears that the landlords are among the
virtuous citizens of the ideal Islamic society as long as they do not commit any
of the vices enumerated in *Barnameh.*

The shopkeepers and artisans would be living in a world of total harmony
with the wealthy and fortunate merchants, while the corrupt and arrogant
capitalist thieves and embezzlers of public funds would be done away with. In
this society whoever lacks capital can acquire it thanks to the generosity of the
wealthy. "In the mosque, the poor and the rich will sit together as brothers,
and the rich will give capital to the poor. The rich trust the poor as Muslims
and know that the poor will pay them back as they make profit in their busi-
nesses."[81] The government would be responsible for providing employment
for the poor and unemployed. It would be among the responsibilities of the
Ministry of Interior to build shopping centers (*pasazh*) to provide space for

the poor and unemployed, who "would receive sufficient capital, in amounts befitting their abilities, from the no-interest loan funds (*qarzolhasaneh*) or charity, to open a business (*kasb*)."[82]

Nowhere in *Barnameh* does Navvab Safavi deal with the well-being of wage earners, their wages, work conditions, or unionization. This neglect of wage earners is consistent with the mercantile (*kaseb*) outlook toward labor. There is an abundance of authoritative religious sources for justifying this position. Imam Sadeq (the Sixth Imam) said "whoever works for wages has limited his livelihood."[83] The degradation of wage labor is complemented with statements in praise of commerce. Imam Sadeq said that "trade adds to your wisdom," and Imam Mosa (the Seventh Imam), declared, "In the morning go to the bazaar, where you acquire dignity."[84] Prophet Muhammad himself has promised special places in heaven to merchants.[85] When in the post-revolutionary years the *modarressin* (professors) of the Qom seminaries wrote an official treatise on Islamic economics, they expressed the opinion that in an Islamic society "the individuals who possess the necessary aptitude and background would own their needed means of production to work independently, or in partnership with others in the cases that large capital is needed."[86]

In this land of benevolence, civil servants "from custodians to ministers, should receive sufficient monthly incomes to pay for their necessities of life and to provide for their well-being at a legitimate level."[87] The officials who have higher expenses than their salaries may draw "an amount equal to their legitimate expenses from the charity fund,"[88] which every ministry would have one for its employees. The source of charity funds would be the contribution of the generous individuals and the payment of *zakat*, which would be compulsory and collected under the supervision (but not by) the Sources of Imitation.[89]

Once these institutions are set up, the economy may be left to the invisible hands of the market. *Barnameh* ridicules economics, economists, and economic planning as elements of a scheme to deceive and rob people and add to their misery. It states that the best way of increasing the wealth of the country is to run it as a grocery store, and adds, "The best lessons in economics, for which many universities have been established in the world, are the careful and scientific calculations of Iranian shopkeepers, who always figure their exports and imports carefully, buy at the proper time and sell at the opportune moment. . . . They always expand and rarely have seen suffering in business or in their well-being."[90]

In short, the economy is a big bazaar composed of many grocers, other shopkeepers, and artisans and civil servants with some generous and charitable, wealthy merchants, much like those whom Navvab Safavi knew, associated with, and received financial support from. Those who could not make it on their own would be helped through the generosity of others. The government would carry on certain responsibilities. It would maintain law and order and would make sure that Islamic codes of conduct are strictly enforced. It would educate the youth (public education by government is accepted) and carry out other social responsibilities. The shah would rule with fatherly care and affection over a nation of happy, virtuous people. And the market, the bazaar, would be left on its own to operate smoothly and efficiently. The welfare of the *kasebs* would result in the welfare of all. After all, "*kaseb habib-e khodast*" (*kaseb* is God's friend).

Conclusion

With the execution of Navvab Safavi, the activity of the Fada'ian-e Eslam ceased. But the political movement leading to the June 1963 uprising in opposition to the shah's White Revolution brought the sympathizers of Navvab Safavi together and in association with Ayatollah Khomeini. In the same year they formed the Allied Islamic Associations (Hey'at-ha-ye Mo'talef-ye Eslami) and took part in some political activities as the grassroots organizing force for Ayatollah Khomeini and other politically active clerics. There were three neighborhood associations, which organized the mourning ceremonies in commemoration of Imam Hosein's martyrdom in the month of Moharam. Haj Mehdi Araqi (one of Khomeini's main organizational arms in the 1979 revolution, who was assassinated a few months after the revolution by Forqan, a rival Muslim group), Habibollah Asgaroladi (the minister of commerce for many years in the Islamic Republic, and deputy in the Majles), and Seyyed Asadollah Lajevardi (the director of the infamous Evin Prison in the Islamic Republic and the central figure in execution and indoctrination of the members of Marxist groups and the Mojahedin) were among the founding members of the alliance. The alliance had some association with Mortaza Motahhri, the ideologue of the Islamic Republic, and Ayatollah Beheshti, the chief architect of the Constitution of the Islamic Republic. The alliance had only brief periods of political activity between the 1963 uprising and the 1979 revolution, but it nevertheless served as the historical link between Navvab Safavi's movement and the Islamic Republic. For a short while after the 1963 uprising, the alliance carried out some underground activities that led to the assassination of Prime Minister Hasanali Mansour on January 21, 1965. Immediately the shah's regime arrested and executed a number of alliance leaders. By the early 1970s, the political agitation of Ali Shariati attracted young Muslim intellectuals to a politicized Islam, which was viewed by some of his critics as no better than Kasravi's *pakdini*. At about the same time, the Mojahedin Khalq promoted an interpretation of Islam viewed by the Islamic orthodoxy as not too distant from Marxism. Then, the Alliance of Islamic Associations turned into the Allied Islamic Parties. These loosely formed, small associations constituted the organizational nucleus of the Islamic movement in the revolutionary and postrevolutionary years.

In the decades between the political activities of Navvab Safavi and the formation of the Islamic Republic much had changed in Iranian society. In the latter period Islam entered the political arena as a leading force riding on the power of the revolution. Therefore, undoubtedly, the character of the Islamic revolutionary movement was different from that of the terrorist movement of the 1940s. There are, however, distinct similarities in the populist–utopian character of both movements. The attempt of the Islamic Republic to create a nation of small shopkeepers alongside a powerful state that would be engaged in managing modern enterprises was the logical evolution of the Navvab Safavi's utopian plan. By the 1970s the number of "capitalist thieves," "corrupt bureaucrats," and "embezzlers of public funds" had multiplied many times; "vices" had reached epidemic proportions; women had gone far beyond the acceptable domain of "maidenhood"; and there was no longer any possibility, or need, to call the shah back as the father of the nation's family. Therefore, there was much more to be done by the Islamic Republic of the 1980s than could be imagined in the 1940s. There were more liquor stores to be smashed in the first days of the revolutionary movement, more theaters and cinemas to become Islamic. There was much more wealth to be confiscated and put in the hands of the associations of the "pious merchants" of the bazaar to put to appropriate use as revolutionary foundations to lend a hand to the oppressed (*bonyad-e mostaz'fan*) or for the family of martyrs (*bonyad-e shahid*), or the needy (*bonyad-e panzdah-e khordad*). The words of Islam could be placed on the flag, mosques could be established in every ministry and governmental office, and public officials could be required to conduct daily payers at the place of work. The universities could be turned inside out by a cultural revolution and cleansed of the ideals of "idol worshippers." The thieves' hands could be cut off, and the fornicators could be stoned. Men and women could be made to sit in different sections of buses, *hejab* could become compulsory, and the moral police could apprehend the violators. There was a historical link connecting the Islamic Republic to the Fada'ian-e Eslam, as demonstrated by Ayatollah Khomeini's preference to sit under *a howal'aziz* sign in his public appearances. It all began with Khomeini's Kashf al-Asrar.

Notes

An earlier version of this chapter was published in *Middle Eastern Studies* 33, 1 (January 1997).

I would like to express my appreciation to Denison University for supporting this project through a faculty development grant. I am also grateful to Bahram Tavakolian for comments and corrections. The opinions expressed and the errors remaining are all mine.

1. See, among many others, Nikki Keddie, *The Roots of Revolution: An Interpretative History of Modern Iran* (New Haven, Conn.: Yale University Press, 1981); Misagh Parsa, *Social Origins of the Iranian Revolution* (New Brunswick, N.J.: Rutgers University Press, 1989); Mansoor Moaddel, *Class, Politics, and Ideology in the Iranian Revolution* (New York: Columbia University Press, 1993); and Ali Rahnema and Farhad Nomani, *Secular Miracle* (London: Zed Press, 1990).

2. Ali Rahnema and Farhad Nomani have made a major contribution in analyzing the essentials of Navvab Safavi's thought. See their "Competing Shi'i Sub-Systems," in Saeed Rahnema and Sohrab Behdad, eds., *Iran after the Revolution: Crisis of an Islamic State* (London: I. B. Tauris, 1995). The literature available in Persian dealing with the political career of Navvab Safavi is cited throughout the analysis that follows.

3. Seyyed Hosein Khoshniyyat, *Seyyed Mojtaba Navvab Safavi: Andisheh-ha, Mobarezat va Shahdat-e O* (n.p.: Manshor-e Baradari, 1982), p. 15.

4. Ibid. Ervan Abrahamian in *Iran between Two Revolutions* (Princeton, N.J.: Princeton University Press, 1983), p. 258, suggests that Seyyed Mojtaba adopted his last name "to identify with the founders of the Shi'i state in Iran." The choice, however, seems to be a matter of Seyyed Mojtaba's childhood circumstances.

5. Haj Mehdi Araqi, *Nagofteh-ha* (Tehran: Khadamat Farhangi Rasa, 1991), p. 18.

6. In many cases, particularly in the cases of clerical garb and unveiling of women, coercive measures were used. For example, civil servants were required to wear Western clothing and to bring their wives to official ceremonies without a veil. In many cases the police attacked and derobed male or unveiled female "violators." See Houchang Chehabi, "Staging the Emperor's New Clothes: Dress Codes and Nation-Building under Reza Shah," *Iranian Studies* 26, 3–4 (1993): 209–29.

7. Araqi, p. 20

8. Araqi, pp. 20–21.

9. Nasser Pakdaman, "Darbareh-ye Qatl-e Kasravi," *Nameh-ye Kanoon-e Nevisandegan-e Iran dar Tab'id* 2 (1990). *Kifaya* is a reference to the book with this title by Sheikh Mulla Kazem Akhond-e Khorasani, one of the required readings in the intermediate level of religious training. See Michael Fischer, *Iran: From Religious Dispute to Revolution* (Cambridge, Mass.: Harvard University Press, 1980), pp. 247–48.

10. Khoshniyyat, p. 17.

11. Nasser Pakdaman, "Bazham Darbareh-ye Qatl-e Kasravi," *Nameh-ye Kanoon-e Nevisandegane Iran dar Tab'id* 4 (1994).

12. Ali Abolhasani (Monzer), *Shahid Motahhari, Afshagar-e Tote'eh* (Qom: Entesharat-e Eslami, 1983), pp. 172–73.

13. Ahmad Kasravi, *Dar Piramoun-e Eslam* (Tehran: Payedar, fifth printing, 1969), p. 4.

14. Ali Shariati, *Mazhab 'Aleyh-e Mazhab, Majmo'eh-e Asar*, vol. 22 (Tehran: Entesharat-e Qalam, 1981) and Sohrab Behdad, "A Disputed Utopia: Islamic Economics in

the Revolutionary Iran," *Comparative Studies in Society and History* 36, 4 (October 1994).

15. Fereydoun Adamiyat, *Andisheh-ye Tarrqqi va Hokomat-e Qanoon* (Tehran: Entesharat-e Kharazmi, 1972).

16. See Yann Richards, "Shari'ati Sangalaji: A Reformist Theologian of the Rida Shah Period," in Said Amir Arjomand, ed., *Authority and Political Culture in Shi'ism* (Albany: State University of New York Press, 1988).

17. Richards, p. 161

18. Pakdaman, "Darbareh-ye Qatl-e Kasravi" (1990), p. 184.

19. *Mahnameh-ye Peyman* announces the forthcoming publication of *Homayoun* and praises its publisher and editor, encouraging its readers to read it. See Abolhasani, p. 315.

20. Abolhasani, pp. 302–3.

21. Richards, p. 160.

22. Ibid.

23. Richards, p. 161. I have used Richards's translation of the title of Khomeini's book and that of Hakamizadeh Qomi.

24. Rohullah Khomeini, *Kashf al-Asrar* (Qom: Entesharat-e Azadi), p. 73.

25. Rohullah Khomeini, p. 74.

26. A reference to Ahmad Kasravi, *Shi'igari* (Tehran: 1942).

27. A reference to Kasravi's use of language. He introduced many ancient Persian words in his effort to de-Arabize the Persian language.

28. Rohullah Khomeini, p. 74.

29. Rohullah Khomeini, pp. 104–5.

30. Araqi, p. 20.

31. Hussein Heykal, *Iran: Koh-e Ateshfeshan* (Qom: Adiyyat, 1987), a collection of articles translated into Persian, quoted in Platform-e Chap, *Fada'ian-e Eslam va Maqalat* (Los Angeles: Platform-e Chap, second printing), p. 99. See also Pakdaman "Darbareh-ye Qatl-e Kasravi," p. 182.

32. Allameh "is the title of respect for one who knows all the Islamic sciences" (Fischer, p. 289).

33. Khoshniyyat (pp. 18–19) suggests Amini was the *mojtahed* who ordered Kasravi's death. Abolhasani, p. 176 states that Navvab Safavi assassinated Kasravi with a permission issued by Khonsari. Araqi (p. 22), however, states that when Navvab Safavi asked the Najaf *mojtaheds* their views about Kasravi, Haj Hosein Aqa Qomi declared him a heretic, but Amini "who realized why the Seyyed was asking the question" did not express an opinion.

34. Ali Rabbani Khalkhali, *Shohada-ye Rohaniyyat Shi`eh dar Yeksad Sal-e Akhir*, vol. 1 (Qom: Entesharat-e Maktab-e Alhosein, 1982), pp. 570–74.

35. Platform-e Chap, p. 100.

36. Pakdaman, "Darbareh-ye Qatl-e Kasravi," p. 186.

37. Manochehr Qaem-maqami, "Nakhostin Didar Dar Kelas," *Nabard-e Mellat* (8 May 1980). The author of this article states that Navvab Safavi was his classmate in the fall of 1945, when he told the author that he had come from Najaf "to defend Islam" against Kasravi. Obviously the date stated by the author is incorrect. Navvab Safavi

could have been a student at the Faculty of Theology only sometime between the fall of 1944 and the early spring of 1945.

38. Araqi (p. 22) refers to Navvab Safavi's meeting with "Aqa-ye Taleqani." At the time that Araqi was writing his memoirs, Ayatollah Seyyed Mahmood Taleqani was well recognized as one of the leaders of the revolution, therefore it is most probable that Araqi's reference is to Ayatollah Taleqani.

39. Araqi, p. 22.

40. For a careful scrutiny of the details of Kasravi's assassination see Pakdaman, "Darbareh-ye Qatl-e Kasravi" and "Bazham Darbareh-ye Qatl-e Kasravi."

41. Araqi, p. 26.

42. Khoshniyyat, p. 19.

43. Araqi, pp. 28, 30.

44. Araqi, p. 26.

45. Ibid.

46. Abrahamian, p. 259.

47. Khoshniyyat, p. 21.

48. Khoshniyyat, p. 22.

49. See for example, 3:5, 6:96,16:60, 31:27, 39:5, and 39:37.

50. Khoshniyyat, p. 22.

51. Khoshniyyat, pp. 22–23.

52. Khoshniyyat, p. 32.

53. Platform-e Chap, p. 139.

54. Platform-e Chap, p. 140.

55. Khoshniyyat, p. 30.

56. Khoshniyyat, p. 58.

57. Khoshniyyat, p. 57.

58. Ibid.

59. Ibid.

60. Platform-e Chap, 20.

61. Khoshniyyat, pp. 84–88.

62. Khoshniyyat, pp. 127–28.

63. Khoshniyyat, pps. 122, 129, 149–50.

64. Khoshniyyat, p. 128

65. [Khomeini], "Islamic Government," pp. 25–166.

66. Navvab Safavi, *Barnameh*, pp. 16–17.

67. Navvab Safavi, *Barnameh*, pp. 51–52.

68. Abrahamian, 267.

69. Navvab Safavi, *Barnameh*, p. 53.

70. Navvab Safavi, *Barnameh*, pp. 55–56.

71. Navvab Safavi, *Barnameh*, p. 18.

72. Navvab Safavi, *Barnameh*, pp. 19–20.

73. See Sohrab Behdad, "Islamization of Economics in Iranian Universities," *International Journal of Middle East Studies* 27, 2 (1995).

74. Navvab Safavi, *Barnameh*, p. 238.

75. Ibid., p. 238.

76. See, for example, Sohrab Behdad, "Property Rights in Contemporary Islamic Economic Thought: A Critical Perspective," *Review of Social Economy* 47, 2 (1989).

77. Behdad, "A Disputed Utopia."

78. [Rohullah Khomeini] *Imam Khomeini's Last Will and Testament*, English translation (Washington, D.C.: Interest Section of the Islamic Republic of Iran, Embassy of Algeria, n.d. [1990]), p. 36.

79. Jean Charles Léonard Sismonde de Sismondi, *Nouveaux principes d'économie politique* (Paris: Chez Delaunay, 1819) vol. II.

80. Navvab Safavi, *Barnameh*, pp. 43–44.

81. Navvab Safavi, *Barnameh*, p. 4.

82. Navvab Safavi, *Barnameh*, pps. 13, 31.

83. Daftar-e Hamkari-ye Hozeh va Daneshgah, *Daramadi bar Eqtesad-e Eslami* (n.p.: Salman-e Farsi, 1984), p. 301.

84. Daftar-e Hamkari, p. 288; see also Behdad, "'A Disputed Utopia," pp. 798–99.

85. For statements in praise of merchants in the Quran, see Maxime Rodinson, *Islam and Capitalism* (Austin: University of Texas Press, 1978), pp. 16–17.

86. Daftar-e Hamkari, p. 303.

87. Navvab Safavi, *Barnameh*, p. 34.

88. Ibid.

89. Ibid.

90. Ibid.

III

INTELLECTUAL DISCOURSES
OF MODERNITY

7

Blindness and Insight:
The Predicament of a Muslim Intellectual

Hamid Dabashi

AFTER THE SUCCESS OF THE ISLAMIC REVOLUTION in Iran in the late 1970s, it has now become something of an academic exercise in futility to give an account of the secular disposition of the country at large in the immediate decades preceding that cataclysmic event. When Ahmad Shamlu, the most distinguished secular intellectual of his generation, died on July 24, 2000, his funeral had an air of an archaeological excavation about it, something quite mummified and eerie about the most elegant poetic voice of the last two centuries dying in his homeland now officially called "the Islamic Republic of Iran." From participant observers, suddenly an entire generation of secular intellectuals turned into chronographers and historians of their own demise. As the fortunes of the Iranian secular intellectuals declined, the stars of a new constellation of religious intellectuals were on the rise. With an Islamic shadow now cast on the entire history of the Iranian colonial encounter with modernity, these religious intellectuals excavated a long and illustrious pedigree for themselves. From Mulla Ahmad Naraqi, early in the nineteenth century, all the way to Ali Shariati in the wake of the Islamic Revolution of 1979, the religious intellectuals sought and found a sustained and legitimate genealogy for themselves. The secular intellectuals went into hiding or left the country; some of them were brutally murdered. The religious intellectuals became prominent, occupying official positions, and a vast spectrum of government-sponsored forums was put at their disposal. Secular intellectuals no longer dared speak the truth to power. Religious intellectuals were in power.

Practically all the major religious intellectuals today have had official affiliations, in one capacity or another, with the Islamic Republic. But, as it is in the very texture of critical intelligence, religious intellectuals soon parted ways with the clerical circle in power. They assumed oppositional postures, and very soon they became subject to official censure, periods of incarceration, vicious attacks by hoodlums hired by the religious Right, and even assassination attempts. A quarter of a century into the successful institutionalization of the Islamic Republic, the term "Religious Intellectuals" (Roshanfekran-e Dini) has now assumed complete discursive legitimacy.

What does it exactly mean to be a "religious intellectual"?[1] How can an intellectual be religious, and how can one metaphysically committed to a set of doctrinal certainties be a free thinker, an autonomous subject, a critical intelligence, an intellectual? No single person embodies this series of contradictions in contemporary Iran better than Abdolkarim Soroosh.[2] The most eloquent and controversial public intellectuals in postrevolutionary Iran, Soroosh, trained as a pharmacologist in England in the 1970s, soon emerged as the leading theorist of the Islamic Revolution. He went so far as being a leading member of the Advisory Council of the Cultural Revolution, appointed by Ayatollah Khomeini to "purify" Tehran University of all its "undesirable" elements, that is, secular members of the faculty incompatible with the brutal Islamization of the curriculum. But very soon after the successful institutionalization of the Islamic Republic, Soroosh began to articulate theoretical positions on Islam that have come against severe criticism by the clerical establishment.

The predicament of Abdolkarim Soroosh as a religious intellectual is thus symptomatic of a larger phenomenon, at once liberating and arresting, in the colonial history of encounter with modernity. By far the most significant public intellectual of postrevolutionary Iran, Soroosh personifies the predicament of a much larger universe of failed ideas. Understanding him is thus not yet another exercise in futility, a Monday morning quarterbacking after the game of the Islamic confrontation with modernity is over. In his blindness and in his insights, Soroosh represents some two centuries of bewildered attempts to locate a historical agency for the Muslim subject in modernity. The colonial integration of Islamic societies at large into the project of capitalist modernity necessitated countercolonial responses that could not but adopt global modes of social mobilization (Nationalism and Socialism) or create its own nativist sites of resistance (Islamism). The intellectual pedigree that Soroosh now represents claims such illustrious luminaries as Seyyed Jamal al-Din Asadabadi, "al-Afghani" (1838–1897); Muhammad Abduh (1849–1905); Rashid Rida (1865–1935); Ali Abd al-Raziq (1888–1966); Abu al-Ala al-Mawdudi (1903–1979); Shaykh Mahmud Shaltut (1892–1963); and, perhaps most significantly, a protégé of Sir Seyyed Ahmad Khan named Chiragh Ali (1844–1895). Soroosh is the very last metaphysician in the Islamic colonial encounter with modernity, the very last ideologue in whose blindness and insights we can see the decline and fall of the most massive mutation of Islam in its long and languid history into an "Islamic Ideology."

The Islam of Soroosh's birth and breeding was an Islam invented in colonial encounter with modernity. Gradually code-named "Islamic Ideology," the Islam of Soroosh's world and vision was coined and made current to match and balance "the West," by far the most massive manufacturing of a categorical concept in modern history. "The West" was the categorical conception of a world that had emerged in modernity to replace medieval "Christendom," substituting, ipso facto, its dynastic components with the aggressive formation of the European national cultures. As the most dominant categorical imperative of colonizing modernity, the selfsame "West" was in dire need of its alternating Others in order to authenticate and believe itself. "The East" in general and "Islam" in particular were invented by Orientalism, as the intelligence arm of colonialism, to match and mate "the West." Muslims themselves in turn categorically bought into this colonial game, whether they opposed "the West" and aggressively mutated Islam into a site of ideological resistance to it or else collaborated with it and sought to ape and emulate its manufactured ethos.

Soroosh is the last in a long and illustrious line of Muslim ideologues who have remained blissfully oblivious to this dialectical constitution of their ancestral faith and have categorically failed to disengage its systematic counter-essentialization: "Islam and the West." But where Muslim ideologues have failed, history has succeeded. It is the fate of Abdolkarim Soroosh to have articulated his particular conception of Islam in silent conversation with "the West" at a time that "the West" no longer exists. As the polar opposites of "the West" and "the Rest" are collapsing because the rapid globalization of labor and capital can no longer sustain their once-ideological necessity, Soroosh has been busy dehistoricizing "Islam" in a mute dialogue with an absent interlocutor. As the world and all its binary oppositions dissolve into the modular formation of one singular empire, Abdolkarim Soroosh has been hard at work saving an essential Islamic noumenon to allow its phenomenological variations to have an historical conversation with a modernity that has long since vacated the scene. He is so late in the last round that some have taken him as early in the next and call him "The Muslim Martin Luther"!

Saving the Sacred from Its History

Soroosh's principal proposition in his massive output is what he has called the "Theoretical Contraction and Expansion of Religious Knowledge" (Qabz-o-Bast

Theoric-e Shari'at). This theory is predicated on a metaphysics that he considers entirely innovative, which is to say "hermeneutic" (*ma'refat-shenasaneh*) and "historical" (*tarikhi*), as opposed to "theological" (*motekallemaneh*) and "interpretative" (*mofasseraneh*).[3] The critical proposal of the theory of the "Theoretical Contraction and Expansion of Religious Knowledge" is to separate "Religion Itself" from the knowledge of religion, and to put forward the proposition of "the historicity" or "the subjectivity (*tabe'iyyat*) of the religious knowledge to other forms of human knowledge."[4] In this theory, Soroosh argues for the contemporaneity of religious knowledge, its accountability, as it were, to its historical presence. According to Soroosh, the purpose of his theory is to "give a new space and possibility to religious democracy."[5] He also admits that he has sought to "predicate the religious government on the religious society."[6] Epistemologically, and Soroosh does consider his proposition epistemological in nature, he wishes to predicate what he calls "the current and collective hermeneutics" on "the collective reason," and "religious knowledge" on "anthropology and jurisprudence," and "religion on justice" and not "justice on religion." In principle, he wishes to propose "the fallibility of religious knowledge" but safeguard "Religion Itself."

Soroosh's conception of the "Theoretical Contraction and Expansion of Religious Knowledge" is linked to an equally significant notion he calls the "Historical Constriction and Dissipation of the School of Thought" (Laff-o-Nashr-e Tarikhi-e Maktab). What he means by that is that religious knowledge not only theoretically contracts and expands by being in dialogue with its contemporary modes of knowledge but that it also fluctuates in response to its historical vicissitudes. Religious knowledge, to be carefully separated from "Religion Itself," is tested both theoretically and practically by being placed, ipso facto, in an historical location. Thus, he proposes that

> the perception that our contemporaries have of religion is at once a creature of history of the religious life and is placed in the geography of human knowledge. Tomorrow, when the book of history is turned again to a new page, and upon the soil of knowledge newer flowers have grown, religious knowledge too will assume a different pigmentation and aroma. And this transformation of colors and aromas is an inevitable and endless phenomenon."[7]

Equally related to both conceptions of the "Theoretical Contraction and Expansion of Religious Knowledge" and the "Historical Constriction and Dissipation of the School of Thought" is Soroosh's insistence on an "Ennobling Understanding of Religion" (Dark-e Azizaneh-ye Din). What he means by that is the proposition that a religion can as much advance a people toward progress and dignity as it can compel them toward backwardness and misery. One's understanding of a religion must thus be geared toward an ennobling of its adherents, their being propelled into an active role in history. The religious hermeneutician, as a result, will have to have a *soda-ye sarbala*, or "the ambition of upper-mobility."[8]

Finally, the "Theoretical Contraction and Expansion of Religious Knowledge," the "Historical Constriction and Dissipation of the School of Thought," and the "Ennobling Understanding of Religion" are all capped by the "Collectivity and Currency of Religious Knowledge" (Jam'i and Jari Budan-e Ma'refat-e Dini). What Soroosh means by that is the historical facility of providing a "multiplicity of human understanding of the Silent Religion, [and thus] preventing the possibility of the ideologization of religion, and inhibiting the propensity to give one final, exclusionary, and official interpretation of it."[9]

Thus separating "Religion Itself" from the knowledge of religion, the principal task of Soroosh is to place the production of such knowledge in what he calls "the general geography of human knowledge." Hermeneutic in its stated ambition, Soroosh's project is targeted toward a systematic epistemology. With a trace of Thomas Kuhn's conception of scientific progress, with the obvious exception of his paradigmatic constitution of the scientific truth, Soroosh believes that human knowledge does not progress cumulatively, but exponentially and qualitatively. "The knowings do not accumulate unit by unit, but, instead, constitute a composition, atom by atom. The resulting composition is constantly in qualitative increase."[10] Any new "intrusion" into human knowledge requires other modes and modalities of accumulated and systematized knowledge to negotiate a new position for themselves. Thus new discoveries in physics, for example, or in cosmology, or in astrophysics, require substantial epistemological remodulations in religious and philosophical thought. There is a domino effect to the neighborly relations among human and religious sciences. More specifically, we may conclude from Soroosh's concern about the qualitative changes in human sciences that the Copernican revolution in particular and the substitution of a heliocentric conception of universe for a geocentric one has had enduring consequences for religious knowledge by having a destabilizing effect on its entire epistemological foregroundings.

The result of this challenge to the continued viability of religious knowledge is that unless one has a current anthropology predicated on a host of related sciences that animate and inform that anthropology, one cannot have a legitimate and current theology. But since in addition to anthropology, not in the disciplinary but in the etymological sense of the term, a whole host of other sciences are in a constant process of progression and development, then so must be the understanding of a religion.[11] Resorting to the sixteenth-century Shi'i philosopher Mulla Sadra Shirazi's theory of "Transsubstantial Motion" (al-Harakah al-Jawhariyyah), Soroosh suggests that the changing notions of belief in accordance with the changing topography of human knowledge does not diminish the continued legitimacy and authority of religious knowledge. Quite to the contrary, it contemporizes and further authenticates the sanctity of religious knowledge. The medieval Islamic metaphysics was predicated on a historically specific physics. Now that that physics has changed, so must the metaphysics respond to and correspond with it.

For the progress of the profane, human knowledge, Soroosh believes in its reality sui generis. Man is constitutionally disposed to discover things, and that is compatible with the Divine Will too.[12] If in "the West" people have abandoned their faith, it is because they could no longer cultivate a legitimate theology that was compatible with their emergent, scientifically based anthropology. In Iran, Soroosh points out, those who want to safeguard their faith and secure it against all historical odds and those who argue for a progressive theology are both responding to the onslaught of modernity and its threatening postures against the historically received understanding of their ancestral faith.

As man is constitutionally disposed to progress in his discovering of new things, so is he also in possession of an absolute and abstract reason, Soroosh adamantly believes. He accuses those who believe in the historicity of reason of Hegelianism. "Their judge is history not Reason. Because they have followed the command of the god-of-history and beheaded Reason."[13] Soroosh exonerates himself from any attachment to Hegelianism or historical determinism. He believes reason and the progress contingent upon it are realities sui generis and immune to any subjugation to history. He denounces the Hegelians for the principality of history in their understanding of reason and of rationality. He maintains that his argument for contemporizing religious knowledge is not tantamount to collapsing his hermeneutics into what he considers to be the Hegelian historical determinism.

> The theoretical development of the religious knowledge (Shari'at) thus assumes an acceptable meaning. The proposition is not to add an item to what is doctrinally enjoined, or subtract an item from what is doctrinally forbidden, nor is it to abrogate a Qur'anic verse, or to distort a Prophetic or Imami Tradition. That which is being changed is the human understanding of the religious knowledge, and that which remains constant is the Religion Itself.[14]

Soroosh then proceeds to suggest that the philosophical, juridical, or even literary orientations in Islamic intellectual history are precisely such examples of multiple readings of one Singular Sacred Reality. History is silent, but historians make it sing different songs. Nature is silent, but physicists and biologists make it tell different stories. One needs to have a theoretically consistent awareness of these multiple readings. It is useless to compare a stagnant jurisprudence with a progressive jurisprudence when we still lack the principles of a hermeneutics that inform us as to what exactly is stagnant and what is progressive and why. Soroosh considers himself as having provided that hermeneutics.

From this premise Soroosh concludes that so far as the nature and function of religious knowledge is concerned, it cannot remain indifferent to changes that occur in other modes of knowledge. Since the knowledge of the material world is changing, so must our knowledge of the "Religion Itself." There ought to be a dialogue between religious and nonreligious forms of knowledge. Here, Soroosh gives primacy of action to the knowledge of the world at large and not to the religious knowledge, because

> that which rationally and practically comes first and stands first and designs the geography of knowledge in general are the human forms of knowledge, that is to say, one first has to have a conception of the world and of the humanity in it before one can place the function of prophethood in it. In other words, it is the human Weltanschauung which gives the permission of entrance and issues the license of legitimacy to the religious Weltanschauung, and not vice-versa.[15]

Upon this extraordinary suggestion, Soroosh then proceeds to argue that a comprehensive understanding of the human condition is the function and responsibility of what he calls "the religious intellectual" (*roshanfekr-e dini*),[16] who is to make peace between the two worlds and lead them to benefit from each other. Soroosh obviously considers himself an example of that prototype of "the religious intellectual," operating on the borderline of religious and nonreligious modes of knowledge. Guiding the religious intellectual in this project is what Soroosh calls *aql-e parsa*, or "the pious intellect." "The pious intellect" does not lead to the periodization or to the relativization of "Truth," the charge against which Soroosh is particularly adamant, but to an active dialogue between the multiplicity of human knowledge and the singular, but ever-changing, nature of the religious knowledge. That task, Soroosh confesses, is not easy. It is much easier to shut the doors and windows to one's fortress of belief and keep a simple conviction in certain eternalities, safe and sound against all active intrusions of doubt. But it is much more courageous and indeed inevitable to dwell in the transsubstantial motion of a religious knowledge that fluctuates and keeps itself afloat against the tumultuous sea of intergalactic changes in human forms of knowledge. To formulate a hermeneutic that corresponds to that difficult task, the religious intellectual must be as diligent, serious, comprehensive, and principled as the functionaries of the human sciences are.

Soroosh summarizes the principles of his hermeneutics in three major steps: (1) a description of the developmental nature of religious knowledge,

(2) a causal analysis of the reasons of and the mechanics behind this development, and (3) an encouragement that Muslims should engage actively in advancing this development.[17] He points out that a cursory look at any form of knowledge, or even a literary tradition, demonstrates that man's understanding of things is constantly on a course of steady progress. Without admitting as much, Soroosh's is an essentially Hegelian teleology in which man's knowledge of things is on a perpetual course of progress. Soroosh is emphatic that the kind of "progress" he proposes pertains to what he calls the "secondary" forms of knowledge that are produced on the "primary" sources of the religious tradition. This he emphasized so that his clerical critics would not accuse him of considering the sacred texts and the sacred knowledge of the "Faith Itself" to be subject to historical progress. When the heavenly sanctity of the sacred revealed itself to mortals, Soroosh argues,[18] then it inevitably became sullied by human reality, and it is a reading of the vicissitude of the dialogue between the sacred and the profane that is the subject of investigation for religious hermeneutics.

Soroosh is equally careful to separate the essence of belief and the religious rituals related to it from the subject of his hermeneutic investigations.[19] These are eternal, sacred, and the signs of divine attention to the mortal creatures. The subject of Soroosh's concern, on the contrary, are the worldly, earthly, and historical vicissitudes of a knowledge of that sacred essence in the context of what he repeatedly calls "the geography of human knowledge." Here he demands an extraordinarily diligent observance from the religious intellectuals who ought to be both aware of the nonreligious knowledge and actively read them against the principality of their "Religion Itself" and the forms of religious knowledge pertinent to it. Man, as a result, ought to be seen in the mirror of the faith, the faith in the mirror of man, but in both these cases, it is the developmental and progressive nature of the knowledge of the world that are the deciding factors. Soroosh's theory of knowledge is neither accumulative, nor completely Kuhnian. He does not believe that knowledge is incrementally accumulated, nor does he believe, as does Kuhn, that there are epistemic breakthroughs in the production of knowledge. He believes that every new item of knowledge that is added to our inventory of knowledge forces the other accumulated ones to resituate, redefine, and replace themselves.

Scientific discoveries, as a result, do not ipso facto discredit the accumulated forms of knowledge, but force them to redefine and replace themselves in accordance with the factual and epistemic assumptions of the new findings. This principle is as much applicable to religious knowledge as to nonreligious knowledge. The Ptolemaic geocentric cosmology, for example, required one kind of consistency in all other related and nonrelated forms of knowledge, whereas the Copernican heliocentric cosmology another. If the climactic condition of the world, Soroosh adds,[20] was limited to one season, there were logical consistencies of one sort operative in it. But as soon as the second, third, and the fourth season appear, all such consistencies need to be reworked. On the basis of this epistemological stipulation, Soroosh then proceeds to examine some of the most recent Quranic commentaries by such contemporaries of his as Seyyed Mahmud Taleqani and 'Allamah Tabataba'i in order to begin to map out their underlying, but never articulated and theorized, hermeneutic principles.[21] These principles are presumed and followed by these Quranic commentators and yet not completely thought through or actively theorized. Such deliberate and conscious theorization and articulation of the already practiced incorporation of contemporary nonreligious forms of knowledge into religious knowledge is the principle hermeneutic task of Soroosh. In doing so, he does not occasionally hesitate[22] to demonstrate how such contemporary luminaries of Shi'i thought as 'Allamah Tabataba'i would hold one specific epistemological position in their Quranic commentaries and yet do not think through a systematic account of their hermeneutics, and as a result would have to hold totally unacceptable doctrinal positions. Because 'Allamah Tabataba'i, Soroosh contends, did not think through a systematic and consistent hermeneutic apparatus, then in such problematic places as the male and female children of Adam and Eve he would run into difficulties. When Tabataba'i has to address the Quranic assertion that from Adam and Eve their male and female offspring emerged, and thus when they married then sisters and brothers must have been able to marry, Tabataba'i must believe, as he does, in the conventionality of religious laws and not in their essentiality (*fitri*).[23] This is a constitutional problem in Tabataba'i's position, Soroosh contends, because we cannot believe in the mere conventionality of religious laws. They are, Soroosh believes, natural, quintessential, and essential. Tabataba'i falls into the trap of having had to consider incestuous or even homosexual relationships as potentially acceptable to a religion the moment he conventionalizes and de-essentializes the sanctity of the religious laws. He falls into that trap because he does not think through the implications of one epistemological assertion for the rest of his hermeneutic system. A hermeneutic "system" is precisely what Tabataba'i and all other religious thinkers of Islam have hitherto lacked and what Soroosh is henceforth providing them with. In short, there is a juridical Islam, and there is a philosophical Islam. There is a mystical Islam, and there is a theological Islam.[24] The function of a hermeneutician like Soroosh is not to judge between 'Allamah Majlisi, a tenth/sixteenth-century Shi'i traditionalist, and 'Allamah Tabataba'i, a fourteenth/twentieth-century Shi'i philosopher. The task of a hermeneutician is to see upon what hidden and unarticulated assumptions their respective readings of the faith are predicated upon, and then set himself the task of monitoring and articulating those principles. Soroosh is that hermeneutician that the Shi'i (and the Islamic) intellectual history has lacked and now achieved.

> To summarize: religious knowledge is a humanly achieved form of understanding and, as such, quite similar to other forms of knowledge in a constant state of flux. The Contraction and Expansion of Religious Knowledge is always contingent on fluctuations in other forms of knowledge. Religious knowledge, in other words, is not independent of our growing knowledge of nature. Thus in the same way that non-religious knowledge is progressing constantly so must religious knowledge.[25]
> This sets an active responsibility of contemporizing the religious knowledge. To have a "contemporary" knowledge of a religion means a four-fold task: (1) Our understanding of religion must be compatible with the current status of knowledge of the time; (2) Our understanding of religion must be influenced and aided by the current status of knowledge; (3) It must be responsive to the theoretical questions of the time; and (4) It must be responsive to the practical questions of the time.[26]

To elucidate further his distinction between "Religion Itself" and the knowledge of religion, Soroosh gives an account of historiography,[27] in which he argues that what remains constant is the historical events themselves, and what is changing is the reading of those events in light of new theoretical developments in historiography. In his account of the theoretical changes in historiography, which though without any footnote are nevertheless modestly informed by the current status of the discipline, Soroosh in fact goes far beyond anything achieved in the theoretical sophistication of Islamic historiography in either Persian or in Arabic. His principal purpose here, though, is to strike a similarity between the theoretically informed historian and the "Silent" nature of historical events, and the suggestion of a similar relationship between the changing character of religious knowledge and the immutability of "Religion Itself." As historical events and texts

> Religion, too, is sitting silently, waiting for us to question It. We will get to know It in correspondence with responses It gives to our questions. Imagine a scientist who is sitting silently, not uttering a word. It is our questions and his answers that gradually reveal his character to us. This character is constantly subject to re-constitution. The person who asks him only philosophical questions (because he himself is philosophically oriented), would get to know him as a philosopher, and the person who asks him only literary questions and hears in response literary answers puts upon him a literary cloak.[28]

Soroosh's most ambitious intention is to argue for a similarity between nature and religion, and thus between the changing logic of knowledge produced on one and on the other. Natural laws are constant, but our understanding of them is subject to progress. God is unchanging and perfect, but our understanding of God is changing and imperfect. Religion and religious dogma are immutable, but our interpretation of them is subject to historical mutation. This is the principal proposition of the theory of "the Theoretical Contraction and Expansion of Religious Knowledge."[29] Religious knowledge is itself a human knowledge, despite the fact that its object of study is a nonhuman reality. This knowledge has a collective and current status, and is in a constant state of progress. Religious knowledge is located in the midst of other forms of human knowledge and has (or ought to have) a persistent dialogue with them. The more legitimately a religious knowledge is sitting among other forms of human knowledge, the more intelligent, current, and relevant the questions it can ask from the otherwise "Silent Religion." In addition, there must be a consistency between the interpreters' current understanding of nature and their understanding of religion. Religion and nature are the products of one creator.[30] Thus the understanding of them ought to be concurrently consistent. The religious intellectual must begin with a universal understanding of the history and the geography of contemporary knowledge of the historical person and the world in which she or he lives. The evolving understanding of religion must then be compatible with those other forms of knowledge. The concurrent correspondence of religious knowledge with nonreligious knowledge will thus constitute the epistemological foregrounding of asking new, pertinent, and liberating questions from religion and making it continuously relevant to the contemporary modes of knowledge. Identical facts, such as the rising of the sun,[31] have different meanings when they are read in the context of different theories of cosmology, for example. The world is thus like a written text: "No written text reveals its own meaning. It is the language-knowing mind that reads meaning into it. Sentences are hungry for meaning, not pregnant with them."[32]

The simpler a mind, the simpler the meaning it reads into the-world-as-the-text (this Soroosh calls "raw realism"), whereas the more complicated the mind, the more sophisticated the meaning it reads into the world-as-the-text (this he calls "complicated realism"). How exactly is a text to be well understood? Soroosh takes his readers through three successive steps. First, we need to understand the world and the worldview of the author; second, we need to understand the logical and historical antecedents of the subject of the text; and third, we bring our own theories and knowledge to the text.[33] This hermeneutic system anticipates and concludes a religious knowledge that originates in this world but targets the sacred, the "Religion Itself," that Soroosh has delegated to the other.

Divesting Agency from the Subject

Two sets of interrelated anxieties inform Abdolkarim Soroosh and his elaborate attempt to take Islam itself out of history: (1) the general anxiety of facing modernity itself, intensifying (2) the particular anxiety of being party to a political triumph of Shi'ism, which in the classical Shi'i paradox is tantamount to its moral defeat.[34] Understanding Soroosh, as a result, is understanding the end of Islamic ideology, the collapse of its political viability, the defeat of its aspirations to posit a legitimate location for itself once it was dragged into a conversation with modernity. When today we look at Soroosh's proposition about the "Theoretical Expansion and Contraction of Religious Law," more than two decades into the success of the Islamic Revolution in Iran and more than two centuries into the meandering history of modernity in the region, we see that his project comes at the tail end of some 200 years of actively mutating Islam into a site of ideological resistance to colonialism, the venue from which we received the European project of Enlightenment modernity. Responding to those two anxieties, Soroosh has two simultaneous projects, one global to Islam, the other local to Iran: first, to dehistoricize what he calls "Islam Itself" in order to safeguard it for posterity and make it immune to political catastrophe every time it has to have a conversation with modernity, and second to separate the political success of Shi'ism from its instantly manifested moral collapse.

The paradox of Shi'ism is constitutional to its doctrinal origin and has scarcely anything to do with its particular predicament in modernity, while the predicament of modernity is circumstantial to its colonial periphery, where Soroosh receives it. Shi'ism is paradoxical. It morally fails at the moment of its political success. Soroosh's attempt to separate "Islam Itself" from its history is to save it from its success. Modernity, meanwhile, is paradoxical on its colonial edges, so Soroosh has to save Shi'ism from its failures. Saving Shi'ism from its success (in order to break its constitutional paradox) and from its failure (in order to sever its link with modernity) combine to lead Soroosh to suppose and suggest a "Religion Itself," which is immune to its own political success and moral failure internally, as it is immune to its ideological failure and moral success externally. If we take Shi'ism as the unfulfilled promise of Islam, as we may, Soroosh's project as a Shi'i Muslim intellectual is to save Islam from a paradox constitutional to its formative doctrines and a predicament accidental to its modern history. He has been too busy articulating his theory to recognize these subterranean anxieties that inform and sustain this ambition. That he ultimately fails is less an indication of his theoretical limitations than evidence of his historical tardiness. Soroosh is late, and he does not see it.

The most significant aspects of Soroosh's work are his acute, however inarticulate, awareness of the constitutional paradox of Shi'ism, that it morally fails at the moment of its political success, and his attempt to break it. His entire hermeneutic apparatus is targeted toward an active separation of the political success of Shi'ism from its moral failure and thus safeguarding Shi'ism from its own success. Soroosh's proposition to separate "Religion Itself" from the knowledge of religion is to keep "Shi'ism Itself" intact and yet subject the religious state, as a manifestation of the religious knowledge, to a historical dialectic. He believes that Iranian society is constitutionally religious and thus needs a religious government, and that religious government, by definition, will have to be Shi'i. But he does not want the political failings of an Islamic republic discrediting "Islam Itself" or "Shi'ism Itself." Thus "Islam Itself," or "Shi'ism Itself" will have to be segregated, quarantined, from the political failures of an Islamic republic. The critical move of Soroosh to achieve that end is to expand the hermeneutic circle in charge of the historical articulation of religion. To do that, he deauthorizes the clerical establishment as the sole custodians of the sacred. The clerical establishment has been the exclusive organ of interpretation in charge of making the sacred accessible to its social constituency. Soroosh, on the trail of a genealogy that includes Ali Shariati, wishes to dismantle that privilege. But this time he does so from the middle of his historical hermeneutics

> The [assumption of] the silence of the religious knowledge, contrary to what is imagined, will not render it susceptible to the whimsical imagination of intruders. But of course it will prevent [its interpretation] from becoming the exclusive prerogative of a single group who thus have a claim on it, and who having reached one interpretation wish to prevent or proclaim as blasphemous all the others. Thus, understanding religion, and indeed understanding it well, is incumbent upon everyone, everyone being equally a participant in and responsible for the construction of religious civilization and of civility, which belong to everyone and which constitute a commonly received Divine Gift. The understanding of no one and no group excludes others from understanding religion and understanding it well, nor does [shrugging from that responsibility] excuse his ignorance. "We all stand alone in front of God."[35]

That expansion of the hermeneutic circle achieved, Soroosh heralds and unleashes an avalanche of lay interpretations to usher his ancestral faith onto the battleground of modernity and yet save it from its historical failures. He has fully recognized that the premodern discourses authenticating the faith or fortifying it to face modernity are just too much invested in the "Religion Itself," and he wishes to dislodge that investment. He has a far more accurate conception of the devastating power of modernity and its ability to corrode into the very fabric and texture of "Religion Itself." Left to decompose with its historical dismantling, the very core of the sacred will equally lose its metaphysical claim to legitimacy. Soroosh wishes to save the "Religion Itself" against its successive failures to face modernity, while saving Shi'ism in particular, which as a religion of protest is the very soul of Islam, from its incidental political success.

Soroosh fails to achieve his objectives. That failure is less a matter of theoretical blindness than a measure of historical belatedness. Soroosh is the last Muslim ideologue, the very last layer in a variegated site that was actively cultivated in colonial response to modernity, and precisely in its representation of the very last gasp for an air of legitimacy his writing marks the death of Islamic ideology. The Islam of Soroosh's captive imagination was invented in modernity, in response to colonialism, and as such it matched and countered "the West," the other, more pernicious, invention of modernity. As a global, and increasingly globalizing, movement, the European project of modernity abstracted and universalized its bourgeois point of origin and code-named it "the West," and in turn unleashed an army of Orientalists to invent a succession of Eastern Others to originate and authenticate the otherwise false assumption of "the West," chief among them "Islam." Soroosh does not know that. He takes the Islam of his colonized imagination for his ancestral faith. The result is a double jeopardy: the metaphysical foregrounding of what he calls "Islam Itself" and the equally metaphysical underpinnings of modernity (itself), which to aggravate the result even more and make it more deadly he receives through the petrified imagination of a colonial subject, combine to give his expansive prose an absolutely terrorizing certainty. But the problem is that with the dawn of globalization, the Islam of Soroosh's colonized imagination no longer has an Other against which it can articulate itself, nor does it have the imperial power with which to assert itself. In the absence of that binary opposition ("Islam and the West"), which made both its parties possible, Soroosh is in effect carrying on a heated debate with a dead interlocutor, with the ghost of an apparition once called "the West." What has remained after the death of that interlocutor is the phantom pain of "Islam and the West," still haunting the perturbed imagination of a Muslim intellectual long since rendered irrelevant by the world at large.

The reason that Soroosh fails in his stated objective is that he is proposing what he calls a "progressive theology" in conversation with a modernity that no longer exists. Conversation with modernity is what Muslim intellectuals have been conducting over the last 200 years. Today that conversation is no longer viable or even possible, because one side of the dialogue is no longer there. The European project of modernity has now imploded epistemically from within, by its own inner self-negation, long after it had already contradicted itself externally at its colonial borders. At the colonial edges of its claim to universality, Enlightenment modernity never had any claim to legitimacy. But now even for the European intellectuals, constitutionally blind to the colonial catastrophes of modernity, it is obscene to believe in the promises of a modernity that had the Holocaust up its sleeve. Soroosh does not realize that the Islam that he now has in his mind is a dialectical outcome of a conversation under duress with a modernity that no longer exists. So in effect, that Islam that came into conception by virtue of that dialogue no longer exists, because it no longer corresponds with the lived realities of living Muslims. That Islam is dead. What Islam will emerge in a globalizing context where all binary oppositions have melted away is yet to be seen. "Islam and the West" mirrored, originated, and authenticated each other in the speculum of each other's reflection. Take one away, the other no longer exists. Soroosh himself, as a result, is the phantom body of an intellectual who can only make sense of the presumption of two transparent realities that used to mirror each other. Those two mirrors removed, the entire oeuvre of Soroosh's writing is an exercise in futility, a ghostly apparition, real only in the mirror of a dialectical negation that no longer is. The world has moved beyond the presumption of a Western center and its peripheries. The viability and usefulness of the categorical imperative code-named "the West" has now dissolved into the global formation of an empire that can no longer sustain the legitimacy of any nation-state, any national culture, or any civilizational thinking.[36] Soroosh does not know any of these and as a mobile piece of archaeological curiosity can only simulate a dead duel, an outdated and stale redoux of once a furious debate between "Islam and the West," as a particular brand of the entirely bogus game of "Tradition versus Modernity." We can no longer think in those terms. The world has left that false opposition behind.

Even if its ghostly interlocutor was not dead, the "progressive hermeneutics" that Soroosh proposes is simply too petrified by the European project of Enlightenment modernity to take it to task. It takes modernity ahistorically for granted, divests itself of its most sacrosanct, and thus most viable, elements, and punches with vacant gloves. In fear of modernity destabilizing Islam, Soroosh deposits Islam itself in a metaphysical safe box and in the process inadvertently cross-essentializes modernity out of its own history. Modernity is modern. It is very recent in its invention and coinage. The fiction of reason and progress that it invented was entirely recent in its coinage and currency. Michel Foucault in *Madness and Civilization* thought that it was needed to imprison the unreason in mental asylums in order to define itself in reasonable terms. But we know that it needed a much bigger space to deposit its shadowy nightmares and that it invented the Orient as a much larger abode of unreason and backwardness in order to ascertain itself in reason and progress. So the interlocutor that Soroosh wishes to engage is really a moving target, amorphous in nature—it may feign an existence in the peripheral anonymity of its colonial translations, but it has lost all credibility in its original claim to authenticity. We can no longer take it seriously, let alone be intimidated by it and hide our innermost vulnerabilities from its ferocious fangs. Disillusioned European intellectuals like Foucault, at their best, may seek in vain to detect a prophetic resistance (alternative) to the catastrophe of modernity that Khomeini once personified and Soroosh now theorizes. But our historical facts no longer allow for any such illusions. Such illusions lead to the eloquent articulation of an "Islam Itself" that aggressively mutates in ever more miasmatic spaces—this at a time of predatory globalization of capital and labor. Taking modernity too belatedly seriously, Soroosh is letting loose the self-abstracting metaphysical underpinnings of "Islam Itself," colonially conditioned, exactly at a time when the material world is expanding in ever larger disproportionality of globalized capital exploiting impoverished labor. Soroosh, as a result, is pushing "Islam Itself," so far as it can have any meaning in a postmodernity beyond its feeble control, toward a metaphysical metastasis, a theological mutation, an epistemic vaporization, where it can signify absolutely nothing because it can mean just about anything.

In awe of modernity, Soroosh is petrified into a numbing positivism that lacks any conception of not just the range and topography but in fact the content and epistemic foundations of sciences being predicated on institutions of power outside their claims to autonomy. Absent in Soroosh's conception of social and biological sciences, with which he believes the religious sciences ought to converse, is any awareness of the presence, force, and ferocity of power in their very epistemic and operative parameters. He has a numbingly positivist conception of knowledge formation devoid and independent of all human interests, completely autonomous in its operation, so much so that if the military conquest of space is epistemically conducive to the advancement of a certain astrophysics as opposed to others, Islamic theology becomes contingent on the whims of American generals at the Pentagon. This does not concern Soroosh in the slightest. He believes that Islamic sciences need to be conversant with the changing discourses of scientific modernity. What constellation of global power and class interest informs and sustains the production of such scientific modernity is not of immediate concern to Soroosh. His is an essentialized and dehistoricized conception of science as solid and eternal as his Religion Itself. By essentializing "Religion Itself" as a noumenon sui generis, Soroosh equally essentializes modernity as a transhistorical reality. Blindfolded by modernity itself (otherwise how could he think of Islam itself?), Soroosh sees the dual imperatives of reason and progress as immutable and does not even see them as modern inventions in the course of Enlighten-

ment modernity and in the full service of a certain mode of the economic production of reality. Tucking away "Religion Itself" from the slings and arrows
of outrageous fortune, Soroosh is also, negationally, dehistoricizing the
modernity that has scared the sacred witless, as if modernity is now so triumphant that the sacred has no recourse except running away into the bosom
of the absolute. Soroosh is far too Hegelian for his own benefit.

All of these failures, in having a critical grasp of the origin and vicissitude of
the European project of modernity, pale in comparison to the catastrophic anthropology that is contingent on Soroosh's theology. Changing, he suggests,
would be the human understanding of religion and constant "Religion Itself."
In proposing this, Soroosh is categorically oblivious to what will happen to the
historical agency of the subject he has thus in his implicit anthropology de-
pleted of all his sacred certitude rooted in historical experience, and waving in
the air by the fluctuating wind of his ever-changing understandings. What use
would that "Religion Itself" have for the historical person once it is ritually and
piously tucked away in some sacred safe-deposit box? What an empty shell of
wavering beliefs would man be without his most sacrosanct convictions put on
the line, exposed to historical elements? Faith, as in hope for an alternative to
human misery, becomes a matter of private piety, publicly irrelevant. A pre-
cious piece of antiquarian interest, perhaps, a museum piece of incidental curiosity, but inconsequential on the battlefield of the person's presence in the
world. Trying to save "Islam Itself" from its doctrinal paradox and historical
predicament constitutes the constellation of a very good set of intentions,
paving the way for some catastrophic consequences. Soroosh's project certainly succeeds in saving "Religion Itself" both from its political success and its
ideological failures, but in the process he squarely manages to deplete Muslims, qua Muslims, from historical agency. Once their "Religion Itself" is
squarely essentialized and safely deposited in some extraterrestrial domain,
Muslims, qua Muslims, will have no historical investment in their faith or any
historical agency in their world. Soroosh's theology may indeed be quite clever,
but his anthropology is positively disastrous. The "Religion Itself" is not particularly saved from this theology either. It too is cut off from its worldly presence, its historical relevance, as it is irrelevantly saved and deposited in the museum of dead certainties. Saving the sacred from its history means
manufacturing an empty shell instead of a historical person with moral
agency. The sacred that is saved from profanity of the historical person is a
museum piece of exotic curiosity, quite expensive among the antique dealers
of historical pieties, worthless in the streets and deserts of human suffering.

Soroosh is no Martin Luther (1483–1546) of his faith, as some have suggested him to be. Soroosh is the Mulla Sadra (1571–1640) of his time, with half

his philosophical genius, twice his metaphysical certainty. Like Mulla Sadra, Soroosh has the creative courage of trying to combine two opposing forces in Islamic intellectual disposition, law and philosophy, the nomocentric and the logocentric proclivities effectively at war against each other throughout the Islamic intellectual history. He equally inherits from Mulla Sadra his poetic prowess to fuse the nomocentricity of the Islamic law and the logocentricity of the Islamic philosophy, with the homocentricity of Islamic mysticism. Soroosh's fascination with Rumi is not a belated addendum to the massive output of his restless, yet alarmingly poised, writings. It is constitutional to his hermeneutically breaking the back of Islamic law by subjecting it to a philosophical distinction between its essence and its attributes, its noumenal certainty and its phenomenal doubts, its metaphysical otherworldliness and its historical mutations. The catastrophic difference between the two is that Mulla Sadra did most of his serious philosophizing in the privacy of his exile in a remote village in central Safavid Iran, whereas Soroosh does his in the full publicity of an increasingly globalized space that is checked only by the obscurantism of his writing in Persian. The result might be irrelevant for the rest of the world that does not read Persian but is deadly for those who do—the captive audience of some 70 million Iranians who having barely survived a retrograde monarchy are now collectively tormented by a medieval theocracy, falsely promised by an eloquent prophet, while in the throws of the globalizing terror of capital and labor, of which they know very little, to which they have no choice but be victim. At a time when Iranians at large need to recognize the bestial barbarity of the globalizing terror of capital on labor, Soroosh is intellectually leading them to ever more expansive spaces of a metaphysical thinking that evaporates the reality of Muslims themselves into the paradisiacal nonity of "Islam Itself." Instead of responding to the globalizing terror of the postmodernity of capital and labor, Soroosh's "hermeneutics" corresponds to its metaphysical constitution of a digitized empire of abstractions (I understand that Soroosh's followers have established an Internet site for him!).

The entire spectrum of Soroosh's discursive universe is a locally outdated, globally irrelevant nativism rendering the very philosophical culture that generates and sustains it epistemically self-absorbed and universally exotic. Soroosh is the very last relic from the "Islam and the West" archaeological site in whose insights we can see how the pathology of power divides to conquer, and in whose blindness we can imagine otherwise than being trapped in a false binary opposition. Separating the historical readings of Islam from "Islam Itself" seeks to safeguard an iconic conception of religion in order to save it for posterity and then offer a carbon copy conception on which history can leave its footsteps and traces. This, in a simpler language, is to try to have your cake and eat it too. This also is the final fear in facing modernity, the anxiety of a colonized, petrified mind writ large, and all of that at a time when the project of modernity itself has self-destructed. Having failed to face modernity, and having mutated itself into the rotating mirror of realities originated elsewhere, Islam is finally made by Soroosh to run for cover and leave behind a conceptual surrogate, a historical shadow, to face the world. This is worse than trying to have your cake and eat it too. This is postulating an agential impossibility, where historical agency is impossible because we are no longer real when we have checked ourselves out of history, imagined a hidden metaphysical haven to run to, where we never face the real because we are not real. We are the shadow of our own former faith.

"So Hallow'd and So Gracious is that Time"

Islam can no longer speak. It has no particular interlocutor. Its once Western interlocutor has now vaporized into the thin air of globalization. Islam has become mute. Molla Omar and Osama bin Laden are its last silent soliloquies, its very last, violent, gasp for air. Faceless, voiceless, suicidal, they face an enemy beyond their imagination. But precisely in their amorphous anger they mirror the phantasmagoric violence of a mode of globalization that the most devastating military machinery in human history, now led by George W. Bush, can barely begin to claim or control. The war is no longer, if it ever was, between "Tradition and Modernity," between "the East and the West," or between "Islam and the West." The war is not between U.S. imperialism and the Taliban, or al-Qaeda either. The war is between a monstrous apparition called globalization and the mirror reflection of the terror it visits upon the world, now code-named "Terrorism." The U.S. army may now fashion itself to become the military arm of globalization, as al-Qaeda is made to represent its carbon copy, "Terrorism." But the battle lines are far too amorphous and porous to yield their imaginative geography so early in the game.

The very ideas of the nation-state, of cultural identity, and of civilizational boundaries have long since lost their categorical legitimacy. After the events of September 11, 2001, the retrograde ideas of such instruments of power as Samuel Huntington and Bernard Lewis were once again dusted off and taken for yet another tired ride. But they are wrong. Even louder speakers can be given to Huntington and Osama bin Laden. But civilizational thinking is over. Bernard Lewis can frequent the Pentagon even more often and Molla Omar may go into hiding to resurface again. But "Islam and the West" is today more an inane binary opposition than it ever was. The battle was never between "Islam and the West." Kuwaiti sheikhs and Enron executives are of the same ilk, culture, and disposition; so are the inner city kids from Harlem and Bronx who join the U.S. army and the Taliban fighters from Kandahar. Islam of the Saudi princes is not the Islam of Algerian migrant laborers in France, and there is no Western corner of any globe in universe that can bring together Park Avenue in New York City and the slums of Newark, New Jersey.

"Islam and the West" was one particularly malicious invention of modernity. With modernity dead and the postmodern infusion of globalization rampant, that ghostly opposition means nothing. Globalization means nothing other than the lifting of that smoke screen of civilizational divides that covered the vertical and horizontal colonization. What difference does it make if the British colonized India or Ireland, the Italians Mezzogiorno or Libya, or the French bourgeoisie the French or Algerian laborers? Colonization is colonization is colonization. Colonization is integral to the operation of capital. The capital colonizes labor, not cultures. Nike will sell shoes to American marines and the Afghan Taliban alike—no discrimination here. Formation of national cultures (the British, the French, the Germans, etc.) succeeded the European dynastic histories by way of giving ideological cohesion to the emerging national economies as the optimum unit for the maximum abuse of labor by capital. Formation of civilizational divides (constituting "the West" and separating it from the Islamic, the Chinese, the Indian, etc., all invented by an army of mercenary Orientalists) succeeded the medieval idea of Christendom and thus expanded the ideological cohesion of national economies to their colonial divides. The Germans thought they were Germans against the French so that they would not see the brutal class division that internally pulled them apart, as the Westerners saw themselves as Westerners against Muslims, Chinese, or Indians so the structural similarities between the ravages of capital on labor whether in Paris or in Cairo would not reveal itself. This was the historical smoke screen that is now lifted from the global face of desperation and destitution that the brutality of capital on labor has visited upon the world. It is far more than theoretical blindness to perpetuate and authenticate inanities such as "Islam and the West" by forgetting that the "Islam" of that opposition, as indeed its "West," is the figment of a tormented, colonized, and captive imagination.

From its very inception, Islam has been a religion of protest. What is called "Shi'ism" is nothing other than the very soul of Islam as a religion of protest. But Shi'ism has succeeded precisely because, as the very soul of the Islamic message, it is a paradox. It can never, and should never, succeed. It should always speak the truth to power. It can never be in power. A "Muslim ruler" is, as it has always been, a contradiction in terms. All the current rulers in the Islamic Republic of Iran who have not been democratically elected are usurpers of power. The very constitution of the Islamic Republic, the very idea of Velayat e Faqih, is the usurpation of power. Democracy, as the will of a people to self-governance, is constitutional to Shi'ism and by extension to Islam as a religion of protest. The confirmation or denial of authority to their leaders is always the sole prerogative of Muslims. The source of legitimacy is from the ground up and not the other way around. The fancy footwork of belated and blind ideologues notwithstanding, the Shi'i Muslims in the streets of Tehran, Cairo, Peshawar, or Ramala, whether or not they even consciously recognize themselves as believing Muslims, are the sole source of revolutionary energy and moral aspiration. That has always been the case, before and after modernity. That will always be the case, before and after postmodernity.

Notes

1. There is an excellent essay on the paradigmatic shifts in the ideas and practices of religious intellectuals by Sohrab Razaqi, "Paradigm-ha-ye Roshanfekri-ye Dini dar Iran-e Mo'aser" (Paradigms of Religious Intellectualism in Contemporary Iran), in *Majmu'eh Maqalat-e Motale'at-e Irani* 2 (1378): 160–89.

2. For a brief account of Soroosh's ideas in English, see John Cooper, "The Limits of the Sacred: The Epistemology of 'Abd al-Karim Soroosh," in John Cooper, Ronald Nettler, and Mohamed Mahmoud, eds., *Islam and Modernity: Muslim Intellectuals Respond* (London: I. B. Tauris, 1998), pp. 38–56. For a more thorough reading of Soroosh, see Afshin Matin-Asgari, "Abdolkarim Soroosh and the Secularization of Islamic Thought in Iran," *Iranian Studies* 30, 1–2 (1997): 97. Valla Vakili's "Abdolkarim Soroosh and Critical Discourse in Iran," in John L. Esposito and John O. Voll's *Makers of Contemporary Islam* (Oxford: Oxford University Press, 2001), pp. 150–76 is a thorough and sympathetic account. Thanks to Mahmoud Sadri and Ahmad Sadri now we have a sound and sympathetic introduction to Soroosh's thoughts in English. See their edited volume, *Reason, Freedom, and Democracy in Islam: Essential Writings of Abdolkarim Soroosh* (Oxford: Oxford University Press, 2000). All of these introductory essays benefit from a close and careful reading of Soroosh and yet suffer from a categorical absence of any critical stance.

3. Abdolkarim Soroosh, *Qabz-o-Bast-e Theoric-e Shari'at* (The Theoretical Contraction and Expansion of Religious Knowledge) (Tehran: Mo'assesseh-ye Farhangi-ye Serat, 1991), p. 31.

4. Soroosh, p. 31.

5. Soroosh, p. 32.

6. Soroosh, pp. 32–33.

7. Soroosh, p. 33.

8. Soroosh, p. 34.

9. Soroosh, p. 34.

10. Soroosh, p. 165.

11. Soroosh, p. 170.

12. Soroosh, pp. 173–74.

13. Soroosh, p. 180.

14. Soroosh, p. 181.

15. Soroosh, p. 190.

16. Soroosh, p. 192.

17. Soroosh, p. 201.

18. Soroosh, p. 205.

19. Soroosh, p. 206.

20. Soroosh, pp. 214–15.

21. Soroosh, pp. 220–24.

22. Soroosh, pp. 231–32.

23. Soroosh, pp. 234–35.

24. Soroosh, pp. 239–44.

25. Soroosh, pp. 245–46.

26. Soroosh, p. 247.

27. Soroosh, pp. 252–59.

28. Soroosh, p. 264.

29. Soroosh, p. 276.

30. Soroosh, p. 280.

31. Soroosh, p. 285.

32. Soroosh, p. 287.

33. Soroosh, pp. 289–98.

34. I have extensively argued and outlined this Shi'i paradox in my "End of Islamic Ideology," *Social Research* 67, 2 (Summer 2000).

35. Soroosh, p. 34. The quotation is from a Quranic phrase.

36. Michael Hardt and Antonio Negri's *Empire* (Cambridge, Mass.: Harvard University Press, 2000), though still pathologically Eurocentric in its narrative, remains the best assessment of the emergence of this nascent globalized empire. I have addressed the causes and conditions of the end of civilizational thinking and its last gasp for air in the works of Samuel Huntington, et al. in my "For the Last Time: Civilization," *International Sociology* 16, 3 (September 2001).

8

The Varieties of Religious Reform: Public Intelligentsia in Iran

Ahmad Sadri

Intellectuals Are Hot

IN HIS *THE VARIETIES OF RELIGIOUS EXPERIENCE*, William James refers to ideas as either hot or cold, dead or alive.[1] By this standard, the idea that committed intellectuals are agents of social change is fairly cool in the United States and lukewarm in Europe. In Iran, however, this notion has been red-hot throughout the twentieth century and remains so today. Twice in the last century Iranian intellectuals acted as catalysts of cataclysmic revolutionary change—during the Constitutional Revolution of 1905–1906 and the Islamic Revolution of 1978–1979. Thus, it is not surprising that intellectuals (in the general sense of producers and synthesizers of ideas) have spearheaded the process of reform of the Islamic Republic.

The intelligentsia is usually conceived of as the transmission belt that reinterprets and conveys the ideas of intellectuals to the public. While it is true that Iranian reformers include lay as well as clerical public intellectuals (e.g., Abdolkarim Soroosh, Mohammad Mojtahed Shabestari, Mohsen Kadivar, etc.) it is not so clear that the "intelligentsia" can be regarded as a "second division," or as a stratum of consumers and transmitters of ideas. Such reform leaders as Abbas Abdi, Akbar Ganji, Saeed Hajjarian, Hamid-Reza Jalie Pour, Shahla Sherkat, and Mashallah Shamsolvaezin are, to varying degrees and often in very crucial ways, both producers and disseminators of ideas. It would be neither hyperbolic nor redundant to call them a "public intelligentsia" since they straddle the fence between intellectual production and political agitation. In this chapter we shall examine the ideal typical varieties of religious intelligentsia who are the carriers as well as the agents of reform. But first a note on the current political situation in Iran is in order.

A House Divided

Twenty-three years after its establishment, the Islamic Republic of Iran is a house divided. Abbas Abdi, whose newspaper's closing in August 1999 heralded the current right-wing backlash, paints the national schizophrenia in bold strokes. According to Abdi, mutually exclusive and utterly incompatible interpretations of the Islamic Republic overlap on Iran's contested political map. He points out that the mainstream of the reform movement that is formally headed by President Khatami operates on the assumption that it has ascended to the leadership of a democratic republic. The conservative establishment headed by the Supreme Leader Seyed Ali Khamenei, however, acts as though it is running a modern theocracy. The parliament in the eyes of the reform is what it was for its liberal framers in the summer of 1978: a genuine, elective legislator. Meanwhile, the conservative right wing prefers to view the same institution in the light of a revised and amended constitution, as a consultative body of the Ummah managing its practical affairs under the absolute tutelage of the Supreme Leader/Juristconsult. Like other proponents of radical reform, Abdi holds government by election to be irreconcilable with government by appointment from above. More moderate reformers prefer a less black-and-white picture, but few would dispute that the republican and Islamic components of the Islamic Republic are undergoing a binary fission along the reform/conservative divide.

The above ideological disagreement is anything but academic. The history of the Islamic Republic has fleshed out both sides of the argument. On the Right, a conservative core of mid-ranking clergymen with roots in a few seminaries in Qom (e.g., Haghani and Bagher-ol Ulum) controls enormous economic resources, including a sizable portion of the government budget and government-owned "charitable" foundations. In addition it enjoys political leverage (the Office of the Supreme Leader, Assembly of the Experts, the Council of Guardians, and the Expediency Council), judiciary prerogative (Ministry of Justice), and sheer military muscle (Revolutionary Guards and its youth mobilization organization). For the last ten years this powerful coalition has also waged a "dirty war" by proxy of operatives of the Information Ministry to liquidate its enemies within the borders of Iran and without. It also operates a variety of media outlets ranging from influential top secret *Bulletins* to the enormous monopoly of "National Radio and Television of Iran" and a dozen official as well as semiofficial newspapers (e.g., *Jomhouri-e Eslami, Keyhan, Resaalat*).[2]

In the face of such overwhelming odds, what are the chances of success for the reform movement that only controls the elective offices of parliament and presidency? The last three years of right-wing backlash that started with the attacks of the summer of 1999 on the dormitories of the University of Tehran have landed the leaders of reform in jail or in wheelchairs and made a mockery of the parliamentary process. If this last act of the reform history is anything to go by, the chances of its success are slim indeed. Yet, the reform legislators continue their strident polemics and defiant gestures. Even the imprisoned reform journalists continue to support a president too impotent to keep them—or his own cabinet for that matter—out of jail.[3] The main capital of the reform appears to be the currency of legitimacy: it has decisively won four consecutive elections (presidential, municipal, parliamentary, and again presidential) in as many years. Reform's advantage, however, lies as much in its actual political power as it does in the historically based national consciousness of Iranians that an idea expressing the collective will can reverse formidable political fortunes. Those who articulate such ideas (or master it as a Culture of Critical Discourse[4]) are called *roshanfekr* or "intellectual/intelligentsia."[5]

The conservative right wing enjoys an apparent ideological continuity dating back to Ayatollah Khomeini's radical speeches, precipitous actions, and extreme positions on electoral, legal, and civil matters. But given the rapid aging of the ideological slogans of the revolution, this continuity is a mixed blessing. By contrast, the more minimalist ideology of reform that only dates back to the termination of the Iran–Iraq war is in sync with the massive disenchantment of the public. Reform was founded by a cadre of young revolutionaries who had witnessed the disastrous mismanagement of the conflict with Iraq and the contempt in which the regime's éminence grise held the publicly touted ideals of the eight-year war. One needs only to consider the chilling effect of episodes like the Iran–Contra Affair on the idealistic Iranian warriors who had been told that in fighting Saddam they were indeed waging war against the real enemy, "The Great Satan." By "quaffing the chalice of poison" that was Ayatollah Khomeini's euphemism for finally capitulating to U.N. Security Council Resolution 598 for ending the war, he also unwittingly launched the reform movement. Put differently, the reform was born with the postwar cooling of a central core of the Islamic Republic that was expressed in a new interest in liberal democratic ideals and a turning away from charismatic authority. Soon after the war many of the founding members of the radical and political reform found each other in a think tank called the Center for Strategic Studies that was affiliated with the office of the president. Among those who were attracted to the Center was a group of former radicals ranging from a lay leader of the students that had precipitated the hostage crisis (Asghar Zadeh) to the wunderkind of the intelligence community and the early architect of the notorious Ministry of Information (Hajjarian). Those who would form the press arm of the reform movement gelled around the offices of the new intellectual "Little Magazine" of Tehran, *Kian* (*Ganji*).[6]

The ideal typical member of the reform public intelligentsia in fin de siècle Iran was a journalist who had left a high or sensitive post in the apparatus of the Islamic Republic around the last decade of the century. For the purposes of the present chapter we define him or her as lay (nonclerical) and unattached to political organizations that are identified with the reform movement.[7]

Radical Reform: The Ex-Editor

Abbas Abdi, today's reformist, was once a young man who scaled the walls of the American Embassy in Tehran in search of hostages. He is not the first among his cohort of ex-radicals to ponder the ultimate incorrigibility of the conservative establishment. But he is one of the first to come clean. The number of openly radical religious intellectuals remains small. But the continued relentlessness of the right-wing backlash is teasing out the kind of expressions that could lead one to believe that Abdi is the tip of the radical reform iceberg.[8] He recently called on the reform politicians to consider withdrawing from politics and thus deny the right wing the fig leaf of legitimacy. It is noteworthy that, although Abdi believes that the right wing's totalitarian interpretation of the constitution is self-serving, he does not claim that it is wrong. Abdi knows that Iran's eclectic constitution supports the diametrically opposite claims of both the reform and the right wing. Like the fabulous elephant of the stories, the Iranian constitution is different things to the tactile denizens of a dark room.[9] Until, that is, a subversive like Abdi throws the switch. The radical reform deems that the true reform can be achieved only by revising the constitution. This suggestion, however, is so radical in the context of the current politics of Iran that even President Khatami, who in a recent address implicitly admitted that his office had been eviscerated by the existing constitution, felt compelled to also disavow attempts at revising the constitution as "treasonous."[10]

Abdi is neither a utopian idealist nor a jaded defeatist. His call to his comrades to retreat from politics also means that they must sit tight. Despite its enormous powers, the right wing is spent—not only because its tired, xenophobic, and conspiratorial rhetoric is unpopular and not only because the once flashy anti-Israeli and anti-American claptrap sounds hollow to a war-weary, increasingly isolationist, and disillusioned Iran. Even the fact that the puritan policies of the conservatives irritate the ubiquitous Iranian youth is not the main reason why the radical reform is optimistic. The Achilles' heel of the theocratic ideology in Iran is that it lacks institutional and ideological support among the clerical intellectual aristocracy of Qom. The obscurity and eccentricity of Ayatollah Khomeini's theory of "Mandate of the Juristconsult"[11] combined with Shi'a Islam's notoriously amorphous ecclesiastical structure provide an unsteady foundation for an Islamic theocracy or even clerocracy. Despite much essentialist ado about Islam's political nature, Ayatollah Khomeini's formula of the "Mandate of the Juristconsult" (Velayat-e Faghih) and its implementation are puny in comparison to theocracies and clerocracies that a sister Abrahamic religion (Christianity) has had the chance to establish from Constantinople and Rome to Geneva and Salem.[12] Shi'i Islam has surely failed to produce the theocratic structure that undergirded the Byzantine Empire. Nor can Islam boast the kind of theocratic rigor one finds in the impressive body of Christian apologetics from the works of Eusebius of Caesarea[13] to those of Manegold of Lautenbach[14] and William Dell.[15] Shi'i Islam cannot even compete with the rudimentary groundwork for a clerocracy that would guarantee the orderly process of succession of a pontiff (e.g., the Vatican's College of Cardinals). No wonder then that the election of the current Supreme Leader (Ali Khamenei) was neither directed nor blessed by Qom. Rather, it was the result of wheeling and dealing by a cabal of the lieutenants of the late Ayatollah Khomeinei, including his son.[16] It is not a surprise that the clerical Assembly of Experts that is formally charged by the constitution to check the power of the reigning Supreme Leader and oversee the election of the next one has degenerated to a patronage system run by the invisible hand of Supreme Leader Khamenie. The same is true of the Council of Guardians and the Expediency Council: they all act as oligarchic knots made of strands of filial, economic, and ideological interests. In short, among many weather signs pointing in their direction, the radical reform counts on the inherent instability and lack of legitimacy of the right-wing "theo-oligarchy."[17]

Muckraking Reform: The Investigative Journalist

Akbar Ganji started his career as an intelligence officer in the Revolutionary Guards and continued his career as a press attaché at the Iranian embassy in Turkey. Later, he worked for the progressive daily *Hamshahri* before joining *Kian*. At the outset of President Khatami's landslide victory Ganji and his firebrand editor and publisher (Mashallah Shamsolvaezin) left *Kian* to propagate their ideas through the enormously popular and rapidly mushrooming newspapers of the reform movement. Ganji branched out of reporting to lecture on a topic that would be a turning point in his intellectual odyssey and which landed him in a closed session of the press court. He had identified the ideology and tactics of the religious Right with classical fascism.[18] Although the charge was not new, it was the first time someone living within the borders of Iran had openly made it. Ganji's reporting was no less controversial. He started a series of investigative reports on the "dirty war" the right wing had waged (through the agency of what was later called "rouge elements" of the Ministry of the Information) against dissidents.[19] A number of "deep throats" must have assisted Ganji, and his comrade, ex-clergyman Emade-Din Baghi,[20] in connecting the dots and getting to the bottom of the vast conspiracy of murdering the dissidents. Ganji had discovered the crucial links that connected the operatives to the reigning right-wing clergymen (Fallahian, Mohseni-Egeay, Mesbah-Yazdi) who had issued the fatwas legitimizing the assassinations. Tantalizing hints at these discoveries in Ganji's articles led many moderate members of the political reform to conclude that following the cases of more than eighty disappearances and murders would destabilize the regime and endanger the long-term project of peaceful and gradual reform. Many believed that such discoveries could implicate the Supreme Leader Khamenei, the powerful head of the Expediency Council, and former two-term president Rafsanjaani. But Ganji was not about to heed the advice of his more moderate friends against rocking the boat. On the contrary; he actually opened a new front against Rafsanjani both for his culpability in the "dirty war" and for the involvement of his flamboyant sons in the Iran's crony capitalism. This had the predicted result of a crushing defeat for Rafsanjani in the parliamentary elections of 2000 and his boundless wrath against Ganji and the reform movement. Ganji was consequently tried on trumped-up charges of planning to overthrow the government by participating in a public conference in Berlin and received a stiff sentence of ten years in jail to be followed by five years of internal exile. It is noteworthy that other reform politicians who had gone to the same conference and expressed roughly the same sentiments either received more lenient sentences or were exonerated. Ganji remains defiant in jail.

In his writings, collected and published in best-selling books that have been reprinted dozens of times, Ganji has helped shape the reform's Culture of Critical Discourse by contributing to the "reform speak." Ganji has coined phrases like "follower of a different life style" (*degar-baash*) as a companion to the phrase "different thinker" (*degar-andish*). Phrases like these challenge the cultural hegemony of the clergy and the stratum of the pious believers and help legitimize pluralism by foregrounding the second-class status of those citizens who wish to think and live by standards not sanctioned by the state.

Naming can legitimize, but not always. Ganji's giving a name to the despicable tactics of the right wing has gone a long way to expose the unsavory nature of these practices. Two of Ganji's coinages related to the show trials demonstrate his contribution to the antitotalitarian language of the reform movement in contemporary Iran. He calls the *1984* style of interrogations of the right-wing forces "manufacturing repentants" (*tavvab saazi*). The actual practice of self-recrimination in forced televised interviews finds expression in Ganji's "self-inflicting TV interviews" (Mosahebeh-ye Televisioni-e Khod-Zani). The effective and popular appellations of "mafia" for the right-wing power elite and that of "godfather" for the urbane, soft-spoken Rafsanjaani are also Ganjisms.

The son of an unskilled laborer, Akbar Ganji is the typical ex-radical who joined the revolution with high hopes and served it single-mindedly. The ideas he has expressed about fascism, freedom of expression, and human rights attest his genuine intellectual transformation. Noble as his intrepid reporting at the risk of his life and freedom and his moral courage in reexamining his beliefs are, he is not unique. Ganji is representative of the fearless journalistic counterculture that has led the reform's campaign against the conservative establishment beyond the point of no return. Ganji's uncompromising attitude in what was designed as his show trial and his heroic perseverance under the psychological and physical hardships of confinement has been legendary. But it is a sign of the maturity of the new reform movement in Iran that, while admiring a triumvirate of jailed heroes (Nouri, Kadivar, Baaghi) as well as Ganji and Shamsolvaezin, it does not require all its leaders to be heroes. The tolerant attitude of the public toward the less heroic reform journalists and political activists (e.g., Ghoochani, Nabavi, Behnood, Afshari, and Sahabi) and toward others who are currently under pressure to "confess on camera" is the case in point.

Political Reform: The Inveterate Editorialist

Saeed Hajjarian's resume would not endear him to the Iranian opposition in diaspora. A radical Islamist at the prestigious faculty of engineering of the University of Tehran in the days of the shah, Hajjarian rapidly rose in the ranks of the revolutionary counterintelligence. Along the way, however, the autodidactic Hajjarian had somehow taught himself Western social sciences and taken extensive lessons in Islamic jurisprudence and philosophy. This preparation and his prodigious talents enabled him to court success as a leader of the postwar opposition. It was during his tenure at the Center for Strategic Studies that Hajjarian emerged as the creative genius behind the ideology of reform in Iran. His newly revived interest in the democratic ideals of the revolution and a resolve to fight the right-wing ideology is reflected in his influential, long-running editorials in the Tehran daily *Asr-e Ma*. In these articles, later published as a book entitled *Republic: Demystifying Political Power,* Hajjarian articulated his democratic and liberal interpretation of the Islamic Republic and challenged the autocratic and oligarchic tendencies of its existing institutions. Hajjarian's didactic crusade against the Islamic authoritarianism of the right wing is informed by his encyclopedic command of both Islamic and Western learning.

Hajjarian calls those who challenge the democratic basis of the Islamic Republic invoking the authority of God, "Kharejite Anarchists,"[21] thus combining traditional and modern images of violent extremism. In another editorial he defuses the right wing's demagogic binary opposition of the divine as opposed to democratic rule. Instead Hajjarian offers a taxonomy of theocracies: theo-autocracy, theo-aristocracy, and theo-democracy. For him Iranians need not choose between God and people as the ultimate source of authority. The more genuine choice would be between varieties of theocracy.[22] Hajjarian argues that the clerical Assembly of Experts that is charged with electing the Supreme Leader could be conceived of as autocratic, aristocratic, or democratic without ceasing to be a clerical body under the constitution of the Islamic Republic. On yet another front, Hajjarian tries his very best to soften the autocratic implications of the adjective "absolute" that was later added before the phrase "mandate of the Supreme Leader" in order to weaken the elective offices of the Islamic Republic. If the office of the Supreme Leader is divine, and if the mandate of the person occupying it is "absolute," then democratic procedures promulgated by the constitution would appear to be redundant, trivial, and ultimately absurd. Some reformers stop right there: since the constitution cannot be an exercise in absurdity, the term "absolute" must not mean what it appears to means.[23] Hajjarian's sophisticated theoretical prestidigitations offers a more subtle formulation. Instead of the self-contradictory formulation that defines the Supreme Leader's power as "absolute within the limits of law," Hajjarian maintains that the absolute power of the leader is in essence a "law-governed" power that originates in both divine and democratic sources.[24]

Byzantine formulations such as the ones outlined above might strike those outside of the cosmos of the Islamic republic—and even many of the religious radicals within it—as conformist embroidery. But if politics is the art of the possible, it would make sense for the political reform to try to operate within the limitations of the constitution and the political atmosphere of the Islamic Republic. The reader might recall the search for Marxism with a human face in the pre-1989 Eastern and Central European countries.[25]

One must note that without the gossamer web of such delicate formulations as presented by Hajjarian, the government of President Khatami and the irreversible achievements of the reform in Iran would have been inconceivable.

Now in his late forties, Hajjarian has been confined to a wheelchair for the past two years due to neurological damage caused by a botched assassination attempt. The perpetrators, who had loose connections to the revolutionary guards, were captured, but the investigations and the trials that were handled by the right-wing controlled Ministries of Information and Justice were predictably perfunctory. The right wing is openly jubilant;[26] Hajjarian was one the reform's most formidable exponents. He grew up in an impoverished slum of southern Tehran (Naziabad) where he absorbed the revolutionary Islamic liberation theology of Ali Shariati and later the radical revolutionary message of Ayatollah Khomeini's Islamic Revolution. He served the revolution at the most sensitive posts conceivable and when he broke with the establishment he was once more at the cusp of a movement that brought seven out of every ten eligible Iranian men and women to the polls. The fact that the powerful right wing regards the potential assassination of Hajjarian with rapt silence—broken with occasional yelps of joy—shows at the very least, the myopia of Iran's revolutionary elite. Elimination of a leader of the enormously popular reform movement might postpone the end but it will also make it more painful.

The Future of Reform

A few years ago, the foreign policy circles of the United States were wondering whether a moderate Iran under the cloak of Rafsanjaani was an illusion. Today's Iranian reformers are wondering whether a moderate or at least rational tendency in the right wing is a chimera. The answer in both cases is yes. By turning a deaf ear to the logic of reform and by attempting to demonize the immensely popular reform movement, the right wing has undertaken a lemmings' expedition. The conservatives' unimaginative use of decades-old rhetorical devices to confront the powerful discourse of the reform shows their ideological bankruptcy. They don't seem to see that the now threadbare revolutionary newspeak is old hat for the generations of Iranians who were born after the revolution. They do not wish to believe that their ideology can no longer bear the weight of the national, international, and even demographic realities and that public brutalization of symbols of the religious reform[27] like Ganji, Baaghi, Shamsolvaezin, and Hajjarian will only quicken the pace of their ineluctable demise.

Notes

A related version of this chapter was published as "Varieties of Religious Reform in Iran," in *Politics, Culture, and Society* 15, no. 2 (winter 2001).

1. *The Varieties of Religious Experience* (New York: Modern Library, 1999), p. 217.
2. These media outlets have been effectively choreographed to launch massive anti-reform investigative serials (e.g., *Identity* and *Carnival of Ashoura*), show trial-confessions and cover-up infomercials (e.g., *Lantern*). A cadre of powerful functionaries operates this powerful arm of the right wing in fluid roles of newspaper editor, writer of top-secret bulletins, and interrogator.
3. Akbar Ganji's open letter to President Khatami on February 27, 2001 (www.iran-emrooz.de/khabar/ganjio1208.html).
4. Gouldner adopts the term from Basil Bernstine's sociolinguistic studies. Alvin W. Gouldner, *The Future of Intellectuals and the Rise of the New Class* (New York: Seabury, 1979) pp. 28–43.
5. Iranian intellectuals, like their comrades everywhere else in the modern world, have to conform to local "templates" that define who they are supposed to be (status) and what they are expected to do (mission). In Iran being an intellectual is a "master status" that carries significant role expectations at the price of considerable personal sacrifices. Thus the Iranian intellectuals may be idolized by the people and scrutinized, prosecuted, and persecuted by the state, but they are never ignored.
6. The staff of *Kian* had been earlier fired from a government-subsidized publication named the *Cultural Keyhan* (*Keyhan-e Farhangi*) for their liberal editorial policies.
7. Deserving as they are of particular attention, members of such reform organizations as the Combative Clerical Organization, the Organization of the Mojahedeen of the Islamic Revolution, and the Office for Fostering Unity between the University and the Seminary are not included in the ideal type of the intellectuals here.
8. The letter of the most radical Islamic student organization (The Office for Fostering Unity between the University and the Seminary) to the Supreme Leader (March 1, 2001) is the case in point. This letter was so strident that the remaining reform newspapers refrained from publishing it (www.iran-emrooz.de/khabar/tahkim1210.html).
9. The duality of the Islamic Republic's constitution is almost as old as the republic itself. The first Assembly of Experts revised the democratic constitution, lacing it with theocratic ideas. These ideas hatched like so many fledglings of a cowbird and starved the legitimate progeny of the revolution that had been conceived in the idea of liberty. The charisma of Ayatollah Khomeini was invoked by the conservative faction in the assembly to suppress opposition to its revision (during the meetings and in the process of constitution's popular ratification) unthinkable. The gradual implementation of the weak and flawed constitution in absence of democratic checks and balances and in the context of an authoritarian political culture made concrete the oligarchic potentials of the revised constitution.
10. *Hamshahri*, 12/7/2000.
11. Grand Ayatollah Montazeri, who is one of the architects of the present theocratic system in Iran, has criticized its present applications as entirely illegitimate. The

reform Mohsen Kadivar has recently echoed the older critique of Ayatollah Khomeini's theory of the Mandate of the Juristconsult first articulated by the Grand Ayatollah Khouie. Ayatollah Khouie's response to Ayatollah Khomeini's contentions at the time of the latter's lectures in the early 1970s in Iraq was published at the time under the title of *Al-Ijtihad wa al-taghlid*.

12. See Peter Iver Kaufman's worthy study of the subject: *Redeeming Politics* (Princeton, N.J.: Princeton University Press, 1990).

13. The fourth-century bishop of Caesarea, Eusebius, wrote the first authoritative history of the church, not only interpreting the enthronement of the first Christian emperor, Constantine, as divine ordination but also reinterpreting the previous three centuries of the Roman Empire as a foreshadowing of the Holy Roman Empire. See Eusebius, *The History of Church from Christ to Constantine*, trans. G. A. Williamson. (New York: Penguin, 1989). Also see Garth Fowden, *Empire to Commonwealth: Consequences of Monotheism in Late Antiquity* (Princeton, N.J.: Princeton University Press 1993), pp. 85–97 and Richard Rubenstein, *When Jesus Became God* (New York: Harcourt, 1999), pp. 65–66.

14. An eleventh-century papal apologist, Manegold defended papal political autonomy against the scriptural text and Christian practice by arguing that the injunction to follow one's emperor was valid but only "if" the emperor honored the church (Kaufman, p. 86, 87). Also see Brian Tierney, *The Crisis of Church and State 1050–1300* (Toronto: University of Toronto Press, 1988), pp. 127–39.

15. The seventeenth-century Puritan preacher of William Cromwell's New Model Army who believed that the pulpit was superior to the altar. See Kaufman, pp. 62–73.

16. Revelations in Ayatollah Montazeri's memoirs, recently published on the Internet, indicate that the disgruntled son of the late Ayatollah may have been subsequently murdered for his lingering ambitions to succeed his father (www.montazeri.com/html/KAHTER49.html).

17. This is a category in Saeed Hajjarian's classification of the types of theocracy, to which we will return later in this chapter.

18. Ganji's lecture at Shiraz University was entitled "Satan Was the First Fascist" (May 1996). He was charged with defaming the Islamic Republic and tried in a closed court. His defense was later published under the title of "Fascism Is One of the Mortal Sins," *Kian*, Number 40, February 1997.

19. Ganji's gambit would have been impossible before the tenure of President Khatami, not only because of the freedom he enjoyed in publishing the results of his investigations but mainly because it was Khatami who withstood the pressure of the Right to brush the scandal under the rug. Khatami insisted that at least four murders that were committed under his watch be solved and prosecuted. This was possibly the most decisive departure of Khatami with the modus vivendi of his predecessors.

20. Baaghi, who is also a political prisoner in Iran, has published two volumes on the subject of the Iranian "dirty war" entitled *The Tragedy of Democracy in Iran*.

21. Saeed Hajjarian, *Republic: Demystifying Political Power* (Jomhooryat: Afsoonzedaie Az Ghodrat) (Tehran: Tarh-e No Publishers, 1999), pp. 659–69. On a concise account of the Kharejites history, see John Esposito's *Islam: The Straight Path* (New York: Oxford University Press, 1998), pp. 41–43.

22. Hajjarian, pp. 659–69.

23. One of the most prominent leaders of the reform and the current vice speaker of the parliament, Behzad Nabavi, is quoted as saying: "Absolute mandate of the Supreme Leader/Juristconsult is absolute only within the framework of the law, for if it were otherwise, there would be no point in having any kind of law to begin with." The obvious tautological tenor of this statement and the violence it does to the meaning of the word "absolute" were hidden neither to the secular critics of the Islamic Republic nor the right-wing critics of the reform. Quoted in *Asr-e Ma*, Number 61, 1995.

24. Hajjarian, p. 677–88.

25. Leszek Kolakowski, *Toward a Marxist Humanism* (New York: Grove, 1968).

26. Masood Deh-Namaki, The Retreat of the Reform Started with the Elimination of Hajjarian, Interview with ISNA (www.iran-emrooz.de/khabar/namaki1214.html), March, 6, 2001.

27. The subject of this chapter does not allow addressing the plight of the Iranian secular intellectuals and intelligentsia upon whom measures of brutal repression have been visited with terrible regularity.

9

The Homeless Texts
of Persianate Modernity

Mohamad Tavakoli-Targhi

Modernity and Heterotopia

THE REEXAMINATION OF THE Eurocentric definition of modernity has been
at the center of recent historical *reactivations* of "modern times."[1] The
conventional Enlightenment story treats modernity as a peculiarly European development and as a byproduct of "Occidental rationalism."[2] Viewed
from within this hegemonic paradigm, non-European societies were "mod-
ernized" as a result of Western impact and influence.[3] Thus Westernization,
modernization, and acculturation were conceived as interchangeable concepts accounting for the transition of "traditional" and "non-Western" societies.[4] These assertions have been reevaluated by scholars examining the
cultural genealogies and etiologies of modernity.[5] Locating the West in a
larger global context beginning with the Age of Exploration, Stuart Hall
suggests that the so-called uniqueness of the West was, in part, produced by
Europe's contact and self-comparison with other, non-Western societies
(the Rest), very different in their histories, ecologies, patterns of development, and cultures from the European model.[6] Demonstrating the critical
importance of the Rest in the formation of Western modernity, Hall submits that without the Rest (or its own internal "others"), the West would
not have been able to recognize and represent itself as the summit of
human history.[7] Hall's revised conception of modernity allows for an expanded framework of analysis encompassing what I call the formative role
of *heterotopic* experiences for the Age of Exploration in the formation of
the *ethos* of modernity.

In contrast to *utopias*, the imaginary places in which human societies are depicted in perfect forms, Michel Foucault explored *heterotopias* as alternative real spaces. As existing loci beyond the everyday space of experience, heterotopias "are something like counter-sites, a kind of effectively enacted utopia in which the real sites, all other real sites that can be found within the culture, are simultaneously represented, contested, and inverted." These loci of alterity served the function of creating "a space of illusion that exposes every real space . . . a space that is other, another real space, as perfect, as meticulous, as well arranged as ours is messy, ill-constructed, and jumbled." Calling the latter type a "compensatory" heterotopia, Foucault speculated that "on the level of the general organization of terrestrial space" colonies might have "functioned somewhat in this manner."[8] He offered as historical examples the regulated colonies established by Jesuits and Puritans. Similarly, sixteenth-century reports of European exploration of exotic heterotopias deepened the Renaissance humanists' understanding of human motives and action and enlarged their framework of understanding. As late as the eighteenth century, according to Stephen Toulmin, Montesquieu and Samuel Johnson still found it helpful to present unusual ideas by attributing them to people in a far-off land like Abyssinia or Persia.[9] The attribution of "unusual ideas to people in a far-off land" was not merely a "literary device."[10] For instance, the physical presence of the Persian ambassador Muhammad Riza Bayk (d. 1717) in France in 1715–1716 provided the pertinent context for the imaginary scenarios informing the "unusual ideas" and the central question of *The Persian Letters*: "How can one be Persian?"[11] As spectacles and as native informants of exotic heterotopias, travelers like Muhammad Riza Bayk inspired native European spectators who in turn provided them with a space of self-recognition and self-refashioning. Considering the material significance of the "Rest" in the formation of "Western modernity," such attributions can be considered as residues of a genesis amnesia in European historiography. Such a historiographical amnesia has made possible the fabrication of a coherent and continuous medieval and modern "Western Civilization." As Maria R. Menocal has demonstrated, the "European Awakening" was "an Oriental period of Western history, a period in which Western culture grew in the shadow of Arabic and Arabic-manipulated learning."[12]

By recovering the significance of heterotopic experiences in the formation of the ethos of modernity, the lands beyond Europe, instead of being the reverse image of enlightenment and modernity, served as "laboratories of modernity," as sites of earliest sightings of "the hallmarks of European cultural production."[13] This has been explored in the historiographical works of Paul Rabinow, Sidney Mintz, Timothy Mitchell, Uday Mehta, Benedict Anderson, Gwendolyn Wright, and Nicholas Dirks, among others.[14] Summarizing the contribution of these scholars, Ann Stoler observed that: "These reconfigured histories have pushed us to rethink European cultural genealogies across the board and to question whether the key symbols of modern western societies—liberalism, nationalism, state welfare, citizenship, culture, and 'European-ness' itself—were not clarified among Europe's colonial exiles and by those colonized classes caught in their pedagogic net in Asia, Africa, and Latin America, and only then brought 'home.'"[15] For instance, in his study of French colonialism in Morocco Paul Rabinow observed that "[t]he colonies constituted a laboratory of experimentation for new arts of government capable of bringing a modern and healthy society into being."[16] In *Imagined Communities* Anderson demonstrated that Creole communities developed "early conceptions of their nation-ness—*well before most of Europe.*"[17] Locating Foucault's *History of Sexuality* in a larger trans-European context, Stoler contends, "One could argue that the history of Western sexuality must be located in the production of historical Others, in the broader force field of empire where technologies of sex, self, and power were defined as 'European' and 'western,' as they refracted and remade."[18] I have also explained how the "founding" of historical linguistics by Sir William Jones was informed by the works of Persianate scholars and scholarship in India.[19]

In light of these recent studies it can be argued that modernity was not a homemade product of "Occidental rationality," as asserted by Max Weber and universalized by "modernization" theorists.[20] Alternatively, modernity can be viewed as a product of a global network of power and knowledge that emerged initially around the sixteenth century. The heterotopic experiences of crisscrossing peoples and cultures provided multiple scenarios of modernity and self-refashioning. Whereas Europeans constituted the modern Self in relation to their non-Western heterotopias, Asians and Africans redefine the Self in dialogic relations to Europe, their new significant Other.

What Toulman calls the "counter-Renaissance" search for certainty[21] constituted European modes of self-refashioning as archetypically universal, rational, and modern. This dehistoricizing universalist claim enabled European rationalists to obliterate the heterotopic context of their self-making and thus constitute themselves as the originators of modernity and rationality. This amnesiac or forgetful assertion gained hegemonic currency and thus constituted "non-Western" modernity as "Westernization." The universalist claims of European enlightenment have blackmailed non-European modernity and debilitated its historiography by engendering a tradition of historical writing that used a dehistorized and decontextualized "European rationality" as its scale and referent. Iranian historians and ideologues, like their Indian and Ottoman counterparts, developed a fractured conception of historical time that viewed contemporary European societies ahead of their own time. This conception of historical time parallels the time-distancing devices of European and American anthropologists who denied *coeval-ness* to contemporary non-Western societies.[22] Such a schizophrenic conception of history informs the nationalist historiography of Iranian modernity, a historiography that assumes the noncontemporaneity of the contemporaneous Iranian and European societies. In a recent expression of this dehistoricizing and detemporalizing presumption, Daryush Shayegan, a leading Iranian critic, inviting his readers to be rational for once and claiming to stay with the facts argued, for more than three centuries we, the heirs of the civilizations of Asia and Africa, have been "on holiday" from history. We succeeded so well in crystallizing time in space that we were able to live outside time, arms folded, safe from interrogation.[23] Informed by the same temporal assumption of non-simultaneity with Europe, Reza Davari, an Iranian philosopher who has set himself the task of transcending Western humanism, asserted that "the past of the West is our future."[24]

The temporal comprehension of these critics is genealogically related to the ironic and self-Orientalizing rhetorical argument of an early twentieth-century Iranian constitutionalist who contended that if Adam, the forefather of humanity, would return today, he would be pleased with his Iranian descendants who have preserved his mode of life for many millenniums, whereas his unfaithful European children have totally altered Adam's tradition and mode of life. With the exception of a short-lived ancient cultural efflorescence, this rhetorical argument was similar to the Hegelian postulate of the fundamental similarity of the ancient and contemporary Persian mode of life, a postulate that Hegel shared with his contemporary Orientalists. Such Hegelian and Orientalist temporal assumptions have been reinforced by Iranian historiographical traditions that equate modernity with Westernization.

Affinities of Nationalism and Orientalism

Recognized as the heterotopia of modernity and scientific rationality, Europe was constituted as the horizon of expectation for the Iranian passage to modernity. Thus European history, as the future past of the desired present, functioned as a normative scenario for the prognosis or forecasting of the future Iran. This anticipatory modernity introduced a form of historical thinking that narrated Iranian history in terms of the European past. By universalizing that past, historical deviations from the European norm have been misrecognized as abnormalities and national illnesses.[25] Thus, the development of feudalism, capitalism, the bourgeoisie, the proletariat, democracy, freedom, scientific rationality, and industry in the "well-ordered" Europe informed the diagnoses of their lack, absence, retardation, and underdevelopment in Iran.[26] In other words, alternative non-European historical processes have been characterized as the absence of change and as unhistorical history. For instance, John Malcolm (1769–1833), the author of an influential Orientalist *History of Persia* (1815), which was translated into Persian in 1876, observed

> Though no country has undergone, during the last twenty centuries, more revolutions than the kingdom of Persia, there is, perhaps, none that is less altered in its condition. The power of the sovereigns, and of the satraps of ancient times; the gorgeous magnificence of the court; the habits of the people; their division into citizens, martial tribes, and savage mountaineers; the internal administration; and the mode of warfare; have continued essentially the same: and the Persians, as far as we have the means of judging, are at the present period, not a very different people from what they were in the time of Darius, and the Nousheerwan.[27]

In a more concise statement, Hegel (1770–1831) similarly asserted that the Persians retained, on the whole, the fundamental characteristics of their ancient mode of life.[28] This dehistoricizing assumption—that is, the contemporaneity of an early nineteenth-century "mode of life" with that of ancient times—informed both Orientalist and nationalist historiographies that constituted the heightened period of European colonialism and imperialism as the true beginning of rationality and historical progress in Iran. Whereas a progressive conception of time informed the modern European historiography from the late eighteenth century to the present, the accounts of modern Iran, like that of other non-Western societies, were unanimously based in a regressive conception of history. Thus the passage to modernity constituted a radical break with the stagnant and eternally recurring Iranian mode of life.

Malcolm viewed Islam and "the example of the prophet of Arabia and the character of some of the fundamental tenets of his faith" as the most prominent factors "in retarding the progress of civilization among those who have adopted his faith." These "retarding" factors explained why "every country inhabited by Mahomedans" never "attained a state of improvement which can be compared with that enjoyed by almost all those nations who form the present commonwealth of Europe." He concluded his recounting of the Iranian past with a reflection on its future. "The History of Persia, from the Arabian conquest to the present day," he claimed, "may be adduced as a proof of the truth of these observations: and while the causes, by which the effects have been produced, continue to operate, no material change in the condition of that empire can be expected." Malcolm wondered whether "the future destiny of this kingdom" could be altered with "the recent approximation of a great

European power." The experience of the Ottomans who "wrapped up in the habits of their ancestors and . . . have for a̱g̱e̱s̱ resisted the progress of that civilization with which they were surrounded did not seem promising to him. Thus the proximity with European powers and the "consequent collision of opposite habits and faith, was more likely to increase than to diminish those obstacles which hitherto prevented any very intimate or social intercourse between Mahomedan and Christian nations."[29] This prognosis, a forerunner of *The Clash of Civilizations?*[30] was grounded in the epistemological differentiation of the progressive Christian "commonwealth of Europe" and the stagnant "Mahomedan nations" of Asia.

With the global hegemony of "the West," this binary opposition became an ever more significant component of an Iranian national historiography venerating progress, development, and growth. With these concerns, a celebratory history of Europe provided the normative manual for deciphering the abnormalities of Iran's past and for promoting its modernization, that is, Westernization. For instance, Ervand Abrahamian, the author of one of the most sophisticated accounts of modern Iran, offers a paradigmatic view of the nineteenth century, a view that is embedded in Persian historical writings.[31] "Traditional Iran," in his estimation, "in sharp contrast to feudal Europe, thus had no baronial rebellions, no Magna Carta, no legal estates, and consequently no representative institutions." These and other lacks constitute the foundation for explaining a series of reformist failures of the nineteenth-century Qajars: "The attempt to construct a statewide bureaucracy failed. . . . The Qajars were equally unsuccessful . . . in building a viable standing army . . . [and] even failed to recapture the full grandeur of the ancient shah-in-shahs." By narrating a failed version of European history, this progressive historian of Iran assumes a typically Orientalist vantage: "the Qajar dynasty was an epitome of ancient oriental despotism; in fact, it was a failed imitation of such absolutism."[32] Such a characterization is a common feature of Orientalist, nationalist, and also Marxist historiography of nineteenth-century Iran.[33] The opening paragraph of Guity Neshat's *The Origin of Modern Reforms in Iran, 1870–1880* is likewise a testimony to the centrality of Europe in the horizon of expectation for "traditional" Iran.

> In 1870 a young Iranian of modest background, Mirza Huseyn Khan, was presented with an opportunity to regenerate Iran. During the next ten years he introduced regulations that were designed to transform the country's traditional political, military, and judicial institutions to resemble Western models. He also attempted to introduce Western cultural innovations and Westernized modes of thought.[34]

Viewed as a "Western model" used to transform "traditional" societies, "the modern," as in the above case, was commonly understood "as a known history,

something which has already happened elsewhere, and which is to be repro-
duced, mechanically or otherwise, with a local content."[35] As a mimetic plan,
Iranian modernity, like its non-Western counterparts, can at best be hailed as
a "project of positive unoriginality."[36] An eternally recurring Iranian premodernity was thus superseded by an already enacted "Western" modernity.

Viewing modernity as the belated reduplication of "Western models," historians of Iran often invent periodizations that are analogous to standard European historical accounts. Recognizing Descartes's *Discours sur la Méthode*
and Newton's *Principia* as two founding texts of modern thought in Europe,
Iranian historians have the same expectations for the Persian rendering of
these texts. In a modularized periodization of the Iranian "discovery of the
West" and the "dissemination of European 'new learning,'" Mangol Bayat, a
historian of modern Iran, writes that a Persian translation of René Descartes's
Discours was commissioned by Arthur Gobineau and published in 1862.[37] Referring to I'tizad al-Saltanah's *Falak al-Sa'adah* (1861),[38] she adds that only
one year earlier Isaac Newton and the idea of heliocentricity had been "introduced to the Iranian public."[39] This periodization concerning the introduction of modern European philosophical texts is similarly advanced by Faraydun Adamiyat, Elie Kedouri, Nikki Keddie, Jamshid Bihnam, and Alireza
Manafzadeh.[40] Adamiyat, a pioneering historian of Iranian modernity, contended that *Falak al-Sa'adah* and the Persian translation of *Discours* provided
the "context for rational transformation" (*zaminah-'i tahavvul-i 'aqlani*) of
nineteenth-century Iran. To dramatize the historical significance of
Descartes's translation, he speculated that all copies of an earlier 1853 edition
of the text might have been burned.[41]

In these narratives, the Comte de Gobineau, a French diplomat in Tehran
as well as an infamous anti-Semite,[42] was credited as the initiator of the rationalizing tasks of translating Descartes's generative text of European modernity into Persian. Although Gobineau commissioned this translation, he
doubted whether Iranians and other Asians were capable of absorbing modern civilization.[43] Like Gobineau, Iranian nationalist historians of scientific
modernity often assumed that "the defense of geocentricism was of greatest
importance for Muslim traditional scholars, just as it was for the medieval
church."[44] In such accounts the endeavor for modernity was often depicted as
a contention between the rational European astronomy and the irrational
Muslim astrology. For example, Bayat wrote that I'tizad al-Saltanah "rose in
defence of Newton and other European scientists' theories, and he declared
obsolete the 'knowledge of the ancients.'"[45] Likewise, Arjomand argued that
I'tizad al-Saltanah's work was "the first book of its kind, aimed at combating
the belief in traditional astronomy and astrology and bringing what might be
termed scientific enlightenment to 19th-century Iran."[46]

Recounting the contentions for scientific rationality, historians of modern Iran often selected scholars who endorsed astrology and opposed heliocentrism as Muslim representatives, ignoring those who did not fit into this schema. By claiming that the Persian publication of Descartes in the 1860s was the beginning of a new age of rationality and modernity, these historians provided a narrative account that accommodated and reinforced the foundational myth of modern Orientalism, a myth that constitutes "the West" as ontologically and epistemologically different from "the Orient."[47] This Orientalist problematic was validated by a nationalist historiography that constitutes the period prior its own arrival as a time of decay, backwardness, and despotism. By deploying the foundational assumptions of Orientalism for the enhancement of its own political project, in this sense, Iranian nationalist historiography participated in its own Orientalizing.[48] As self-designated vanguards of modernity and national homogenization, both official and counterofficial Iranian nationalists naturalized and authenticated Orientalists' temporal assumption of the noncontemporaneity of the contemporaneous Iranian and European societies.[49]

Homeless Texts

In the mid-seventeenth century a purely self-congratulatory view of European civilization as the paragon of universal reason and the concurring "blackmail of the Enlightenment"[50] had not yet been formed. Similarly, Europe's Oriental-Other had not yet been dehistoricized as only "traditional," "static," and "unchanging," and Muslims were not viewed as "anti-scientific." More significantly, historical thinking had not yet been confined to the boundaries of modern nation-states. It is during this period that an alternative account of a Persianate modernity can be retrieved. Predating the consolidation of modern nation-states and the co-optation of modernity as a state-legitimating ideology, following Foucault, modernity may be envisaged as an *ethos* rather than a well-demarcated historical period.[51] By envisaging modernity as an ethos, historians of Iran and India may imagine a joint fact-finding mission that would allow for reactivating what the poet Mahdi Akhavan Salis aptly recognized as "stories vanished from memory" (*qissah-ha-yi raftah az yad*).[52] These vanished stories may be retrieved from a large corpus of texts made homeless with the emergence of *history with borders,* a convention that confined historical writing to the borders of modern nation-states.

The convention of history with borders has created many *homeless texts* that have fallen victim to the fissure of Indian and Iranian nationalism. Although abolished as the official language of India in the 1830s, the intellectual use of Persian continued, and Persian publications in nineteenth-century India outnumbered those produced in other languages. Publishers in Calcutta, Bombay, Lucknow, Kanpur, Delhi, Lahore, Haydarabad, and other cities in the Indian subcontinent also published more Persian books than their counterparts in Iran. Many of the literary and historical texts edited and published in India achieved canonical status in neighboring Iran. Rammahan Roy, the acclaimed "father of modern India," was in fact the editor of one of the first Persian newspapers, *Mir'at al-Akhbar* (1822). This Indo-Iranian intellectual symmetry continued until the end of nineteenth century, when a Persian newspaper, *Miftah al-Zaffar* (1897), campaigned for the formation of Anjuman-i Ma'arif, an academy devoted to the strengthening of Persian as a scientific language.[53] Whereas the notion of "Western civilization" provided a safety net supplementing European national histories, no common historiographical practice captures the residues of the colonial and national conventions of historical writing that separates the joint Persianate literary culture of Iran and India—a literary culture that is irreducible to Islam and the Islamic civilization. A postcolonial historiography of Indian and Iranian modernity must begin to reactivate the concurring history that has been erased from memory by colonial conventions and territorial divisions.

The conventional account of Persianate acquaintance with the Cartesian notion of "I think, therefore I am" differs radically from an account retrievable from the *Travels* of François Bernier (b. 1620), a French scholar who resided in India for a few years. Approximately 200 years prior to Arthur de Gobineau, Danishmand Khan Shafi'a Yazdi (1578–1657), a Mughal courtier and Iranian émigré who was aware of current intellectual developments in Europe, dared to be wise (in Kant's sense of *sapere aude*) and commissioned Bernier to translate into Persian the works of René Descartes (1596–1650), William Harvey (1578–1657), and Jean Pecquet (1622–1674).[54] Bernier, a student of the philosopher Gassendi and a recipient of a doctor of medicine in 1652, who is also considered to be a founding figure of modern Orientalism,[55] was an employee of Mirza Shafi'a, who was granted the title *danishmand* (scholar/scientist) for his intellectual endeavors. Illustrating the intellectual audacity and curiosity of Danishmand Khan, Bernier wrote, "[M]y Navaab, or Agah, Danech-mend-khan . . . can no more dispense with his philosophical studies in the afternoon than avoid devoting the morning to his weighty duties as Secretary of State for Foreign Affairs and Grand Master of the Horse. Astronomy, geography, and anatomy are his favorite pursuits, and he reads with avidity the works of Gassendi and Descartes."[56] Danishmand Khan was known by his contemporaries to have espoused and disseminated many of the innovating principles of that [European] community (*aksari az ahkam-i tahrifat-i an jama'at tikrar minimud*) and desired to know European sciences (*'ilm-i ahl-i farang*) at a time when Europe was still plagued with religious wars.[57] His sustained interest in European intellectual developments is evident from his securing of a promise from Bernier to send him the books from *farangistan* [Europe].[58] It was within the dynamic intellectual community around Danishmand Khan that Bernier became familiar with Persian translations of classical Sanskrit texts, including the *Upanishads,* which he brought back to Paris.[59] But the writings of Danishmand Khan and his cohorts who trained Bernier—this pedagogue of educated society in seventeenth-century Europe—have remained virtually unknown. This is in part because of the stereotypical perception of the period of the Indian Mughal emperor Aurangzayb's rule (1658–1707) as the age of Muslim bigotry and medieval decline. Confined within the grand narratives of historical stages and countercolonial Hindu nationalism, historians of medieval India have mostly found facts of decline, all too often the only facts that they have searched for. During the same period, François Martin, a friend of Bernier who visited Iran in 1669, observed that Persians love the sciences, particularly mathematics. Contrary to received ideas, Martin reported, "It is believed that they [the Persians] are not very religious."[60] Likewise, Pietro della Valle (1586–1652) could still confide that the Persianate scholar Mulla Zayn al-Din Lari, who has remained unknown to historians of Iran, was comparable to the best in Europe.[61]

The scholarly efforts of Raja Jai Singh (1688–1743) provide another precolonial example of Persianate scholars' engagement with the modern sciences. Jai Singh built the observatories of Delhi, Banaris, and Jaipur and, based on new observations, prepared the famous Persian astronomical table *Zij-i Muhammad Shahi* of 1728.[62] After the initial draft of his astronomical calculations, he sent a mission to Portugal in 1730 to acquire new observational equipment and to inquire about recent astronomical findings. The mission, which included Father Emmanuel de Figueredo (circa 1690–1753) and Muhammad Sharif, returned with an edition of Phillipe de La Hire's *Tabulae Astronomicae* from 1702.[63] Mubashshir Khan provides a brief account of Jai Singh's scientific mission in his *Manahij al-Istikhraj,* an eighteenth-century guide for astronomical observation and calculations. He reported that Mirza Muhammad 'Abid and Mirza Khayr Allah were two Muslim engineers who assisted Raja Jai Singh in the building of observatories. He had met Mirza Khayr Allah, who explained to him how Jai Singh, with the assistance of Padre Manuel, acquired European observational equipment and a copy of de La Hire's *Tabulae.* La Hire's calculations were used by Jai Singh in a revised edition of his *Zij-i Muhammad Shahi.*[64] This astronomical table, which was well known to eighteenth-century Iranian scholars, has remained virtually unknown to historians of Iran.[65] It is significant to note that almost a century earlier Shah 'Abbas II (1642–1666) had also sent a mission to Rome to learn

European painting techniques. The delegation included Muhammad Zaman Paulo, whose macaronic style left a long-lasting imprint on representational art in both India and Iran.[66]

Works of Tafazzul Husayn Khan (d. 1800), well known to his Iranian friends and associates, are among other homeless texts that are elided from both Indian and Iranian annals of modernity. Hailed as an 'allamah (arch-scholar), he was an exemplary figure of the late eighteenth century who interacted closely with the first generation of British Orientalists in India and actively promoted vernacular inquiry into modern science. In the 1780s he translated Sir Isaac Newton's *Principia*, Emerson's *Mechanics*, and Thomas Simpson's *Algebra*.[67] In his obituary in 1803, *The Asiatic Annual Register* remembered Tafazzul Husayn Khan as "both in qualities and disposition of his mind, a very remarkable exception to the general character of Asiatic genius." Taking an exception to William Jones's assessment that "judgment and taste [were] the prerogative of Europeans," the obituary stated, "But with one, at least, of these proud prerogatives, the character of Tafazzul Husayn unquestionably interferes; for, a judgment at once sound, clear, quick, and correct, was its indistinguishable feature."[68] To document the accomplishments of this Asiatic who had "cultivated ancient as well as modern European literatures with ardor and success . . . very uncommon in any foreigner," *The Asiatic Annual Register* published letters received from Ruben Burrows (1747–1792),[69] David Anderson,[70] and Lord Teignmouth (1751–1834). Lord Teignmouth remarked that for Tafazzul Husayn Khan, mathematics was his favorite pursuit, and perceiving that the science had been cultivated to an extent in Europe far beyond what had been done in Asia, he determined to acquire a knowledge of European discoveries and improvements; and with this view, began the study of the English language. He further noted that in two years, Tafazzul Husayn Khan was not only able to understand any English mathematical work, but to peruse with pleasure the volumes of the best historians and moralists. From the same motives he afterward studied and acquired the Latin language, though in a less perfect degree; and before his death had made some progress in the acquisition of the Greek dialect.[71]

Well-acquainted with Tafazzul Husayn Khan, the British Orientalists Sir William Jones, Richard Johnson, and Ruben Burrows utilized his knowledge of classical Indo-Islamic sciences in their Orientalogical endeavors.[72]

Mir 'Abd al-Latif Shushtari (1758–1806), a close associate of Tafazzul Husayn Khan who traveled to India in 1788, provided a synopsis of European modernity, modern astronomy, and new scientific innovations in his *Tuhfat al-'alam* (1216 H/1801).[73] Shushtari constituted the year 900 of Hijrah (1494/5 CE) as the beginning of a new era associated with the decline of the caliphate (*khilafat*) of the pope (*papa*), the weakening of the Christian clergy, the ascent of philosophy,

and the strengthening of philosophers and scientists. Referring to the English
Civil War, he explained the decline of religion. While both philosophers and
rulers affirmed the unity of God, they viewed prophecy, resurrection, and
prayers as entirely myths (*hamah ra afsanah*).[74] He also explained the views of
Copernicus and Newton on heliocentricity and universal gravitation. Shushtari
rejected the astrological explanations of earlier philosophers (*hukama-yi ma
taqaddam*) and found affinities between the contemporary British scientific
views and the unbounded rejection of astrologers in the splendid *Shari'ah* (*kah
hamah ja dar Shari'at-i gharra' takzib-i munajimin varid shudah ast*). Critical of
the classical explanation of tides, as recounted by 'Abd Allah Jazayiri (d.
1173/1760) in *Tilism-i Sultani*, he offered a Newtonian account, relating the
tides to gravitational actions of the sun and moon on oceanic waters.[75] Accordingly, he explained why the magnitude of the high tides in Calcutta differed
from that of the coastal cities of the Persian Gulf. Written some fifty years prior
to I'tizad al-Saltanah's *Falak al-Sa'adah* (1861), Shushtari viewed Newton as a
great sage and distinguished philosopher (*hakim-i a'zam va filsuf-i mu'azzam*)
and ventured that in view of Newton's accomplishments all the golden books of
the ancients (*gawharin namah'ha-yi bastaniyan*) are now similar to images on
water (*nimunah-'i naqsh bar ab ast*).[76] Shushtari's critical reflections on European history and modern sciences was appreciated by Fath 'Ali Shah
(1797–1834), who assigned the historian Marvazi Vaqayi' Nigar (d. 1834) the
task of editing an abridged edition of *Tuhfat al-'Alam*, which is known as
Qava'id al-Muluk (Axioms of Kings).[77] Given Shushtari's competence in both
classical and modern astronomy, a periodization of Iranian scientific modernity
that lionizes I'tizad al-Saltanah's *Falak al-Sa'adah* (1861) as the harbinger of scientific modernity needs serious reconsideration. This is particularly important
since I'tizad al-Saltanah was familiar with *Qava'id al-Muluk*.[78]

Aqa Ahmad Bihbahani Kirmanshahi (1777–1819), an Iranian Shi'i scholar
and a friend of Shushtari who visited India between 1805 and 1810, devoted
a chapter of his travelogue, *Mir'at al-Ahval-i Jahan Nama* (1810), to the classification of the universe according to the school of the philosopher Copernicus.[79] In the introduction he explained that eminent philosophers are so numerous in Europe that their common masses (*avvam al-nas*) are inclined
philosophically and pursue mathematical and natural sciences.[80] Like many
other Muslim scholars, Bihbahani linked the new views (*ara'-i jadidah*) of
Copernicus to those of ancient Greek philosophers but emphasized that most
of his beliefs are original (*mu'taqidat-i u aksari tazigi darand*).[81] He explained
favorably the heliostatic system, the sidereal periods for the rotation of plan-
ets around the sun, the daily axial and annual orbital revolutions of the earth,
and the trinary rotations of the moon. This Muslim theologian found no necessary conflict between Islam and modern astronomy.[82]

The corpus of homeless texts of modernity includes Mawlavi Abu al-Khayr's concise account of the Copernican solar system, *Majmu'ah-'i Shamsi* (1807),[83] which appears to have been known in Iran.[84] Like the works of Tafazzul Husayn Khan, *Majmu'ah* is a product of dialogic interaction between Persianate scholars and British colonial officers. Among topics discussed in the *Majmu'ah* are the movements of the earth, the law of inertia, the planetary motions, and universal gravitation. In the introduction Mawlavi Abu al-Khayr noted that his book was based on English language sources and was translated with the assistance (*bi-i'anat*) of Dr. William Hunter (1718–1783).[85] It is significant to note that Hunter had introduced Raja Jai Singh's *Zij-i Muhammad Shahi* to the English reading public in an article appearing in *Asiatic Researches* (1799).[86] It is likely that Mawlavi Abu al-Khayr had assisted Hunter in understanding and translating this highly technical Persian text.

During the first three decades of the nineteenth century numerous other texts on modern sciences were written in Persian that do not appear in accounts of Iranian and Indian modernity.[87] Muhammad Rafi' al-Din Khan's treatise on modern geometry and optics, *Rafi' al-Basar* (1250 H/1834),[88] was one such text. The author was informed by English sources brought to his attention by Rev. Henry Martyn (1781–1812),[89] a renowned Christian missionary and a translator of the Bible into Persian.[90] With an increased mastery of modern science, Persianate scholars become active in the production of scientific knowledge. In *A'zam al-Hisab*, a treatise on mathematics completed in 1814, Hafiz Ahmad Khan A'zam al-Mulk Bahadur (d. 1827) took issue with the Scottish astronomer James Ferguson on reckoning the difference between the Christian and the Muslim calendar. Aware of the self-congratulatory views of Europeans, "particularly among the people of England," A'zam al-Mulk wrote a treatise on astronomy, *Mir'at al-'Alam* (1819), in order to "disprove" the assertion that Muslims were "uninformed of mathematics and astronomy."[91] Based on Copernican astronomy and informed by the most recent observations and discoveries at the Madras Observatory, this treatise likewise remains homeless and among those not yet included in the Indian and Iranian nationalist accounts of modernity.

Orientalism's Forgotten Texts

Similar to the capitalist process of commodification and reification,[92] histories of Orientalism have concealed the traces of creativity and agency of the intellectual laborers who produced the works that bear the signature of "pioneering" Orientalists. The archives of unpublished Persian texts commissioned by eighteenth- and nineteenth-century British Orientalists reveal this underside of Orientalism. Having examined the works of the British who commissioned these unpublished works, it appears that they had "authored" books that closely resemble their commissioned Persian works.

Sir William Jones (1746–1794), who is viewed as the founder of British Orientalism as well as "one of the leading figures in the history of modern linguistics,"[93] relied heavily on the intellectual labor of numerous Persianate scholars. He was supported by an extensive network of scholars whom he labeled as "my private establishment of readers and writers."[94] This network of "readers and writers," included Tafazzul Husayn Khan (d. 1801), Mir Muhammad Husayn Isfahani, Bahman Yazdi, Mir 'Abd al-Latif Shushtari, 'Ali Ibrahim Khan Bahadur, Muhammad Ghaus, Ghulam Husayn Khan Tabataba'i (1727–1814?), Yusuf Amin (1726–1809), Mulla Firuz, Mahtab Rai, Haji Abdullah, Sabur Tiwari, Siraj al-Haqq, and Muhammad Kazim. In addition, Jones was assisted by many pundits, including Radhacant Sarman. In one letter he specified that, "My pendits must be *nik-khu, zaban-dan, bid-khwan, Farsi-gu* [well-tempered, linguist, Vedantist/Sanskrit-reader, and Persophone]."[95] As the manager of an extensive scholarly enterprise, William Jones appropriated as his own the finished works that were the products of the intellectual capital and labor of these Indian scholars.

Jones's connection to Persianate scholars predated his 1783 arrival in India. Mirza I'tisam al-Din, an Indian who traveled to England between 1766 and 1769, reported that during his journey to Europe he helped to translate the introductory section of the Persian dictionary *Farhang-i Jahangiri,* which was made available to Jones when he composed his academic best-seller, *A Grammar of the Persian Language* (1771). As Munshi I'tisam al-Din recounted

> Formerly, on ship-board, Captain S[winton] read with me the whole of the Kuleelaah and Dumnah [*Kalilah va Dimnah*], and had translated the twelve rules of the Furhung Jehangeree [*Farhang-i Jahangiri*], which comprise the grammar of the Persian language. Mr. Jones having seen that translation, with the approbation of Captain S[winton], compiled his Grammar, and having printed it, sold it and made a good deal of money by it. This Grammar is a very celebrated one.[96]

With the publication of his "The Sixth Discourse: On the Persians" (1789),[97] Jones was recognized as "the creator of comparative grammar."[98] While Jones continues to be lionized for his remarks concerning the affinity of languages,[99] the Persian-Indian scholars and texts that informed Jones's work have remained unknown.

A few decades prior to Jones, the Persian lexicographer and linguist Siraj al-Din Khan Arzu (1689–1756) wrote a comprehensive study of the Persian language, *Muthmir* (Fruition), discerning its affinity with Sanskrit.[100] Textual evidence indicates that Jones was familiar with this work and so had used it in writing the lecture that gained him recognition as "the creator of the comparative grammar of Sanskrit and Zend."[101] In his study of phonetic and semantic similarities and differences of Persian, Arabic, and Sanskrit, and the interconnected processes of Arabization (*ta'rib*), Sanskritization/Hindianization (*tahnid*), and Persianization (*tafris*) in Iran and India, Arzu was fully aware of the originality of his own discernment on the affinity of Sanskrit and Persian. He wrote, "Amongst so many Persian and Hindi [Sanskrit] lexicographers and researchers of this science [*fann*], no one except *faqir* Arzu has discerned the affinity [*tavafuq*][102] of Hindi and Persian languages." Arzu was amazed that lexicographers such as 'Abd al-Rashid Tattavi (d. 1658), the compiler of *Farhang-i Rashidi* (1064/1653) who had lived in India, had failed to observe "so much affinity between these two languages."[103] The exact date of the completion of Arzu's *Muthmir* has not been ascertained. But it is clear that Arzu had used the technical term "*tavafuq al-lisanayn*" (the affinity/concordance of languages) in his *Chiraq-i Hidayat* (1160 H./1747), a dictionary of rare Persian and Persianized concepts and phrases.[104] In this dictionary he offered examples of words common to both Persian and Hindi (Sanskrit).[105] Since Arzu died in 1756, *Muthmir* must have been written prior to that date. Arzu's works on the affinity of Sanskrit and Persian certainly predated the 1767 paper by Father Coeurdoux, who had inquired about the affinity of Sanskrit and Latin.[106]

Traces of Persianate texts can be found in many other works of British Orientalists. For instance, Charles Hamilton's *Historical Relation of the Origin, Progress, and Final Dissolution of the Rohilla Afghans* (1787) corresponds closely to Shiv Parshad's *Tarikh-i Fayz Bakhsh* (1776).[107] Similarly, W. Francklin's *History of the Reign of Shah-Aulum, the Present Emperor of Hindustan* (1798) is comparable in content and form to Ghulam 'Ali Khan's *Ayi'in 'Alamshahi*.[108] Likewise, a large set of Persian language reports on Tibet provided the textual and factual foundations for Captain Samuel Turner's *An Account of an Embassy to the Court of the Teshoo Lama in Tibet Containing a Narrative of a Journey through Bootan, and Part of Tibet* (1800).[109] The most fascinating of these textual concordances is William Moorcroft's *Travels in the Himalayan Provinces of Hindustan and Panjab*.[110] Moorcroft is recognized as "one of the most important pioneers of modern scientific veterinary medicine" and is also viewed as "a pioneering innovator in almost everything he touched." In 1812 Moorcroft commissioned Mir 'Izzat Allah to journey from Calcutta to the Central Asian city of Bukhara. Along the way, Mir 'Izzat Allah collected invaluable historical and anthropological information, which he recorded in his *Ahval-i Safar-i Bukhara*.[111] Mir Izzat Allah's findings, similarly, provided the factual foundations for the "pioneering" *Travels* of Moorcroft. A preliminary inquiry indicates that Moorcroft might not have personally made the recounted journey that is praised for its "accuracy of historiographical and political observations."

Based on these and other collated texts, it seems that in the formative phase of the discipline, European students of the Orient, rather than initiating "original" and "scientific" studies, had relied heavily on research findings of native scholars. By rendering these works into English, the colonial officers in India fabricated scholarly credentials for themselves and, by publishing these works under their own names, gained prominence as Oriental scholars back home.[112] The process of translation and publication enabled the Europeans to obliterate the traces of the native producers of these works and thus divest them of authorality and originality, attributes that came to be recognized as the distinguishing marks of European "scholars" of the Orient. In many of these cases, European scholars differentiated their works by adding the scholarly apparatuses of footnotes and references, citations that were already available in the body of the commissioned texts.

In some other cases, scholarly competition helped to preserve the name of the original authors. For instance, Mirza Salih Shirazi served as a guide for the delegation led by Sir Gore Ouseley (1770–1844), the British ambassador extraordinary and plenipotentiary, who visited Iran between 1811 and 1812.[113] Mirza Salih accompanied and kept records of the journey of this delegation, which included leading Orientalists William Ouseley (1767–1842), William Price, and James Morier (1780–1849).[114] Mirza Salih composed a set of dialogues in Persian that were published in William Price's *A Grammar of the Three Principal Oriental Languages*.[115] According to Price, "While we were at Shiraz, I became acquainted with Mirza Saulih, well known for his literary acquirements: he entered our train and remained with the Embassy a considerable time, during which I prevailed upon him to compose a set of dialogues in his native tongue, the pure dialect of Shiraz."[116] In his *Travels* of thirteen years earlier William Ouseley had cited an "extract from some familiar Dialogues, written at my request by a man of letters at Shiraz."[117] The extract offered by Ouseley was the opening of the "Persian Dialogues" written by Mirza Salih.[118] Both Ouseley and Price claimed that the "Dialogue" was written at their request.[119] These competing claims may account for the preservation of the name of Mirza Salih as its author. In the introduction to the "Dialogue," Price humbly noted, "having myself no motive but that of contributing to the funds of Oriental literature, and of rendering the attainment of the Persian language to students; I have given the Dialogues verbatim, with an English [sic] translation as literal as possible."[120] Mirza Salih also assisted Price in the research for his *Dissertation*.[121] William Ouseley likewise credited Mirza Salih for providing him with a "concise description and highly economiastick [sic]" narrative on historical and archaeological sites used in his *Travels in Various Countries of the East, More Particularly Persia.* Having relied on Mirza Salih's contribution, Ouseley viewed part of the work as "the result of our joint research."[122] Oddly enough, Mirza Salih is only remembered as a member of the first group of Iranian students sent to England in 1810 who were supposedly in need of "instruction in reading and writing their own language."[123]

The obliteration of the intellectual contributions of Persianate scholars to the formation of Orientalism coincided with the late eighteenth-century emergence of authorship as a principle of textual attribution and accreditation in Europe. The increased significance of authorship is attributed to the Romantic revolution and its articulation of the author "as the productive origin of the text, as the subjective source that, in bringing its unique position to expression, constitutes a 'work' ineluctably its own."[124] With the increased cultural significance of innovation (*inventio*), European interlocutors constituted themselves as the repositories of originality and authorship. It was precisely at this historical conjuncture that contemporary works of non-European scholars began to be devalued and depicted as *traditio*. This rhetorical strategy authorized the marginalization of Persianate scholarship at a time when the existing systems of scholarly patronage in Iran and India were dislocated. Without stable institutional and material resources that authorized the Persianate scholars, Orientalists were able to appropriate their intellectual works. The institutionalization of Orientalism as a field of academic inquiry, and its authorization of "original sources," enabled European scholars to effectively appropriate the works of their non-Western contemporaries who were denied agency and creativity.

The challenge of postcolonial historiography is to rehistoricize the processes that have been concealed and ossified by the Eurocentric accounts of Orientalism. This challenge also involves uncovering the underside of "Occidental rationality." Such a project must go beyond a Saidian critique of Orientalism as "a systematic discourse by which Europe was able to manage—even produce—the Orient politically, sociologically, militarily, ideologically, scientifically, and imaginatively." Said's *Orientalism* provided the foundation for immensely productive scholarly works on European colonial agency, but these works rarely explore the agency and imagination of Europe's Other, who are depicted as passive and traditional. This denial of agency and *coevality* to the "Rest" provided the ground for the exceptionality of the "West." By reconstituting the intertextual relations between Western texts and their repressed "Oriental" mastertexts, the postcolonial historiography can reenact the dialogical relations between the West and the Rest, a relationship that was essential to the formation of the ethos of modernity. The reinscription of the homeless texts into historical accounts of Orientalism is essential to this historiographical project.

Decolonizing Historical Imagination

The preceding analysis calls for the decolonization of historical imagination and the rethinking of what is commonly meant by South Asian and Middle Eastern modernity. By anticipating a period of decline that paved the way for the British colonization, historians of Mughal India have searched predominantly for facts that illustrate the backwardness and the disintegration of this empire. Mughal historiography in this respect has a plot structure similar to late Ottoman history. In both cases, the dominant themes of decline and disintegration are based on a projection about the rise and progress of Europe. In a similar manner, historians of modern Iran inherited historiographical traditions that militate against the construction of historical narratives about the pre-Constitutional and/or pre-Pahlavi times as anything but an age of ignorance (*bikhabari*), stagnation, and despotism. Anticipating the coming of the Constitutional Revolution of 1905–1909, historians have crafted narratives of intolerable conditions that instigated the coming of the revolution.[125] Written by a participant of the revolution between 1910 and 1912, Nazim al-Islam Kirmani entitles his paradigmatic account of the revolution *Tarikh-i Bidari-i Iraniyan* (The History of the Awakening of Iranians), revealing this prevalent assumption of prerevolutionary dormancy. To legitimate the Pahlavi dynasty (1926–1979) as the architect of Iranian modernity and progress, Pahlavi historians likewise depicted the Qajar period as the dark age of Iranian history. These two Iranian historiographical traditions have been informed by, and in turn have informed, Orientalist accounts of Qajar shahs as absolute Oriental despots and Islam as only a fetter to rationalization and secularization. Inscribing the history of Europe on that of India and Iran, both Indian and Iranian historians have deployed a regressive conception of time that constitutes their respective histories in terms of lacks and failures.

These bordered histories have rendered homeless texts that yield a different account and periodization of Persianate modernity. Historians of modern India often view Persian as a language only of the medieval Muslim Mughal court and thus find it unnecessary to explore the Persian texts of modernity.[126] Viewing Persian as solely an Iranian language, historians of Iran also consider unworthy Persian texts produced outside of the country. The conventional Persian literary histories, moreover, regard poetry as a characteristically Iranian mode of self-expression. With the privileged position of poetry in the invented national *mentalite,* the prose texts of the humanities are devalued and scholarly efforts are infrequently spent on editing and publishing nonpoetic texts. Thus a large body of historically significant prose texts of modernity have remained unpublished. This willful marginalization of prose is often masked as a sign of the prominence of poetry as an intrinsically Iranian mode of expression. These factors account for the elision of texts produced in India, which are stereotypically considered as either linguistically faulty or as belonging to the corpus of the degenerate Indian-style (*sabk-i Hindi*) texts. Consequently, Persian-language texts documenting precolonial engagement with the modern sciences and responding to European colonial domination have remained nationally homeless and virtually unknown to historians working within the confines of modern Indian and Iranian nationalist paradigms. This has led to several historiographical problems. Exclusion of these homeless texts from national historical canons, on the one hand, has contributed to the hegemony of Eurocentric and Orientalist conceptions of modernity as something uniquely European. On the other hand, by ignoring the homeless texts, both Indian and Iranian historians tend to consider modernity only under the rubric of a belated Westernization. Such a conception of modernity reinforces the exceptionality of Occidental rationality and corroborates the programmatic view of Islamic and Oriental societies and cultures as static, traditional, and unhistorical. This historical imagination is simultaneously grounded on two problematic conceptions of historical time. On the one hand it is grounded in the presupposition of the noncontemporaneity of the contemporaneous Western and Oriental societies, and on the other hand it is based on the dehistoricizing supposition of the contemporaneity of the noncontemporaneous early nineteenth-century and ancient modes of life. With the onset of Westernization, consequently, the premodern repetition of ancient modes of life is replaced with the repetition of Western modernity.[127]

Notes

A related version of this chapter was published in *Refashioning Iran: Orientalism, Occidentalism, and Nationalist Historiography* (Houndmills, U.K.: Palgrave, 2003).

1. For instance, see Enrique Dussel, "Eurocentrism and Modernity," *Boundary 2* 20, 3 (1993): 65–76; Enrique Dussel, *The Underside of Modernity: Apel, Ricoeur, Rorty, Taylor, and the Philosophy of Liberation,* trans. Eduardo Mendieta (Atlantic Highlands, N.J.: Humanities, 1996); Dipesh Chakrabarty, *Proventializing Europe: Postcolonial Thought and Historical Difference* (Princeton, N.J.: Princeton University Press, 2000).

2. Max Weber, *The Protestant Ethic and the Spirit of Capitalism* (New York: Scribner, 1958), p. 25; Jürgen Habermas, *The Philosophical Discourse of Modernity: Twelve Lectures,* trans. Frederick G. Lawrence (Cambridge, Mass.: MIT Press, 1987), p. 1.

3. For instance see Bernard Lewis, "The Impact of the West," in *The Emergence of Modern Turkey,* 2nd ed. (London: Oxford University Press, 1961), pp. 40–73; Leonard Binder, "The Natural History of Development Theory, with a Discordant Note on the Middle East," in *Islamic Liberalism: A Critique of Development Ideology* (Chicago: University of Chicago Press, 1988), pp. 24–84.

4. According to G. E. von Grunebaum

Acculturation, or more precisely Westernization, in the Near and Middle East has gone through distinct typical phases. After the shock caused by the discovery of inadequacy, there followed an almost complete surrender to foreign values and (not infrequently misunderstood) aspirations; then with Westernization partially realized, a recoiling set in from the alien, which however, continues to be absorbed greedily, and a falling back on the native tradition; this tradition is restyled and, in some instances, newly created with borrowed techniques of scholarship to give respectability to the results. Finally, with Westernization very largely completed in terms of governmental reforms, acceptance of the values of science, and adoption of Western literary and artistic forms, regained self-confidence expresses itself in hostility to the West and in insistence upon the native and original character of the borrowed product. (*Modern Islam: The Search for Cultural Identity* [Berkeley: University of California Press, 1962], pp. 248–88; quote on 248).

5. Stuart Hall, "The West and the Rest: Discourse and Power," in Stuart Hall, David Held, Don Hubert, and Kenneth Thompson, eds., *Modernity: An Introduction to Modern Societies* (Cambridge, Mass.: Blackwell Publishers, 1996), pp. 184–227; J. M. Roberts, *The Triumph of the West* (London: British Broadcasting Corporation, 1985), particularly pp. 194–202.

6. Hall, p. 187. The dichotomy, the West and the Rest, was originally formulated by Marshall Sahlins in his *Culture and Practical Reason* (Chicago: University of Chicago Press, 1976).

7. Hall, p. 221.

8. Michel Foucault, "Of Other Spaces," *Diacritics* 16, 1 (Spring 1986): 22–27, quotes on 24 and 27.

9. Stephen Toulmin, *Cosmopolis: The Hidden Agenda of Modernity*, 2nd ed. (Chicago: University of Chicago Press, 1992), p. 28.

10. For instance, see Judith Shklar, *Montesquieu* (Oxford: Oxford University Press, 1987), p. 30.

11. The first edition of *The Persian Letters* was published in 1721. In Letter 91, documenting this evocative pertinent context writing about Muhammad Riza Bayk, Montesquieu noted, "There has appeared a personage got up as a Persian ambassador, who has insolently played a trick on the two greatest kings in the world." See his *Persian Letters* (1721; New York: Penguin, 1973), pp. 172–73.

12. Maria Rosa Menocal, *The Arabic Role in Medieval Literary History: A Forgotten Heritage* (Philadelphia: University of Pennsylvania Press, 1987), p. 2. Explaining the scholarly resistance to this view of European awakening, Menocal writes, "The tenor of some of the responses to the suggestion that this Arab-centered vision might be a viable historiographical reconstruction for the West has occasionally been reminiscent of the reaction once provoked by Darwin's suggestion (for so was the theory of evolution constructed) that we were 'descended from monkey'" (p. 3).

13. Ann Stoler, *Race and the Education of Desire: Foucault's History of Sexuality and the Colonial Order of Things* (Durham, N.C.: Duke University Press, 1995), p. 15. On "laboratory of modernity," see Paul Rabinow, *French Modern: Norms and Forms of the Social Environment* (Cambridge, Mass.: MIT Press, 1989), pp. 289 and 317.

14. For example, see Paul Rabinow; Sidney Mintz, *Sweetness and Power* (New York: Viking, 1985); Timothy Mitchell, *Colonizing Egypt* (Cambridge: Cambridge University

Press, 1988); Uday Mehta, *Liberalism and Empire: A Study in Nineteenth-Century British Liberal Thought* (Chicago: University of Chicago Press, 1999); Benedict Anderson, *Imagined Communities: Reflections on the Origin and Spread of Nationalism* (London: Verso, 1983); Nicholas B. Dirks, "Introduction: Colonialism and Culture," in *Colonialism and Culture* (Ann Arbor: University of Michigan Press, 1992).

15. Stoler, p. 16.

16. Rabinow, p. 289.

17. Anderson, pp. 47–65; quote on 50 (emphasis in original).

18. Stoler, p. 195.

19. Mohamad Tavakoli-Targhi, "Orientalism's Genesis Amnesia," *Comparative Studies of South Asia, Africa and the Middle East* 16, 1 (Spring 1996): 1–14.

20. According to Jürgen Habermas

> The theory of modernization performs two abstractions on Weber's concept of "modernity." It dissociates "modernity" from its modern European origins and stylizes it into a spatio-temporally neutral model for processes of social development in general. Furthermore it breaks the internal connections between modernity and the historical context of Western rationalism, so that processes of modernization can no longer be conceived of as rationalization, as the historical objectification of rational structures (*The Philosophical Discourse of Modernity*, p. 2).

21. According to Toulmin, "In four fundamental ways . . . 17th-century philosophers set aside the long-standing preoccupation of Renaissance humanism. In particular, they disclaimed any serious interest in four different kinds of practical knowledge: the oral, the particular, the local, and the timely" (*Cosmopolis,* 30).

22. Johannes Fabian defines the denial of coeval-ness as "*a persistent and systematic tendency to place the referent(s) of anthropology in a Time other than the present of the producer of anthropological discourse* [emphasis in original]." See his *Time and the Other: How Anthropology Makes Its Object* (New York: Columbia University Press, 1983), p. 31.

23. Daryush Shayegan, *Cultural Schizophrenia: Islamic Societies Confronting the West*, trans. John Howe (London: Saqi Books, 1992), p. 12.

24. Reza Davari Ardakani, *Shimmah'i az Tarikh-i Gharbzadigi-i Ma: Vaz'-i Kununi-i Tafakkur dar Iran* (Tehran: Surush, 1363 [1984]), p. 88.

25. For a study of the past as illness, see Mohamad Tavakoli-Targhi, "Going Public: Patriotic and Matriotic Homeland in Iranian Nationalist Discourses," *Strategies* 13, 2 (November 2000): 174–200.

26. For instance, see Ahmad Ashraf, "Historical Obstacles to the Development of a Bourgeoisie in Iran," in M. A. Cook, ed., *Studies in the Economic History of the Middle East: from the Rise of Islam to the Present Day* (London: Oxford University Press, 1970), pp. 308–32; Kazim Alamdari, *Chira Iran aqab mand va gharb pish raft?* (Tehran: Nashr-i Gam-i Naw: Tawsiah, 1379/2000).

27. John Malcolm, *The History of Persia from the Most Early Period to the Present Time* (London: J. Murray, 1815), vol. 2, p. 621; for the Persian translation, see *Tarikh-i Iran*, trans. Mirza Isma'il Hayrat (Bombay: Matba'-i Datparsat, 1886).

28. George W. F. Hegel, *The Philosophy of History*, trans. J. Sibree (Buffalo, N.Y.: Prometheus Books, 1991), p. 188.

29. Malcolm, vol. 2, pp. 622, 623, and 624.

30. Samuel Huntington, *The Clash of Civilizations?* (Cambridge, Mass.: Harvard University, John M. Olin Institute for Strategic Studies, [1993]).

31. For instance, see Ahmad Ashraf's renowned work *Mavani'-i Tarikhi-i Rushd-i Sarmayahdari dar Iran: Dawrah-'i Qajariyah* (Tehran: Zaminah, 1359).

32. Ervand Abrahamian, *Iran between Two Revolutions* (Princeton, N.J.: Princeton University Press, 1982), respectively on pp. 35, 38, 39, 40, and 47.

33. Homa Katouzian, *The Political Economy of Modern Iran: Despotism and Pseudo-Modernism, 1926–1979* (New York: New York University Press, 1981), pp. 7–26, 298–300; Homa Katouzian, "Arbitrary Rule: A Comparative Theory of State, Politics and Society in Iran," *British Society for Middle Eastern Studies* 24, 1 (1977): 49–73; Ervand Abrahamian, "Oriental Despotism: The Case of Qajar Iran," *International Journal of Middle Eastern Studies* 5 (1984): 3–31; Ervand Abrahamian, "European Feudalism and Middle Eastern Despotisms," *Science and Society* 39 (1975): 135.

34. Guity Nashat, *The Origins of Modern Reform in Iran, 1870–80* (Urbana: University of Illinois Press, 1982).

35. Meagan Morris, "Metamorphoses at Sydney Tower," *New Formations* 11 (Summer 1990): 10, cited in Dipesh Chakrabarty, "Postcoloniality and the Artifice of History" *Representations* 37 (Winter 1992): 1–26; quote on 17.

36. Morris, p. 10.

37. Mangol Bayat, *Iran's First Revolution: Shi'ism and the Constitutional Revolution of 1905–1909* (Oxford: Oxford University Press, 1991), p. 36

38. Ali Quli Mirza I'tizad al-Saltanah, *Falak al-Sa'adah* (Tehran: Dar al-Taba'ah-'i Aqa Mir Muhammad Tihrani, 1278/1861).

39. Bayat, p. 37.

40. Elie Kedouri, *Afghani and Abduh: An Essay on Religious Unbelief and Political Activism in Modern Islam* (London: Cass, 1966), pp. 44–45; Nikki Keddie, *Sayyid Jamal al-Din "al-Afghani": A Political Biography* (Berkeley: University of California Press, 1972), pp. 197–99; Jamshid Bihnam, *Iraniyan va Andishah-'i Tajaddud* (Tehran: Farzan Ruz, 1375/1996), pp. 32-34; Alireza Manafzadeh, "Nukhustin Matn-i Falsafah-'i Jadid-i Gharbi bah Zaban-i Farsi," *Iran Nameh* 9, 1 (Winter 1991): 98–108.

41. Faraydun Adamiyat, *Andishah-'i Tarraqi va Hukumat-i Qanun: 'Asr-i Sipahsalar* (Tehran: Khwarazmi, 1351/1972), pp. 17 and 18.

42. On Arthur Gobineau's anti-Semitism, see Peter Pulzer, *The Rise of Political Anti-Semitism in Germany and Austria* (New York: Wiley [1964]).

43. Arthur Gobineau, *Les religions et philosophies dans l'Asie centrale* (Paris, 1979), 98, pp. 110–14; Arthur Gobineau, *Trois ans en Asie, Voyage en Perse* (Paris: Métailié, 1980), pp. 322–23, 330–36.

44. Kamran Arjomand, "The Emergence of Scientific Modernity in Iran: Controversies Surrounding Astrology and Modern Astronomy in Mid-Nineteenth Century," *Iranian Studies*, 30, 1–2 (Winter/Spring 1997): 15.

45. Bayat, p. 37

46. Arjomand, p. 17.

47. According to Edward Said: "Orientalism is a style of thought based upon an ontological and epistemological distinction made between 'the Orient' and (most of the time) 'the Occident.' Thus a very large mass of writers . . . have accepted the basic distinction between East and West as the starting point for elaborate theories, epics, novels, social descriptions, and political accounts concerning the Orient, its people, 'mind', destiny, and so on." See his *Orientalism* (New York: Vintage, 1979), pp. 2–3.

48. Writing about the post–World War II developments in the Middle East, Said observed: "despite its failures, its lamentable jargon, its scarcely concealed racism, its paper-thin intellectual apparatus, Orientalism flourishes today in the forms I have tried to describe. Indeed, there is some reason for alarm in the fact that its influence has spread to 'the Orient' itself: the pages of books and journals in Arabic (and doubtless in Japanese, various Indian dialects, and other Oriental languages) are filled with second-order analyses by Arabs of 'the Arab mind', 'Islam', and other myths." See Edward Said, *Orientalism*, 322.

49. Elaborating the function of intellectuals in self-Orientalizing, Said wrote

Its role has been prescribed and set for it as a "modernizing" one, which means that it gives legitimacy and authority to ideas about modernization, progress, and culture that it receives from the United States for the most part. Impressive evidence for this is found in the social sciences and surprisingly enough, among radical intellectuals whose Marxism is taken wholesale from Marx's own homogenizing view of the Third world. . . . So if all told there is an intellectual acquiescence in the image and doctrines of Orientalism, there is also a very powerful reinforcement of this in economic, political, and social exchanges: the modern Orient, in short, participates in its own Orientalizing." Said, *Orientalism*, 325.

50. Michel Foucault, "What Is Enlightenment?" in *Ethics: Subjectivity and Truth*, ed. Paul Rabinow (New York: New Press, 1994), pp. 303–319; quote on 312.

51. Foucault, "What Is Enlightenment?" pp. 309–10.

52. Mahdi Akhavn Salis, "Akhir-i Shahnamah," in *Akhir-i Shahnamah*, 8th ed. (Tehran: Intisharat-i Murvarid, 1363 [1984]), pp. 79–86, quote on 85.

53. "Anjuman-i Ma'arif," *Miftah al-Zaffar* 2, 12 (March 22, 1899): 182–83.

54. François Bernier, *Travels in the Mogul Empire, AD 1656–1668*, trans. Archibald Constable, Rev. Vincent Smith (reprint; New Delhi: Atlantic Publishers & Distributers, 1989), pp. 324–25. Danishmand Khan, also known as Muhammad Shafi', was born in Iran and went to Surat, India, in 1646. Shah Jahan appointed him as a Bakhshi (military paymaster) and granted him the title of Danishmand Khan. Alamgir appointed him as governor of Shah Jahan Abad or New Delhi, where he died in 1670. William Harvey was a lecturer at the Royal College of Physicians and discovered the circulation of blood. Jean Pecquet discovered the conversion of chyle into blood.

55. Raymond Schwab, *The Oriental Renaissance: Europe's Rediscovery of India and the East, 1680–1880*, trans. Gene Patterson-Black and Victor Reinking (New York: Columbia University Press, 1984), pp. 142–46.

56. Bernier, respectively pp. 324–25 and pp. 352–53.

57. Samsam al-Dawlah Shahnavaz Khan, *Ma'asir al-Umara*, ed. Mawlavi 'Abd al-Rahim and Mawlavi Mirza Ashraf 'Ali (Calcutta: Asiatic Society of Bengal, 1892), vol. 2, pp. 30–32; quote on 32.

58. François Bernier to M. Caron (March 10, 1663) in François Martin, *François Martin Mémoires: Travels to Africa, Persia & India*, trans. Aniruddha Ray (Calcutta: Subarnarekha, 1990), pp. 546–66; quote on 548.

59. This Persian translation of the *Upanishads* was rendered into French and Latin by Anquetil-Duperron in 1801–1802.

60. Martin, *François Martin Mémoires*, pp. 441–42.

61. Pietro della Valle, *Viaggi di Pietro della Valle* (Brighton, 1843), pp. 326–28; cited in Arjomand, p. 7; John D. Gurney, "Pietro Della Valle: The Limits of Perception," *Bulletin of the School of Oriental and African Studies* (1986): 103–16.

62. On the *Zij-i Muhammad Shahi*, see William Hunter, "Some Account of the Astronomical Labours of Jaha Sinha, Raja of Ambhere, or Jayanagar," *Asiatic Society* 5 (1799): 177–210. This article includes the preface of the *Zij* and its English translation. Also see G. R. Kaye, *The Astronomical Observatories of Jai Singh* (Calcutta: Archaeological Survey of India, 1918); Eric Forbes, "The European Astronomical Tradition: Its Transmission into India, and Its Reception by Sawai Jai Singh II," *Indian Journal of History of Science* 17, 2 (1982): 234–43; Virendra Nath Sharma, "Jai Singh, His European Astronomers and Its Copernican Revolution," *Indian Journal of History of Science* 18, 1 (1982): 333–44; Raymond Mercier, "The Astronimical Tables of Rajah Jai Singh Sawa'i," *Indian Journal of History of Science* 19 (1984): 143–71; S. A. Khan Ghori, "Development of Zij Literature in India," in S. N. Sen and K. S. Shukla, eds., *History of Astronomy in India* (New Delhi: Indian National Science Academy, 1985), pp. 20–47.

63. Phillipe de La Hire (1640–1718), *Tabulae astronomicae* (Paris: Apud Joannem Boudot, 1702). This was originally published in 1687.

64. Muhammad 'Ali Mubashshir Khan, *Manahij al-Istikhraj* (Unpublished manuscript: Kitabkhanah-'i Astan-i Quds-i Razavi, #12302). On the influence of de La Hire, see Virendra Nath Sharma, "Zïj Muhammad Shahi and the Tables of de La Hire," *Indian Journal of History of Science* 25, 1–4 (1990): 36–41.

65. Many copies of *Zij-i Muhammad Shahi* are available in Iranian libraries. One of the earliest editions is reported "to be extant" in the library of Madrasah-'i 'Ali-i Sipahsalar, which was renamed after the 1979 Revolution as Madrasah-'i 'Ali-i Shahid Mutahhari. See S. M. Razaullah Ansari, "Introduction of Modern Western Astronomy in India During 18-9 Centuries," in S. N. Sen and K. S. Shukla, eds., *History of Astronomy in India* (New Delhi: Indian National Science Academy, 1985), pp. 363–402.

66. 'Abbas Mazda, "Nufuz-i Sabk-i Urupa'i dar Naqashi-i Iran," *Payam-i Nau*, 2, 10 (1325 [1946]): 59–72, particularly 61; Husayn Mahbubi Ardakani, *Tarikh-i Mu'assasat-I tamadduni-I Jadid dar Iran* (Tehran: Anjuman-I Danishjuyan-I Danishgah-I Tihran, 1975–1989), vol. 1, p. 234. The claim of Muhammad Zamman's travel to Europe is refuted by the Russian Orientalist Igor Akimushkin. See Abolala Soudavar, "European and Indian Influences," in *Art of the Persian Courts: Selections from the Art and History Trust Collection* (New York: Rizzoli International Publications, 1992), pp. 365–79, particularly f.n. #16, p. 379. For a critical evaluation of the controversy over Muhammad Zaman's career, see A. A. Ivanov, "Nadirah-'i Dawran Muhammad

Zaman," in *Davazdah Rukh: Yadnigari az Dawazdah Naqash-i Nadirahkar-i Iran*, trans. Ya'qub Azhand (Tehran: Intisharat-i Mawla, 1377/1998), pp. 313–28.

67. Mir 'Abd al-Latif Shushtari, *Tuhfat al-'Alam va Zayl al-Tuhfah*, ed. Samad Muvahhid (reprint; Tehran: Tahuri, 1363/1984), pp. 363–67. See also "An Account of the Life and Character of Tofuzel Hussein Khan, the Vakeel, or Ambassador, of the Nabob Vizier Assof-Ud-Dowlah, at Calcutta, during the Government of Marquis Cornwallis," *The Asiatic Annual Register, or, A View of the History of Hindustan, and of the Politics, Commerce and Literature of Asia for the Year 1803* (London: Cadell and Davies, 1804), Characters, 1–8, quote on 1.

68. "An Account of the Life and Character of Tofuzel Hussein Khan," Section on Characters, 1. Spelled Tofuzel Hussein in the original.

69. Ruben Burrows was supposed to write "notes and explanations" to Tafazzul Husayn Khan's translation of Newton's *Principia*. According to the *Asiatic Annual Register*: "The translation was finished, but it has not been printed; and we believe Mr. Burros never added the annotations he mentions." See "An Account of the Life and Character of Tofuzel Hussein Khan," Characters, 7. Mir 'Abd al-Latif Shushtari noted that Tafazzul Husayn Khan acquired his knowledge of European philosophy (*hikamiyat-i farang*) from Mr. Burrows (*Tuhfat al-'Alam*, 371) On Ruben Burrows see *Asiatic Researches* 2 (1790): 489.

70. Tafazzul Husayn Khan, who "wrote the Persian language with uncommon elegance," had been appointed by Hastings to accompany David Anderson to Mahajee Scindiah. According to David Anderson, Husayn Khan learned English from "my brother, Mr. Blaine" and European mathematics and astronomy "from his communication with the learned Mr. Broome." In 1792, upon a friend's request, Anderson had asked Tafazzul Husayn Khan to inquire about "the ancient astronomy of the Hindus." All quotes are from a letter by David Anderson published in "An Account of the Life and Character of Tofuzel Hussein Khan," Characters, 2–3.

71. "An Account of the Life and Character of Tofuzel Hussein Khan," Characters, 8.

72. For Husayn Khan's acquaintance with Sir William Jones and Richard Johnson, see "An Account of the Life and Character of Tofuzel Hussein Khan," Characters, 4.

73. Juan Cole, "Invisible Occidentalism: Eighteenth-Century Indo-Persian Construction of the West," *Iranian Studies* 25, 3–4 (1992): 3–16.

74. Shushtari, *Tuhfat al-'Alam*, respectively 252 and 255.

75. Shushtari, *Tuhfat al-'Alam*, 36–40, 299-315; particularly 36 and 38.

76. Shushtari, *Tuhfat al-'Alam*, respectively 303 and 307. For an alternative interpretation of this passage, see Cole, pp. 11–12. As it relates to the state of astronomical knowledge, Shushtari mentioned meeting the ninety-year-old Mir Masih Allah Shahjahanabadi, who resided in Murshidabad and had spent most of his life mastering astronomy. He reports studying *Zij-i Muhammad Shahi*, the observations of Chayt Singh, and other astronomical texts which were in the possession of Mir Masih. It would be important to locate the works of these two scholars. See Shushtari, *Tuhfat al-'Alam*, 374.

77. Mirza Muhammad Sadiq Vaqyi' Nigar, *Qava'id al-Muluk* (Tehran: Iranian National Library, MS #F/1757).

78. See I'tizad al-Saltanah's biographical note on Vagayi'nigar in his *Iksir al-Tavarikh*, ed. Jamshid Kayanfarr (Tehran: Visman, 1997), pp. 274–77.

79. Aqa Ahmad Bihbahani Kirmanshahi, *Mir'at al-Ahval-i Jahan Nama*, ed. 'Ali Davani (Tehran: Intisharat-i Markaz-i Asnad-i Inqilab-i Islami, 1996), p. 392.

80. Bihbahani Kirmanshahi, *Mir'at al-Ahval-i Jahan Nama*, 392. For a different rendering, see Cole, p. 11.

81. Kirmanshahi, p. 392.

82. For instance, Kamaran Arjomand claims that "in the second half of the nineteenth century there were serious efforts to defend traditional Islamic cosmology against modern European astronomy." See his "Emergence of Scientific Modernity," pp. 5–24, quote on 10.

83. Mawlavi Abu al-Khayr b. Mawlavi Ghiyas al-Din, *Majmu'ah-i Shamsi: mushtamil-i bar masa'il-i 'ilm-i hay'at mutabiq-i tahqiqat-i 'ulama-yi muta'akhirin-i Farang* (Calcutta: Hindoostani Press, 1222/1807). In the introduction Mawlavi Abu al-Khayr notes that *Majmu'ah-'i Shamsi* is based on English language sources, which he translated with the encouragement and assistance of Dr. William Hunter (1718–1783). *Majmu'ah-i Shamsi* bears the following note in English: "A Concise View of the Copernican System of Astronomy. By Mouluwee Ubool Khuer. Under the superintendence of W. Hunter, M. D. Calcutta. Printed by T. Hubbard at the Hindoostanee Press, 1807."

84. Writing about the status of modern science, particularly astronomy, in Iran, John Malcolm observed: "Efforts have recently been made to convey better information to them upon this important branch of human sciences. An abstract of the Copernican system, and the proofs which the labours of Newton have afforded of its truth, have been translated into Persian; and several individuals of that nation have laboured to acquire this noble but abstruse subject." Macolm then added, "but it is not probable that these rays of light will soon dissipate the cloud of darkness in which a prejudiced and superstitious nation have been for centuries involved." See Sir John Malcolm, *The History of Persia*, vol. 2, pp. 536–37.

85. Abu al-Khayr, p. 2.

86. William Hunter, "Account of the Astronomical Labours of Jaya Sinha, Rajah of Ambhere, or Jayanagar," *Asiatic Researches or Transactions of the Society Instituted in Bengal* 5 (1799): 177–211.

87. Other texts on modern sciences, particularly astronomy, include Muhammad Isma'il Landani's *Tashil al-adrak fi sharh al-aflak*, available at Dar al-'Ulum Nadwat al-'Ulama, radif 3, no. 4; Muhammad Ayyub's *Risalah dar 'Ilm-i Nujum* (1801/1216), available at the Khuda Bakhsh Oriental Public Library, (Acc. 334); Sayyid Ahmad 'Ali's *Muqaddamat-i 'Ilm-i Hay'at* (Calcutta: n.p., n.d.), and Rathan Singh Zakhmi Lakhnavi's *Hadayiq al-Nujum* (1838).

88. Muhammad Rafi' al-Din Khan 'Umdat al-Mulk, *Rafi' al-Basar* (Calcutta: C. V. William Press, 1841).

89. For a discussion of Martyn, see 'Abd al-Hadi Ha'iri, *Nukhustin Ruyaruyiha-yi Andishahgaran-i Iran ba Du Ruyah-'i Tamaddun-i Burzhuvazi-i Gharb* (Tehran: Amir Kabir, 1367), pp. 507–45.

90. For Martyn's Persian translation of The New Testament, see *Kitab al-Muqaddas va Huwa Kutub-i al-'Ahd-i al-Jadid-i Khudavand va Rahanandah-'i Ma 'Isa-'i Masih* [The New Testament of Our Lord Saviour Jesus Christ], (London: The British and Foreign Bible Society, 1876).

91. Afzal-ul-Ulama Muhammad Yousuf Kokan, *Arabic and Persian in Carnatic, 1710-1960* (Madras: Hafiza House, 1974), respectively pp. 340–44 and 345–48.

92. Discussing the "phenomenon of reification," Georg Lukacs explained that "[i]ts basis is that a relation between people takes on the character of a thing and thus acquires a 'phantom objectivity,' an autonomy that seems so strictly rational and all-embracing as *to conceal every trace of its fundamental nature*: the relation between people" (emphasis added). See his *History and Class Consciousness: Studies in Marxist Dialectics*, trans. Rodney Livingstone (Cambridge, Mass.: MIT Press, 1971), 83.

93. From the publisher's "Note" appearing in the reprint edition of Jones's *A Grammar of the Persian Language* (Menston: The Scholar Press Limited, 1969), p. v.

94. *The Letters of Sir William Jones*, ed. Garland Cannon (Oxford: Clarendon Press, 1970), vol. 2, 798.

95. Jones to Charles Wilkins, 17 September 1785, in *The Letters of Sir William Jones*, p. 683.

96. Mirza Itesa Modeen, *Shigurf Namah I Velaët, or Excellent Intelligence Concerning Europe; Being the Travels of Mirza Itesa Modeen, in Great Britain and France*, trans. James Edward Alexander (London: Parbury, Allen, and Co., 1827), pp. 65–66.

97. William Jones, "The Sixth Discourse: on the Persians; Delivered 19 February 1789," in *The Works of Sir William Jones in Six Volumes*, ed. Ann Maria Shipley-Jones (London: G. G. and J. Robinson, 1799), pp. 73–94.

98. Max Müller, *The Sacred Languages of the East*, vol. 4, pp. xx. Hans Aarsleff also views Jones as the founder of modern philology. See his *The Study of Language in England, 1780–1860* (Minneapolis: University of Minnesota Press, 1983), p. 124.

99. The history of linguistics texts often opens with entries on William Jones. For instance, see Thomas A. Sebeok, *Portraits of Linguistics: A Bibliographical Source Book for the History of Western Linguistics, 1746–1969* (Bloomington: Indiana University Press, 1966; Westport, Conn.: Greenwood Press, 1976). The first three articles in this volume are devoted to Jones.

100. Siraj al-Din Khan Arzu, *Muthmir* [*Musmir*], ed. Rehana Khatoon (Karachi: The Institute of Central and West Asian Studies, 1991). According to Rehana Khatoon

> Khan-i Arzu is also the first scholar in both the East and the West who introduced the theory of similarities of two languages [*tavafuq-i lisanayn*], meaning that Sanskrit and Persian are sister languages. His ideas in this regard are contained in his monumental work being discussed here, i.e. the Muthmir. The work has not yet been thoroughly studied and made a subject of serious assessment; [a]nd this has prompted me to undertake and prepare a critical edition of the *Muthmir* (see Rehana Khatoon, "Introduction," in *Muthmir*, 43).

101. Müller, "Introduction," in *The Sacred Books of the East*, vol. 4, xx.

102. The term *tavafuq* literally means concordance or concurrence.

103. Arzu, *Muthmir*, p. 221.

104. Arzu offered a detailed definition of *tavafuq al-lisanayn* under the concept of *ang*. See his *Chiragh-i Hidayat*, published with Ghiyas al-Din Rampuri's *Ghiyas al-Lughat*, ed. Mansur Sirvat (Tehran: Amir Kabir, 1984), pp. 1017–18.

105. Arzu, *Chiragh-i Hidayat*, 1050, 1061, 1068, 1091, 1119, 1020–21, and 1214.

106. Julia Kristeva, *Language—The Unknown: An Initiation into Linguistics*, trans. Anne M. Menke (New York: Columbia University Press, 1989), p. 196.

107. This analysis is based on a comparison with Shiv Parshad's *Tarikh-i Fayz Bakhsh* (Oxford: Bodleian Library, shelfmark: Caps.Or.C.2).

108. William Franklin, *The History of the Reign of Shah-Aulum, the Present Emperor of Hindostaun* (London: Cooper and Graham, 1798). The claim is based on Ghulam 'Ali Khan's *Ayi'in 'Alamshahi* (Oxford: Bodleian Library, shelfmark: Elliot 3).

109. My analysis is based on an examination of a collection of documents belonging to Samuel Turner, which are held at the Bodleian Library (shelfmark 2822.Ms.Pers.a.4). A French translation of the *Account* (London: W. Bulmer and Co., 1800) was published in the same year, *Ambassade au Thibet et au Boutan* (Paris: F. Bussion, 1800). In the following year it was also translated into German, *Gesandtschaftsreise an den hof des teshoo lama durch Bootan und einen theil von Tibet* (Hamburg: B. G. Hoffman, 1801).

110. William Moorcroft, *Travels in the Himalayan Provinces of Hindustan and the Panjab; in Ladakh and Kashmir; in Peshawar, Kabul, Kunduz, and Bokhara . . . from 1819 to 1825* (London : J. Murray, 1841).

111. See Mir 'Izzat Allah, *Ahval-i Safar-i Bukhara* (Oxford: Bodleian Library, Bodl.OR.745).

112. Among other English-language texts that are based on Persian works is Captain William Henry Sleeman, *Ramaseeana or Vacabulary of the Peculiar Language Used by the Thugs,* which is based on *Mustalahat-i Thugan* of 'Ali Akbar.

113. On Sir Gore Ouseley's travel to Iran, see Denis Wright, *The English amongst the Persians during the Qajar Period, 1787–1921* (London: Heinemann, 1977), pp. 12–17.

114. For a fraction of Mirza Salih's report, see Mirza Salih Shirazi, "Safar Namah-'i Isfahan, Kashan, Qum, Tihran," in *Majmu'ah-'i Safar namah-hayi Mirza Salih Shirazi* (Tehran: Nashr-i Tarikh-i Iran, 1364), pp. 5–36. The official *mihmandar* of this delegation was Mirza Zaki Mustawfi Divan-i A'la. See 'Adb al-Razzaq Maftun Dunbuli, *Ma'asir-i Sultaniyah* (Reprint of 1825/1241 edition; Tehran: Ibn Sina, 1351/1972), p. 247.

115. William Price, *A Grammar of the Three Principal Oriental Languages, Hindoostani, Persian, and Arabic on a Plan Entirely New, and Perfectly Easy; To Which Is Added, A Set of Persian Dialogues Composed for the Author, by Mirza Mohammed Saulih, of Shiraz; Accompanied with an English Translation* (London: Kingsbury, Parbury, and Allen, 1823).

116. Price, *A Grammar of the Three Principal Oriental Languages,* p. vi. The text of Mirza Salih's "Persian Dialogues" appear on pp. 142–88, followed by a French translation, "Dialogues Persans et Français," pp. 190–238.

117. William Ouseley, *Travels in Various Countries of the East, More Particularly Persia* (London: Rodwell and Martil, 1819–23), vol. I, xvii.

118. The extract in Ouseley's *Travels in Various Countries of the East,* vol. I, xvii, is identical to the opening of Mirza Salih's text as appeared in Price's *A Grammar of the Three Principal Oriental Languages,* pp. 142–43.

119. The colophon of the manuscript, *Su'al va Javab,* held at the Bodleian Library, which belongs to the Ouseley Collection, notes that it was written for Sir William Ouseley (Oxford: Bodleian Library, Shelfmark Ouseley 390).

120. Price, *A Grammar of the Three Principal Oriental Languages,* p. vii. In a note Price remarked, "Since that period Mirza Saulih came to England with Col. Darsy, in order to learn the English Language, returned to Persia in 1819, and lately arrived on a special Mission from the King of Persia to his Majesty George the Fourth. On my presenting him with a copy of his own dialogues, he expressed himself much pleased, and promised to compose a new set" (p. vi).

121. William Price, *Journal of the British Embassy to Persia; Embellished with Numerous Views Taken in India and Persia; Also, a Dissertation upon the Antiquities of Persepolis,* 2 vols. (London: Thomas Thorpe, 1932).

122. Ouseley, *Travels in Various Countries of the East,* respectively vol. III, p. 363 and vol. II, p. 16.

123. Wright, p. 73.

124. John Binder and David Wellbery, eds., *The End of Rhetoric: History, Theory, and Practice* (Stanford, Calif.: Stanford University Press, 1990), p. 16.

125. For instance, see Buzurg 'Alavi, "Critical Writings on the Renewal of Iran," in Edmond Bosworth and Carloe Hillenbrand, eds., *Qajar Iran: Political, Social, and Cultural Changes, 1800–1925* (Costa Mesa, Calif.: Mazda Publishers, 1992), pp. 243–54, quote on 253.

126. Writing on eighteenth-century Bengal, Richard Eaton has also observed: "Two stereotypes—one by students of Indian history, the other held by students of Islam— have conspired greatly to obscure our understanding of Islam in Bengal, and especially of the growth of a Muslim peasant community there. The first of these is the notion of eighteenth-century Mughal India as a period hopelessly mired in decline, disorder, chaos, and collapse." See his "The Growth of Muslim Identity in Eighteenth-Century Bengal," in Nehemiah Levtzion and John Voll, eds., *Eighteenth-Century Renewal and Reform in Islam* (Syracuse, N.Y.: Syracuse University Press, 1987), pp. 161–85; quote on 161.

127. For further elaboration of issues raised in this article, see Mohamad Tavakoli-Targhi, *Refashioning Iran: Orientalism, Occidentalism, and Nationalist Historiography* (Houndmills, Basingstoke, England: St. Antony's/Palgrave Series, 2001).

IV

MODERNIZATION, GENDER, AND POLITICAL CULTURE

10

Women's Employment in Iran: Modernization and Islamization

Roksana Bahramitash

IN THE YEAR 2000, IN THE HOLY CITY OF MASHHAD—a major site of Shi'a pilgrimage—more than a hundred women started working as taxi drivers—one of the most male-dominated professions in the world. Trained in martial arts, carrying cellular phones, and still wearing their veils, these women work night shifts regularly, protected through a central dispatch office. Even in North America very few women feel safe enough to drive taxis at night.

This phenomenon of Islamic, Iranian women breaking into a profession that is male-dominated around the world—regardless of religious tradition—must surely seem paradoxical in the eyes of most people of the West. It is generally believed in the West that Islam represses female employment and that such a phenomenon of women taxi drivers in an Islamic state can only be credited to the blessings of Westernization and the weakening of Islamization. This dominant view is dangerously simplistic and is based on stereotypical assumptions about the Muslim world in general and Iran in particular.

The example of Iran, in fact, illustrates that modernization of the Western style was very limited in its scope of transforming women's lives. Forced Westernized modernization created a backlash in the form of an Islamic Revolution (1978–1979), which received the support of great numbers of women. The practices of the subsequent Islamist government and its oppressive stand against women had, despite itself, a far greater impact on women entering into the public sphere. Since the 1990s, the employment rate for women has accelerated, and this is because of a proportional increase of those belonging to the lower strata that have sought employment outside their homes. Increased employment has been partly due to the expansion of education for women. Today there are more women in secondary education than there are men. In addition, political participation among women has increased. These new developments show that women have been able to make gains in spite of a regime whose agenda has been to keep women subordinate.

It is important to deal with the realities of women's experience in Iran because the persistence of stereotypical images is not only erroneous and simplistic but has racist implications. The images of oppressed Muslim women portray women in Iran as helpless victims who are the objects of pity—these women need Western saviors. There is no doubt that the Islamist movement and the regime in Iran have been repressive and oppressive toward women. But, ironically, as the regime mobilized women for volunteer work to serve its purposes, these women have in turn made demands on the regime and there have been some concessions for women's rights.

On the contrary, such achievements for women must be analytically examined to determine which forces have been at work. The central point is that shah's Western-style modernization was not nearly as successful in bringing changes to women's employment, education, and political participation as an Islamist regime.[1]

The above-mentioned example of women taxi drivers illustrates an increase in employment in a highly unconventional profession for women that has happened under an Islamist regime and not during the shah's Westernized modernization. To some extent, the Islamization process in Iran has attempted to combine an anti-Westernization political agenda with a development strategy in favor of industrialization and urbanization; two important features of modernization. The Islamist government has attempted to marry Islamist principles with the economic and social structural changes of modernization, which distinguishes it from Westernization. Some may argue that modernization and Westernization cannot be distinguished. For this reason, some clarification of terms is required.

There are different interpretations of modernization, but in the literature of theories of economic development and sociology, the process of modernization has been more generally equated with industrialization. And urbanization has been more generally equated with the rise of bureaucracy and the nation-state. Modernization is a process of change in economic structure and the sociopolitical institutions that go with it. The mainstream interpretation of modernization regards the process as evolutionary, homogenous, and based on Europeanization and Americanization (Levy 1967). Furthermore, it is regarded as inevitable and desirable. To demonstrate the desirability of the process, examples of progressive changes in the nature of women's employment in Europe and America are often cited.

Recent developments in Iran contradict these mainstream assumptions that the evolutionary nature of the modernization process is homogenous. Iran's Islamist government has not put a stop to the industrialization trend of the prerevolutionary period. Iran has, in fact, more recently opened up to the global market, encouraging foreign investment and borrowing from the World Bank and the International Monetary Fund (IMF). Alongside these economic strategies, the government (at least politically) has kept its anti-Western stand.[2]

To understand Iran's anti-Western sentiment while at the same time attempting to embrace industrialization, urbanization, and the global market,[3] it is important to look at some of the major developments of Iran's recent socioeconomic history. By doing this, I hope to show how Iran's concurrent economy—especially as it pertains to women—grew out of opposition to externally imposed modernization of a Western style.

The process of modernization effectively started after the World War II but has progressed much more distinctly since the 1960s. There is little data on the nature of female employment in Iran prior to the 1960s, but as many parts of Iran remained nonindustrialized, agricultural, or tribal, even up until today, it is possible to make some general comments. Much of the nature and structure of female employment in the rural areas has remained untouched by the process of modernization, though urbanization has certainly affected the equilibrium of the rural/urban dichotomy.

Iran has great regional diversity and different modes of production; there are different regional variations, and the extent to which women were part of the production process varied according to local economic forces. Among the pastoral-nomadic, women have been highly engaged in the production process of dairy products and weaving, to name two examples. Women in the agricultural sector have had varying roles; some have been highly involved in fieldwork, such as rice paddy work in Northern Iran (south of the Caspian Sea) while they are less involved in fieldwork in regions such as parts of the northwest. By and large, Iranian women—much like women from other parts of the world—have been part of the agricultural economy. The role of women in carpet weaving throughout the country remains vital. After oil, export of carpets has been among the largest sources of hard currency—thanks to the labor of many women and girls.

Traditionally, female employment in the urban areas has been low. This low participation has been partly because the urban population consists of a larger proportion of wealthy people. It is among the upper class that women have been most excluded from employment. The lower down on the social and economic ladder, the more women have been forced to earn a living for themselves and their families. Urban women of low income have traditionally worked as maids, cooks, prostitutes (that could include those who entered temporary marriages as a profession), handy women, dressmakers, workers in public baths, hairdressers, and door-to-door makeup saleswomen. There are also female religious functionaries who work for pay (or volunteer) to perform religious ceremonies. Other than these, there have been Gypsies, fortune tellers, beggars, and wet-nurses. Some of these traditional occupations have been transformed or simply disappeared; wet-nurses are gone, as there is now powdered milk; but hairdressers and small beauty salons have proliferated throughout major cities.

Revolution, Islamization, and Anti-Westernization, 1979–1988

The shah's downfall had serious implications for the position of women. The new Islamic state gradually adopted an increasingly conservative religious interpretation of the role of women and excluded them from the social and political mainstream even though the regime's rise to power had benefited from women's political activism. The new regime soon marginalized all women's groups except those that adhered strictly to religious codes spelled out by Ayatollah Khomeini (Paidar 1995).[4]

Under the Islamist ideology, women came to be viewed primarily, if not exclusively, as mothers. Their main place was in the home. This was stressed in the new constitution. The state reversed all legal reforms that had favored women during the shah's regime and replaced them with laws in accordance with its orthodox interpretation of "Islam." Any public role for women was mainly regarded as Western and therefore a vestige of colonialism. Women were banned from certain professions, for example, from practicing law, either as judges or lawyers (Afshar 1996). Certain subjects at the university level, such as civil engineering, were closed to women. These changes in women's status and legal position were far more serious for women from the upper and middle classes (those who were from an educated urban background) than women from low-income urban, rural, and tribal groups. It was mainly the upper- and middle-class women who had been brought into the public sphere during the modernization period and not low-income women from often traditional families. It was the upper- and middle-class women who could (and in fact did) adapt to Western ways of life and were suited to be part of the Western-style modernization. The new Islamist regime intimidated and at the time attempted to force upper- and middle-class women to leave their jobs (Poya 1999). The regime, in an effort to Islamize, imposed dress codes, like the *hejab*, which made many modern/Westernized upper- and middle-class women uncomfortable, and many left their jobs.

Many upper-class and middle-class women who had the financial means to leave preferred to withdraw from employment. But for the working class and women of low income, there was no option. In many senses, the new Islamist regime was ideologically traditionalist in the area of female employment and attempted to set the clock back. But turning to traditions only affected those who had been affected by the shah's Western-style modernization. In rural areas, women continued to remain in jobs they had been employed in for many decades. The shah's modernization had changed little for most of the rural population and women's employment. Subsequently, this population remained unaffected by the new shift toward a conservative interpretation of Islam.

Women's participation during the war period increased, but because of falling oil prices and economic sanctions, the state used the Islamist ideology to implement women's volunteer work. Khomeini himself called for religious women to become involved in supporting the revolution's goal. Once again, the ayatollah appealed to women, this time to mobilize women's support in order to deal with the impact of a war imposed by Iraq (and supported by the United States through Israeli arms) (Poya 1999). Khomeini called for millions of Iranian women to join "the army of twenty million," (*artesh bist milliony*) and help the country in any way they could. Women from low-income and traditional families responded to Khomeini in large numbers. During the shah's regime (contrary to common Western stereotypes) coerced adoption of Western customs alienated women from the lower strata of the society. For example, many low-income women and nearly all traditionally religious women did not want to go to work without Islamic dresses and the veil. These women were thus excluded from professional positions or made to feel uncomfortable. Many professions were closed to women who refused to embrace middle-or upper-class codes of conduct. A school headmaster, for instance, would not be chosen from veiled women. Veiled teachers could be tolerated in the impoverished parts of large cities like the south slums of Tehran or in very religious towns. But in the middle-class and upper-class neighborhoods, female headmistresses were often among the most fashionably dressed (in Europe's latest fashions) women imaginable.[5]

When Khomeini came into power, however, looking European and American and being a member of the upper and middle class was stigmatized. The reintroduction of veiling was welcomed by those women who had gone through so much frustration during the shah's regime. Consequently, when Khomeini called for volunteer organizations, many religious women joined. Along with these organizations, Khomeini mobilized mosques to set up literacy campaigns and many middle-class, educated women joined the campaigns as volunteers.[6]

The benefits of the successful literacy campaign were twofold. First the literacy rate among women increased; second, many religious women working as volunteers took an increasingly public role, particularly as the literacy campaign branched into others such as military training for women. The literacy campaign in itself provided increased skills for many women to prepare them for different types of employment.

Modernization and Islamization: Islamic State Second Phase after 1988

The war with Iraq ended in 1988, and one year later Ayatollah Khomeini died. These two events marked the beginning of yet another new era. The state relaxed its regulations against foreign investments and shifted toward neoliberal economic policies such as privatization. This shift brought Iran into the world market as the state borrowed from international creditors such as the World Bank and IMF. Since the late 1980s, Iran has adopted free market policies such as privatization, deregulation, and further devaluation of the *riyal* (Behdad 1995). This new, more liberal policy orientation has increased the participation rate for women, though not for the reasons a neoliberalist might expect.

Labor force participation by women has accelerated since the beginning of the 1990s. However, one of the main reasons for this accelerated increase is increased poverty and income disparity that has been exacerbated by the market economy. As was the case during the war with Iraq, exacerbated conditions of poverty made it imperative for many women with families to find paying work in order to survive. In the 1980s women had to go to work in response to the shock of war and economic sanctions. From the 1990s through today, it is free market policies (and their tendency toward greater income disparity and greater impoverishment of the poor) that have forced women to, once again, take up work outside their homes.

In a response to deteriorating economic conditions, the state started to relax its codes for female participation. The Iranian state realized the economic necessities of women's work both for the economy and for family survival of low-income groups. Also, the extent and the persistence of women's political agitation constantly put pressure on the government to make changes to their initial policy of sending women back home (during the period after the revolution). As an example, it was feminist pressure on the state that finally forced the judiciary to allow women to become lawyers and judges in the 1990s. Incidentally, this battle was fought by religious women as well as secular ones. In fact, a religious man—a graduate from the highly ranked religious education of *Qom*—joined the cause by writing newspaper articles under a female pseudonym. His vast technical knowledge proved to be an important asset in presenting women's arguments from a religious standpoint.

At the same time, the percentage of highly educated women increased; it currently exceeds that of men (52 percent of those who entered university were women by 1999) (Poya 1999: 106.) The increase in the percentage of highly educated women and feminist agitation in turn has had further feedback into the system. The increasing number of female journalists highly critical of the regime is a good illustration of this. (The percentage of female journalists has increased by far from that of the 1970s, when the shah's supposedly more liberal regime was in power.)

Increased poverty and income disparity (the result of opening to the world market and neoliberal policies of privatization and deregulation) have also expanded the informal market. The number of female home-based income generating activities such as hairdressers, seamstresses, food processors, as well as prostitutes and beggars, has increased steadily over the past two decades, but there are no estimates about the extent (Afshar 1996).

Conclusion

A review of women's experience since the Islamic Revolution illustrates that, contrary to commonly held views on the position of women as a result of Islamization, women's education, employment, and political participation had increased, particularly during the 1990s. Though women continue to suffer repression in Iran, simplistic Western prejudices about women are far from the truth. Iranian women have been able to push for improvements in spite of hardships. In fact, under the Islamist regime, a greater number of the female population was able to enter into the labor market (when such advancements are in keeping with religion and traditions) than following Western models. The Western model, as seen with the shah, offered employment opportunities mainly to a middle- and upper-class minority. It would have taken the shah many decades to send women as taxi drivers driving through a major Shi'a pilgrimage city, if ever. But under an Islamist government and with strict veil-keeping codes of sexual segregation, women have been able to enter to such a profession. Western images of oppressed Muslim women portray helpless victims who are the object of pity who need Western saviors. Such prejudicial perspectives must be challenged.

Women in different parts of the world have different strategies, and these local strategies work in particular circumstances. Just as a development strategy based on a Western model turned out not to be appropriate for Iran, Iranian women are fighting their battle to be heard—by their own means.

Notes

1. One area that still remains oppressive much more than during the shah's reign is the position of women in the legal system. After the revolution, some laws, especially those dealing with the family, were changed, taking away some women's rights. Since the initial stage of the revolution some minor modifications have occurred, and women have constantly challenged such laws, but by and large, the legal system has remained one area where there has been little success.

2. Some may argue that modernization without Westernization is not possible and the passage to an industrial society can only take one path. This is a clear mistake. When Japan was transformed from an agrarian to industrial country at the turn of the twentieth century, there was little cultural adoption of the West and the rise of nation-state and bureaucracy was very much within the context of the Japanese cultural heritage. As far as the position of women is concerned, Japanese women's position remained very traditional (subordinate) until very recently.

3. Iran's industrialization remains very much limited as the country relies heavily on the export of oil. But the Iranian experience with industrialization is not unique to Iran, and most developing countries are experiencing very similar economic problems.

4. It is not the first time a male-led revolution and social political movement brought women into its resistance movement for support but then when the movement came into power, it pushed women aside. Many examples exist in the history of the nationalist movement and anticolonial movements throughout the Third World.

5. I went to school during this period. My mother was also a headmistress of several schools; she often felt very uncomfortable that she had to keep up with the fashions. Not only could she hardly afford expensive foreign designs, but the time and energy that went into her appearance was a source of constant frustration for her and several of her friends who were also teachers and headmistresses.

6. I was among those who joined mosque-based literacy campaigns, where many women would drop by with numerous children, and for many of us teachers, helping women to read and write was a way of providing support for low-income women to improve not just their literacy but their overall well-being.

References

Afshar, Haleh. 1996. "Islam and Feminism: An Analysis of Political Strategies." In *Feminism and Islam*, ed. Mai Yamani. New York: New York University Press.

Behdad, S. 1995. "The Post-Revolutionary Economic Crisis." In *Iran after the Revolution*, ed. S. Rahnema and S. Behdad. London and New York: I. B. Toauris.

Levy, Marion J. 1967. "Social Patterns and Problems of Modernization." In *Readings on Social Changes*, ed. Wilbert Moore and Robert M. Cook. Englewood Cliffs, N.J.: Prentice-Hall.

Paidar, Parvin. 1995. *Women and the Political Process in Twentieth-Century Iran*. Cambridge: Cambridge University Press.

Poya, Maryam. 1999. *Women, Work and Islamism*. London: Zed Books.

11

"Islamist" Women Activists:
Allies or Enemies?

Sussan Siavoshi

IRANIAN POLITY IS IN A STATE OF transition and as such its future cannot be easily predicted. Among the unpredictable aspects of a transitional polity is the
situational malleability of its political leaders and activists who might modify
their positions, sometimes even drastically.[1] Hard-liners can become soft-
liners, radical elements might ally themselves with moderate forces, authori-
tarians can move in the direction of openness and inclusion. In Iran, since the
revolution, there have been ample examples of shifting positions on the part
of members of the elite. Women activists have not been immune to this trend.

Women activists come from different ideological, educational, and social
backgrounds. They are uniform neither in their ideas of what goals best address the interests of women, nor in their views of what strategies are most effective in achieving those goals. They also vary in the extent of their own religiosity as well as in their views regarding the extent of religious interference in
politics. In the Iranian transitional polity the challenge for those concerned
with genuine gender equality is to find the meaningful criteria for the
inclusion and exclusion of women activists in a women's rights movement.
For most of the 1980s the prevalent reference categories for such decision was
secularism versus religiosity of women activists, a dichotomy translated automatically into modernism versus traditionalism respectively. No doubt notions of religiosity/tradition and secularism/modernity have a place in the discussion of women in Iran, but this dichotomy does not provide a complete
analytical framework for understanding the differences among women activists and their potential role in the cause of gender equality. The major problem, of course, is with the conceptualization of these terms. What do we mean

when we employ words such as modern or traditional, and what criteria do we use in differentiating between them?

For the modernization theories of the 1950s and 1960s, as grand narratives or totalistic theories, the idea of a modern person was embodied in portrayals made by social scientists such as Gabriel Almond, Daniel Lerner, David Apter, Karl Deutsch, and Lucian Pye. They depicted a modern person as an educated (enlightened), enthusiastic and optimistic, ambitious and active, secular, and urban individual with a universalistic rather than a parochial frame of reference.[2] Politically, almost all the above-mentioned early theorists argued that the logic of modernity requires a modern person to be democratic.[3] On the other hand, a traditional person was defined as one who lacked all these attributes. She or he was religious, pessimistic, passive/fatalistic, parochial, and also authoritarian. However, this comfortable, neat, and dichotomous classification was challenged by the late 1960s.

Politically, some of the challenge came from the *dependencia* theorists with their antiliberal, anti-imperialist worldview. From the perspective of philosophy and epistemology however, the more important challenge came from the postmodern paradigm. Postmodernism took to task the essentialist aspects of modernization theories, including the notion of a modern person. Its approach to the individual as a fractured many, rather than an undivided entity, undermined the neat dichotomy of modern/traditional person or personality.

In the specific case of Iran and in an experiential manner the Iranian revolution and its aftermath played an instrumental role in challenging the dichotomy of modern versus traditional. The attributes of many of the key players and leaders of the revolution destroyed the neat boundaries between modern and traditional person, as depicted by modernization theorists, with relative ease. Among these players were many Islamist women such as Maryam Behrouzi, Zahra Rahnavard, Azam Taleghani, and Monireh Gorgi. In the decades following the revolution, the collapse of the boundaries set by the grand narratives of modernization necessitated a redefinition or at least a revisiting of concepts such as modern, traditional, progressive, and reactionary. The reexamination of these concepts led to a seemingly less exclusive notion of modernity and a modern person. The new classification, although still dichotomous, was narrower in its focus, shying away from totalistic theories. The focus this time was on notions of human subjectivity/agency and democratic polity. The narrower focus allowed for a more inclusive notion of modernity and therefore more tolerance for diversity of beliefs and style of behavior.

In spite of the retreat or revision of early modernization theories, the debate within the field of Iranian women's studies still, to some extent, revolves around the notions of early modernization theories, particularly that of religiosity and secularism. There are many scholars who believe that religiously oriented (read regressive) and secular (read progressive) women's agenda are mutually exclusive. In doing so, they consider religiously oriented women activists as monolithic and on balance against genuine gender equality.[4] Needless to say, this approach has been challenged by others who see differences, nuanced as well as glaring, among these same activists and therefore allow for a more inclusive approach to the issue of coalition building.[5] Mindful of this tension between the two approaches, this chapter intends to focus on the activities and ideas of two Islamist activists, Maryam Behrouzi and Zahra Rahnavard, both members of the religious elite associated with the Islamic Republic since its inception. As elite Islamist women they have shared many experiences and ideas. However, several factors separate them, particularly at this moment of transition. The evolution of the Islamic Republic warrants a rethinking of the old categorization regarding the nature of the regime as well as that of its participants. Maryam Behrouzi, a four-time member of the parliament, is a conservative and religious woman who identifies very closely with the conservative/authoritarian faction within the Iranian political elite. Zahra Rahnavard, also an Islamist and a member of the elite, is affiliated with the reformist faction of the Iranian power holders. These women do not function in a vacuum and, therefore, their similarities, differences, and potential impact can only be understood with some familiarity with the political context within which they operate.

The Iranian polity has been rift with factionalism for most of its existence since the revolution. The factions have been malleable and their numbers, names, and characters have changed overtime. At the time of this writing, factions are broadly divided into two loose clusters of reformist/liberal and conservative/authoritarian. In a simplified manner one can characterize the reformists as supporters of popular sovereignty, expansion of individual rights and domain of privacy, and a more tolerant interpretation of Islamic precepts. The conservatives on the other hand, are suspicious of the reformist stands, and prefer a more restricted political system. They emphasize the role of the elite clergy in governing the country and, therefore, advocate a very limited and elite-guided political participation by the masses. Their interpretation of Islamic precepts is authoritarian and restrictive, particularly in sociopolitical and cultural domains. In their view, responsibility has priority over rights, community over individual, and men over women.

Maryam Behrouzi: The Authoritarian/Conservative

Maryam Behrouzi provides us with an interesting example of an assertive public figure with very conservative religious ideas. Behrouzi was born in

1945 into a religious family. She received her theology degree from Tehran University and later, after the revolution, studied with Ayatollah Khomenei to achieve the highest religious degree, Kharj-e Fiqh. Prior to the revolution, her political activities were limited to teaching Interpretation of Quran (Tafsir) to Muslim women, an activity that seemed harmless enough for the Pahlavi regime to tolerate. But as it gradually became clear that religion was becoming a rallying point for the opposition to the regime, such activities became suspect. Behrouzi was banned from teaching Interpretation of Quran and was eventually arrested and detained for a short period of time. After the revolution, she was one of the very few women who were elected to the first session of the parliament and was able to remain a representative for four consecutive terms. She was also one of the rare examples of women who did not achieve high political status through connection to a male relative, be it a husband, father, or brother, as was the case for most other women who achieved such positions. During her tenure in the parliament, she was selected as the Iranian representative to the international organization of the Union of Parliamentary Women Representatives. She failed, however, to be elected to the fifth session of the parliament. She is now the secretary of the woman's organization Jame'ye Zeynab (Zeynab Society), whose stated goal is "the enhancement of Muslim women's culture and social relations" and whose stated "policy" is to "safeguard the Islamic revolution's achievements . . . [through] absolute obedience to Ayatollah Khomenei."[6] She is also the woman's affairs advisor to the head of the most important charity organization in Iran, the Mostazafin and Janbazan Foundation (MJF), and a member of the organization of Islamic Human Rights and the chair of its Women's Affairs Committee.

In her capacity as a representative of the parliament, Behrouzi pushed through several bills, including one that allows women to retire after twenty years of active service, five years earlier than what is required of men. She was also active in reforming some of the more draconian laws pertaining to divorce, particularly those dealing with compensation settlements.[7] As the advisor to the MJF, she was an advocate for a joint governmental and MJF program to create employment for the wives of the disabled and to pay a monthly salary to these wives for their "guardianship responsibility and nursing of their disabled husbands."[8]

Does this record of activities illuminate all the factors that are required for the secular and/or liberal feminists to make their decision regarding Behrouzi as a potential ally or enemy in their fight for women's emancipation? A closer look at her *ideas* might shed a better light on the question of whether or not she can be considered a partner in a genuine movement for women's rights in the future.

Behrouzi's Views

There is no doubt that Behrouzi is a fierce critic of many of the cherished ideas of modern, particularly liberal Western, feminism. Her overall political views set her far apart from any individual or group that aspires to individual liberty. Labeling liberalism as the ideology of sexual promiscuity, she argues that, in the liberal worldview, women are assigned only two functions, first to provide sexual pleasure and second to serve the advertising industry, which uses women's bodies to promote consumerism. Arguing that women have no control over their lives in such roles, she concludes that liberalism victimizes women.[9] She does not, however, deny the achievements of Western women during the last century. Indeed, she argues that economic exploitation of women in the West in the eighteenth and nineteenth centuries led to the formation of women's movements that ultimately succeeded in providing women access to the public space of financial and industrial centers. As a result, women became somewhat liberated from economic exploitation. But what the West failed to do for women was to create a healthy social trend to protect them from moral dangers and therefore made them victims of sexual exploitation.[10] She blames this situation on the liberal secularism of the West. Her critique of progress in achieving women's rights and freedoms during the previous regime in Iran is also based on her view of Western secular liberalism. She agrees that the Pahlavi regime did bring many women onto the scene, but she immediately questions the public arena that was opened to women. Not surprisingly, Behrouzi portrays this public arena as one of corruption, promiscuity, and worthlessness and argues that Pahlavi's evidence for women's progress was restricted to exhibiting nude women in the streets, on beaches, and in cheap movies, rather than in intellectual, scientific, or political arenas.[11] Any domain of activities, other than the three latter, is beneath the dignity of women. Behrouzi considers women's participation in sports, for example, as frivolous. She took a conservative position in the early 1990s when women's participation in sports was under scrutiny. She declared that women skiing, horseback riding, and biking are the most ridiculous and insulting manifestations of women's presence in public scenes.[12] So what does Behrouzi herself think of as dignified or legitimate areas of women's public presence? To provide answers she turns to the Quran and Islamic history.

In a speech given on the anniversary of the birth of Zeynab (the granddaughter of the Prophet Mohammed and the sister of Hussein, the most revered martyr of Shiite Islam), Behrouzi lays out some of the key components of her views on women. She first argues that, despite historical contempt for women aimed at suppressing their talents in public arenas, women have been present and active at critical moments of history. Western claims to champion women's rights notwithstanding, she argues it is Islam that, since its inception, has provided for the realization of women's political and social excellence. The reason for the obscurity of the Islamic position in the area of women's rights, she argues, is due to the lack of active participation of Muslims in demonstrating and communicating their position to the world.[13] She then tries to make a case for her assertions.

Starting with Quranic verses, Behrouzi argues that since thirteen centuries ago, Islam has provided opportunities for women's political participation, voting rights, and economic rights such as the right to property.[14] Islam demonstrates its stand on equal worth of men and women, according to Behrouzi, through the story of Adam and Eve. First of all, the Quran has explicitly declared that man and woman are created from the same substance "Nafs-e Vahedeh."[15] In the Quran, God addresses both Adam and Eve as equals when He warns them not to get close to the forbidden tree. In addition, unlike some interpretations that blame Eve for seducing Adam into the sinful action, Quranic verses admonished both Adam and Eve for their disobedience to God's order and consider both to be equally guilty. To demonstrate evidence for her assertions about Islam's attitudes toward women, she refers to numerous stories about strong women in the Quran. Hajar and Sara (Prophet Ibrahim's wives); Asiyeh, the wife of an Egyptian Pharaoh who died for her principles; and Belqays, a queen who was not intimidated by King Solomon, are among those women.[16]

After these preliminary arguments Behrouzi reveals Zeynab as her model of a true and active Muslim woman. According to Behrouzi, Zeynab should be emulated by all progressive and faithful Muslim women. She was the assertive sister of Imam Hossein, who, after the martyrdom of her brother, made a fiery public oration against his killers. Her oration has remained a source of pride for Shiite Muslims. Behrouzi, however, focuses not only on the public activism of Zeynab but applauds the latter's dedication as a wife and a mother. To Behrouzi, the public and the private domains can go together. But if for some the mixing of public with the private proved to be costly, she argues that priority should be given to the role of a woman in the private arena: the responsibility to form a family and raise children.[17] As far as public activities are concerned, Behrouzi only allows for the type of works that enable women to actualize their intellectual potential. Women should not seek jobs such as secretarial positions or those that only involve mindless performance of menial services. There has to be a definite benefit for the woman and the community to justify and legitimize her venturing out of the private sphere of the home. The mere presence of women in the public arena is not a "good in itself."[18]

Even though Behrouzi emphasizes the central role of women in forging family life, she considers it more in terms of *responsibility* than of *rights*. Her attitude is clear when she expresses her views on issues of divorce and polygamy. It is true that Behrouzi, during her tenure in the parliament, fought to obtain certain rights for women in the process of divorce, but she generally does not think that the established divorce laws are problematic and therefore does not challenge the current laws that give men a virtually absolute right to divorce. Being aware of the outspoken critics of the current divorce law, however, she makes a distinction between the true purpose of the law, on the one hand, and its practice in the history of Islamic societies, on the other. She argues that in a truly Islamic polity, the right to divorce belongs to the state and not to the individual man, and it is the state that should take over and set the conditions of the settlement to the wife. But, she agrees that in reality, the law has been appropriated and interpreted in such a way that men, as individuals, seem to have the final say in divorce cases. As for the specific practice in the Islamic Republic, she points out that a woman can ask for a divorce and can, in her wedding contract, stipulate her entitlement to half of the family property in case of divorce.[19] One can see the tension between her adherence to the conservative interpretation of the divorce laws and her awareness that they can in fact be quite problematic in the social context of postrevolutionary Iran.

Despite some efforts to improve certain aspect of women's lives, particularly in economic domains, Behrouzi does not challenge the conservative version of the fundamentals of Islam except when it is obvious that no established rule of Islam will be broken. Her activities demonstrate that she is somewhat aware of the miserable condition of most women in Iran but, due to her connection to the conservative forces, she does not ask for foundational changes. Much like her male conservative counterparts, she does not believe in individual autonomy, for women or men. Therefore, in addressing women's problems her solutions are confined to the authoritarian, conservative, and non/anti-liberal positions consistent with a patriarchal worldview. Women, and men for that matter, are not considered as fully autonomous individuals who should take their fate into their own hands. God, through his representatives (the prophet Mohammed, the twelve Imams, and now the supreme leader of the Islamic Republic), has given laws to societies to govern themselves. But active governance is restricted to the leaders, while popular participation is confined to obedience to the leader. People's existence is defined, therefore, more by obligation to fulfill their *responsibilities* than by the assertion of their *rights*.

It is this understanding of human beings and their place in society that has made Behrouzi a natural member of the conservative/authoritarian faction within the Iranian polity. Even before the reformist faction with its emphasis on individual rights and popular sovereignty asserted itself as a viable force in

Iran, Behrouzi was actively hostile toward its budding stands. Her most pub-licized attack on such stands occurred during the third session of the parlia-ment when she participated in a 1992 crusade against Mohammad Khatami, the then minister of culture and Islamic guidance.[20] In her speeches in the parliament she attacked the "lax" cultural attitude of the ministry in its deal-ings with the producers of cultural and artistic products. Her outspoken at-tack contributed to the creation of an atmosphere that led to the resignation of Khatami from the head of the ministry and his replacement with a conser-vative, Ali Larijani, in 1992.

But, as history witnessed, the reform movement achieved a great deal of mo-mentum after the election of Khatami to the presidency of Iran in 1997. And even though the reformist faction is vulnerable, it is evident that the conserva-tive counterpart has not much to offer in terms of addressing women's predica-ments at this juncture in postrevolutionary Iran. The conservatives are adamant in their protection of authoritarian interpretation of Shari'a, including the family law and penal laws.[21] In fact, to many members of the conservative/authoritarian factions, it is precisely in the novel interpretation of these areas of Islamic precepts that the most fundamental danger to an authentic Islamic polity lies. And since Behrouzi has decided to stay within the fold of the con-servative/authoritarian faction, it would be tremendously difficult for her to contradict the authoritarian interpretation. As things stand now, it is not diffi-cult, therefore, to reach the conclusion that Behrouzi, despite her earlier efforts and achievements on women's issues, cannot be considered as a long-term and steady coalitionary partner for the women's movement in Iran. She is restricted not only by her ideological conviction, but by her political affiliations. Can the same conclusion be drawn in the case of Zahra Rahnavard?

Zahra Rahnavard, the Socialist Reformist

Zahra Rahnavard comes from a middle-class background. Her father was a military officer, and her mother was from a religious family associated with Navab Safavi, the founders of the religious oppositional organization Fada'ian Eslam (Devotees of Islam) in 1946. Rahnavard, however, had a sec-ular upbringing. She reports that she did not wear the Islamic *hejab* until her early twenties, when she was a student at Tehran University. There she received a master's degree in fine arts and a Ph.D. in political science. While a student, she became attracted to socialist idealism, particularly in the con-text of Third World politics. But she eventually decided not to join the sec-ular leftist opposition and instead opted for the Islamic movement. Her attraction to socialism, however, colored her view of Islam and the solution for the ills of society.

Prior to the revolution, she focused her political activities on writing and lecturing in different international fora, including many conferences in the United States. Her prerevolution writing included *Payam-e Hejrat-e Zan-e Mosalman* (The Message of Muslim Woman's Migration) and *Tolou-e Zan Mosalman* (The Dawn of Muslim Woman). After the revolution, she continued her political activities, this time as part of the triumphant religious elite, among whom she is considered an Islamic feminist with somewhat leftist ideas. Her husband, Mir Hossein Musavi, became one of the first prime ministers of the young Islamic Republic. Rahnavard's activities after the revolution included the cofounding of a woman's organization, the Islamic Society of Women. She also became the editor-in-chief of a woman's magazine, *The Path of Zeynab*. As an educated woman she fought against some of the new policies aimed at restricting women's access to higher education. She also served as a member of the High Council of Cultural Revolution (HCCR) and was designated as one of the advisors to President Khatami. In her capacity as a member of the HCCR, she pushed for policy statements regarding women in the workplace. When Behrouzi and other female members of the parliament were trying to provide privileges for women in areas such as retirement and leaves of absence during pregnancy, Rahnavard was fighting the same battle in the HCCR. Their efforts, as mentioned previously, had some payoff.

Since September 1998, Rahnavard has been the chancellor of an all-female university, Al Zahra. Within a year of assuming that position, Rahnavard managed to get permission to add twelve new graduate degree programs as well as four new doctorate programs. In the year 2001, she, along with other women academics, set up a newly formed Association for Muslim Academic Women as a nongovernmental organization to address the specific concerns of women in academia. She has also become forceful in her denunciation of the controversial arrests by the judiciary of women such as journalist Fariba Davoudi Mohajer and parliament deputy Fatemeh Haqiqatju. She sharply criticized the judiciary for the "reprehensible" manner by which Mohajer was arrested and considered her arrest as a "stark violation of her privacy."[22] In an open letter to the president of the republic, she condemned the sentencing of Haqiqatju and denounced the ruling as a "violation of the rights of a Majles deputy." She also raised the question of whether these arrests have been attempts to intimidate female members of parliament (MPs).[23] Rahnavard's activities, particularly the most recent ones, seem to go beyond the merely paternalistic demand for protection of women, as might have been the case with Behrouzi's. As I will discuss, this evolution can also be detected in her ideas.

Rahnavard's Views

Rahnavard started as an Islamic feminist with leftist tendencies. She was critical of the gap between rich and poor countries, as well as the gap between rich and poor classes within each country. Her analysis of social classes however, was not based on a Marxist point of view, and in fact she criticized those whose frames of reference were based on concepts such as bourgeois, petty bourgeois, proletariat, or other Marxist terms. Her own classification was based on a simple dichotomy consisting of a class of the corrupt and the wealthy on the one hand, and the rest of the society on the other.[24] In her analysis of societal problems, she argued that structural factors are equally—if not more—important than cultural issues in explaining the fall and rise of societies. In her book *Moz'giri-ye Tabaqat-e Ejtema-i* (The Stands of Social Classes), Rahnavard argued for the creation of an ideal society based on what she considered to be the Islamic ideology. Such a society, she contended, is one that will be built not by the oppressive arms of political, economic, or religious power establishments, but by the hands of the have-nots, by those who are at the lower steps of the ladder of social positions, in a word, by Mostaz'affins.[25]

As a self-declared Muslim woman, Rahnavard shares some of Behrouzi's perspectives. However, she differs from the latter in many areas, particularly with respect to means and method. Rahnavard does not consider herself an antifeminist even though she was outspokenly critical of Western bourgeois or liberal feminism. For her and many other Third World feminists, Western feminism, particularly its liberal strand, is devoid of any understanding of the concrete problems of women in underdeveloped countries. In fact, she accused liberal Western feminists of being part of the overall neo-imperialist, anti-Third World phenomenon and, therefore, useless if not actually harmful to the progress of underdeveloped countries and the liberation of their women.[26]

Rahnavard did, and still does, share Behrouzi's positive view of *hejab*. But, from early on, she was aware of modern criticism of it and felt compelled to provide an elaborate philosophical and sociopolitical justification for her advocacy of *hejab*. In her book *Beauty of Concealment and Concealment of Beauty*, Rahnavard stated that there is a true human essence with a divine origin but argued that modern societies have separated humans from their essence. The reason for this alienation, she argued, is that modern societies have wrapped human beings in many curtains (*hejabs*): curtains of class, status, shape, and reputation, and thus have denied them access to their true selves.[27] The prevalent ideological and economic systems of the West, be they capitalist or communist, have stolen the souls of humans and reduced them to mere economic entities, to spiritless bodies. In the specific case of women, Rahnavard argued that in the West the beauty of the body has long been a key ingredient in defining women's worth and virtue. Connecting ancient Greek mythology and art to the Western Renaissance and ultimately to the practices of modern Western societies, she continued that a modern materialist society seeks beauty in the body and virtue in the concrete and therefore judges the worth and virtue of its women through the exposure of their bodies.[28] Within such a value system, the demand of a society, which includes both men and women, from a woman revolves around her physical, ephemeral, and therefore untrue, beauty.

To recover the essence of women, Rahnavard turned to Islamic *hejab*. What Islamic *hejab* does, Rahnavard argued, is draw the curtains of concealment in modern societies aside and provide women with the possibility of rediscovery of the self.[29] A woman, through Islamic *hejab*, is able to give up the allure of individualism, to become one with the rest of humanity, and to recapture her true self—a self with divine origin.[30] Rahnavard defined the true self (Islamic self) as a seeker of god and of unity, a self that demands justice and opposes amassed force and wealth.[31] She conceded, however, that Islamic *hejab* has a bad reputation in modern societies and wondered why. How did the Islamic *hejab*, as the destroyer of all other oppressing *hejabs*, such as individual status, reputation, and class, became subject to profound misunderstanding? What concealed the liberating impact and, therefore, the beauty of the Islamic *hejab*? She then attempted to answer these questions by targeting two factors: the external factor (imperialism) and the internal weakness of Muslim societies.

In an analysis influenced by the *dependencia* approach, Rahnavard followed the development of imperialism. Growth of capitalism and advancement in technological fields, with their potential for producing unprecedented amounts of commodities, led to the malady of surplus production. Despite the effective advertisement in capitalist countries to create wasteful and consumerist societies, surplus still outweighed demand. To rid itself of surplus production, capitalist countries, first through colonialism and later neocolonialism, looked for markets in the East. To them, viable markets required the cooperation of women in the East as consumers and as alluring tools for advertising commodities for men.[32] Women in the Muslim world had to become like women in the West so they could be judged on the basis of their physical beauty and sex appeal. Both Islam and the Islamic *hejab* were obstacles for the imperialists in achieving their goals.

Rahnavard argued that imperialism, by its nature, is interventionist. In the East, Western imperialism has long been engaged in an attempt to deny and destroy not only the essence of the "Eastern self," but its outward manifestations.[33]

Only through such cultural destruction can imperialism dominate the Eastern political and economic resources. In the Middle East this "Eastern self" is the "Islamic self" manifested through phenomena such as language and dress code. In Algeria, the French colonialists tried to destroy the Arabic language and replace it with French. In Turkey the influence of imperialism caused the change of the script from Arabic to Latin, and in Iran, the subservient and "Westoxicated" founder of the Pahlavi regime decreed the compulsory removal of *hejab* in public. A successful attack on the manifestation of an Islamic self, in the case of Iran the Islamic *hejab*, paved the way for an assault on every other aspect of an autonomous and authentic Islamic identity. Islam and its manifestations were contemptuously, but effectively, connected to backwardness, while the cultural imperialism of the West was portrayed as progress. During the history of cultural imperialism, the intervention of the West and its subordination of the community were legitimized by its advocacy of freedom of the individual, something that Rahnavard considered (until lately) to be harmful.

In affecting this tragedy on the "Islamic self," imperialism was helped by the weakness of Muslim societies. Regarding women, Rahnavard pointed out two problems in Muslim societies. One was the artificial divorce of Islam from social activity, which led to emptying Islam of its true essence. The other was the tyranny of rulers in Muslim countries that disallowed intellectuals and religious leaders to find practical solutions for societal problems. Therefore, the true nature of Islam was and still is buried under the false perception that it not only does not provide women with any system of support, but that it contributes to sanctioning of those laws that allowed the oppression of women by men.[34] Imperialism, with its emphasis on the alluring but faulty idea of individual freedom, could not find a better local condition to realize its goals of cultural domination, particularly among oppressed women.

As stated previously, Iran is in a state of flux and so are its political actors, including Rahnavard. The evolution of Iranian society and polity has compelled many leaders to reevaluate their positions regarding many issues, including women's rights. Rahnavard is affiliated with the reformist movement and has changed or modified many of her views along the way. Whether these modifications are the result of situational imperative or genuine conversion is not clear, and from a pragmatic point of view is not very important. The important thing is that Rahnavard, as an active and influential Islamist woman, has, at this juncture, made certain statements that cannot be easily recanted. Of special importance are her changing views of the individual and his or her domain of freedom. For example, even though she is an advocate of *hejab* and a fierce critic of what she considers Western exploitation of female body, Rahnavard recently has come to argue that the decision to veil must not be forced on women. In an interview with the daily *Bahar*, she stated, "I am of the opinion that anything a person chooses to do must be based on her own free choice. If it is not voluntarily accepted, hejab or no hejab would make very little difference, no matter what a political system tells the person to be like."[35]

Therefore, she opposes the government policies regarding punishment of violators of the Islamic dress code. She states that in her own case she has *chosen* to wear the *hejab*, not because of the force of tradition but after contemplation and when she came to truly accept Islam as her faith.[36] She believes that through education women will develop an awareness of the benefit of veiling and will embrace it.

Rahnavard has also been quite outspoken about genuine equality between men and women in the area of economic and political activities, where she focuses most of her attention. Rahnavard believes that men and women are equal in their intellectual potentials and leadership abilities and laments the fact that in reality this equality, particularly in the area of decision making, is neglected. She is a strong advocate of female representation in political offices at all levels, including city and village councils. She considers women's participation in politics a good thing not only for women, but also for the promotion of democratic practices. Similar to feminists who celebrate "difference" as opposed to "sameness" on gender issues, Rahnavard argues that "if women played a more active role in policy-makings and at managerial levels, the world would have been more developed and life more pleasant and peaceful."[37]

Rahnavard, as a member of the reformist movement, has adopted the language of democracy and openness and argues that only in a nonauthoritarian way can a society progress. This nonpatriarchal stand allows for different groups, including women's groups, to propose diverse views and legitimately assert themselves as autonomous actors. She has understood the dead end that women are cornered into as the result of clinging to outdated and conservative interpretation of Islamic rules, and therefore is making an attempt to address them. For an Islamist such as Rahnavard, however, the moral guidance of Islam can still be presented through democratic methods. What is needed, according to her, is a more dynamic interpretation of Shari'a (*fiqh-e pouya*).

Conclusion

Looking through the totalistic lens of modernization theories, neither Behrouzi nor Rahnavard could play a meaningful role in the project of women's emancipation. With their critique of liberalism and their conviction that religion should be mixed with politics, these Islamists would be automatically placed, by modernization theorists, in the category of traditional and antiprogressive forces. Based on this judgment, there will be no reason for genuine supporters of women's rights to contemplate any cooperative scheme with these women. But this totalistic view of modernity, with its undifferentiated view of either traditional or modern, has been challenged in all fields—including the field of women's studies. Islamist women activists do not constitute a monolithic or static group, but come from diverse ideological backgrounds and political affiliations. Many of them also demonstrate their ability to evolve in their ideas and subsequently in their actions. Some, such as Maryam Behrouzi, adhere to patriarchal views and have close connections with the conservative/authoritarian groups within the political elite. In the early days of the Islamic Republic they were able to address some of the concerns of many women. But due to their ideological conviction and political alliances, they have been unable to go beyond a very limited domain. They address only those aspects of women's predicaments that do not directly threaten what the conservatives/authoritarians consider to be the pillars of Islam and its corresponding Islamic society.

On the other hand, there are Islamist women such as Zahra Rahnavard who, although they have a very tight connection to the Islamic republic, differ from the first group in their interpretations of Islamic precepts as well as in their views about the character of an Islamic society. They have opted to be part of the fast-moving (ideologically speaking) reformist movement that has increasingly made democratic discourse its own. These women hope for a more open polity in which women can participate as citizens of a democratic society. But as Islamist women, they differ from Western secular feminists, particularly from the liberal strand.

There is disagreement among scholars of Iranian women's studies as to whether any Islamist women could or should be considered part of a broad movement to advance women's rights. For me this question can only be answered if the ideological and political affiliations of these activists, over a period of time, are highlighted. This chapter has been an attempt to study the ideas and political positions of two Islamist women, Behrouzi and Rahnavard, and to make a case for their possible inclusion or exclusion in a progressive women's rights movement. Based on this study, it is not hard to make a case for considering Rahnavard as an ally of the women's rights movement in Iran. She has accepted the necessity of evolution in many areas, including women's status. As a result she is much more at ease with the ideas of woman's agency, autonomy, and rights than in the earlier years of the Islamic Republic. As for the case of Behrouzi (as things stand), it is much harder to see her as a long-term and consistent participant in a genuine women's movement. Unlike Rahnavard, Behrouzi has been unwilling or unable to evolve beyond the permitted boundaries set by authoritarian and patriarchal interpretations of Islam and by her political allies.

Notes

1. For a view of Iran as a transitional polity, see Sussan Siavoshi, "Authoritarian or Democratic: The Uncertain Future of Iran," *Journal of Iranian Studies* 32, 3 (Summer 1999): 313–32.

2. For a neat listing of these attributes, see Daniel Lerner, *The Passing of Traditional Society* (New York: Free Press, 1958), pp. 44–46.

3. In the late 1960s, Samuel Huntington diverged from the early modernization theorists by arguing that democracy should not and would not be the natural outcome of the modernization process. See his book, *Political Order in Changing Societies* (New Haven, Conn.: Yale University Press, 1968).

4. For an assertive proponent of this approach, see Haideh Moghissi, *Feminism and Islamic Fundamentalism: The Limits of Postmodern Analysis* (London: Zed Books, 1999), and *Populism and Feminism in Iran: Women's Struggle in a Male-Defined Revolutionary Movement* (London: Macmillan, 1994).

5. See, for example, Parvin Paidar, *Gender of Democracy: The Encounter between Feminism and Reformism in Contemporary Iran* (New York: United Nations Research Institute, Oct. 2001), and her article "Feminism and Islam in Iran," in D. Kandiyoti, ed., *Gendering the Middle East* (Syracuse, N.Y.: Syracuse University Press, 1996). See also Shahla Haeri, "Of Feminism and Fundamentalism," in *Contention* 4, 3 (Spring 1995).

6. www.salamiran.org/Women/Organizations/jz.html.

7. See "Mashruh-e Mozakerat-e Majles-e Shoray-e Eslami"(The Proceedings of the Islamic Consultative Assembly), June 27, 1992, pp. 18–19.

8. *Iran News*, November 19, 1998, Internet version.

9. See *Zanan*, no. 29, June–July 1996, p. 12.

10. Maryam Behrouzi, *Payam-e Zeynab* (The Message of Zeynab), no. 3, pp. 27–28.

11. Behrouzi, *Payam-e Zeynab*, no. 3, p. 27.

12. See *Zanan*, no. 29, June–July 1996, p. 11.

13. Maryam Behrouzi, *Payam-e Zeynab*, no. 2, Tehran, no date, pp. 6–7.

14. Behrouzi, *Payam-e Zeynab*, no. 2, p. 9

15. See Behrouzi's speech "The Role of Women in Development of Mankind," at the Conference on the Role of Women and Family in Human Development, Tehran, May 1995.

16. Ibid., pp. 10–19.

17. Ibid., p. 24.

18. Personal interview, Tehran, Summer 1996.

19. Personal interview, Tehran, Summer 1996.

20. See, for example, "Mashruh-e Mozakerat-e Majles-e Shoray-e Eslami" (The Proceedings of the Islamic Consultative Assembly), August 10, 1992, pp. 23–24.

21. For one of the most influential voices of the authoritarian faction, consult the writing and statements of Ayatollah Mesbah-Yazdi.

22. See IRNA (Iranian News Agency), Internet version, www.irna.ir, March 3, 2001.

23. IRNA, Internet version, Aug 25, 2001.

24. Rahnavard, *Moz'giri-ye Tabaqat-e Ejtema-i* (The Stands of Social Classes) (Tehran, 1978), p. 32.

25. Rahnavard, *Moz'giri-ye Tabaqat-e Ejtema'-I*, pp. 180–81.

26. Personal interview, Tehran, Summer 1996.

27. Zahra Rahnavard, *Beauty of Concealment and Concealment of Beauty*, trans. Sayyid Ali Reza Naqavi (Islamabad: Cultural Consulate of the Islamic Republic of Iran, 1987), p. 5

28. Rahnavard, *Beauty of Concealment and Concealment of Beauty*, p. 6.

29. Rahnavard, *Beauty of Concealment and Concealment of Beauty*, p. 4.

30. Rahnavard, *Beauty of Concealment and Concealment of Beauty*, p. 5.

31. Rahnavard, *Beauty of Concealment and Concealment of Beauty*, p. 13.

32. Rahnavard, *Beauty of Concealment and Concealment of Beauty*, p. 26.

33. Rahnavard, *Beauty of Concealment and Concealment of Beauty*, p. 11.

34. Rahnavard, *Beauty of Concealment and Concealment of Beauty*, p. 15.

35. See the daily *Bahar*, July 2000, p. 10.

36. See interview with Rahnavard in *Zan-e Irani*, no. 1, p. 16.

37. *Tehran Times*, Dec. 22, 1998, p. 30.

12

Power and Purity:
Iranian Political Culture,
Communication, and Identity

Majid Tehranian

One may begin rather than end with the proposition that a nation's identity is derived from ways in which history has, as it were, counterpointed certain opposite potentialities, the ways in which it lifts this counterpoint to a unique style of civilization, or lets it disintegrate into mere contradiction. . . . One must learn, then, to see a dynamic polarity rather than an inner contradiction in what at first looks like a basic inconsistency, such as that between fusion-in-the-mass and utter solitude, between sensual license and compulsive order, or between an utterly a-historical sense of living and inventories of assembled facts.

—Erik H. Erikson[1]

IN THIS CHAPTER, RELATIONS BETWEEN "power and purity" are the focus of a more generalized explanation of Iranian political culture. The concept of "political culture" is clearly narrower than cultural or national identity.[2] It suggests manifest patterns of cultural behavior in the political arena rather than in cultural life in general. In this sense, Iranian political culture is caught between a series of recurrent and dialectical contradictions. At times, these contradictions have led to a synthesis of historical greatness of spirit and achievement. At other times, they have dissipated into irresolvable contradictions, disarray, and despair. Collective memories and actions are made up of changing juxtapositions of recurrent patterns that give them an undeniable uniqueness and surprising turns. Such is the story of the rise and fall of nations, cultures, and civilizations. History repeats itself but never in boring sameness.

In trying to understand the complexities of the Persian mind, foreign observers have often been misled to conclusions that essentialize a presumed

Iranian national character. James Morier's 1828 novel *Haji Baba of Isfahan*, for example, became a source in the nineteenth century for British civil servants to construct an Orientalist image of Iranian "national character" as fickle, clever, and opportunistic.[3] Other studies of Iranian national psychology in the twentieth century have similarly attributed mistrust among the Iranians to fundamental character flaws rather than to the historical circumstances and contradictions shaping it. They have also failed to recognize the intense loyalties that have held Iranian society together for centuries through family and friendship, the bonds of affection, and mutual obligation. As Edward Said has brilliantly argued in *Orientalism,* these portrayals of Iranian "national character" have often revealed more about Western self-projections as well as colonial rationalizations.[4] They have shed little light on their object of study. In other instances, such as the portrayal of Persians and Jews as "flies," they have displayed outright racial prejudices.[5]

This chapter critically reviews the prevailing cycles, archetypes, continuities, and changes in Iranian political culture. Since the problem is of immense interest, extremely complex, and replete with controversy, the chapter should be considered as preliminary and suggestive rather than conclusive, interpretive rather than positivist. Let the reader beware! I happily admit my own interpretive biases for a democratic political culture that allows freedom of speech, freedom of conscience, freedom of assembly, political competition, transparency, and accountability, as well as checks and balances. I believe this political culture may be considered as an extension of Iran's traditional diversity of languages, ethnicities, and religions that has produced relative color-blindness and cultural tolerance. Despite its tradition of absolutist monarchy, since 1905 Iran has had "constitutional" government interrupted by prolonged periods of de facto dictatorship. Iranian political culture, therefore, has to develop tolerance toward competing political ideologies and parties. If this view is called "liberal," so be it.

Cycles of History and Psychohistory

Situated at the crossroads of great population movements, nomadic invasions, and Western penetration, Iran has had a turbulent history during which it has succeeded in maintaining its territorial and cultural continuity through centuries. However, the cyclical patterns of Iranian history from excessive centralization to excessive fragmentation have resulted in conditions of perennial insecurity, mistrust, and adaptability. Every Iranian more or less bears the psychic imprint of the cyclical swings to political extremes, producing a variety of defense mechanisms. The unpredictable fluctuations and discontinuities have produced a political culture with a fourfold set of dialectical responses to the intense insecurities of life and limb. The resulting deep mistrust has often produced extreme polarities. The dialectics of *power* and *purity, imperialism* and *conspiratorial, mysticism* and *nihilism, heroism* and *opportunism,* and *messianism* and *fundamentalism* are the foundations of this political culture. At times, these dialectics have produced a dualism resulting in bifurcation of Iranian society and culture. At other times, the same dialectics have resulted in fruitful syntheses that can be identified as *patriotism, skepticism, pragmatism,* and *ecumenicalism.*

A caveat is in order. This schema for understanding a complex subject should be taken seriously but not too seriously. Clearly, the patterns are not fixed and predictable. However, there is sufficient historical evidence to support their plausibility. This dialectical synthesis has often produced the noblest of human virtues: openness, tolerance, generosity, adaptability, creativity, sensitivity, and hospitality. However, the same set of dialectics has also descended into dualism, dogmatism, intolerance, xenophobia, opportunism, rigidity, rage, and revenge. No wonder that observers are often baffled by the paradoxes of Iranian political culture and behavior. On the one hand, the vast and lofty literature of Iran has provided a spiritual and moral source of inner strength in the Iranian psyche that can withstand the harshest of political conditions. On the other hand, the historical swings to extremist political regimes have produced such enormous conditions of insecurity and mistrust that some Iranians have had to resort to *taqyeh* (dissimulation) and naked opportunism or hero worship to secure their fortune, life, and limb. In this respect, opportunism and hero worship in Iran operate no differently from when Peter denied Jesus three times before the cock crowed. But the same Peter requested his Roman captors to crucify him upside down in a humble act of devotion to his Master. Such are the dialectics of response to conditions of oppression and insecurity.

Power, Purity, and Democracy

Iranian political culture has been historically caught between the dialectics of power and purity. This is characterized by the mundane struggles for power between the indigenous population and recurrent foreign encroachments while utopian yearnings for messianic figures have kept hope and revolutionary movements alive against domination, tyranny, and injustice. Before the Pahlavi dynasty, all Iranian dynasties were tribal in origin. As the fourteenth-century Islamic historian Ibn Khaldun has argued, recurrent tribal incursions on the sedentary population used to be the dominant pattern of most Islamic history.[6] However, every tribal conquest of the sedentary population led to a cultural conquest of the conquerors by the conquered. As the triumphant tribal dynasties settled, they would assume the language, culture, and manners of the sedentary population. The resultant softening process often paved the way for a new round of tribal invasion. However, the Pahlavi dynasty was the first to be based on a standing national army recruited through universal military draft. In modern times, Iran increasingly came under the forces of Western imperialism, igniting national aspirations for national independence, economic development, political democracy, and social justice. The struggles for power divided the nation between a secular, Western-oriented elite and the religious masses, while the yearning for messianic salvation led to the Islamic Revolution of 1979.[7]

The genius of Iranian culture is generally embedded in its openness, diversity, and adaptability.[8] Iranian culture has absorbed elements of Aryan, Greek, Indian, Arab, Turkik, Mongolian, and Western languages, literature, mythologies, and beliefs without losing its own unique but syncretic identity. There is thus no purity of race, religion, language, or culture in Iran. The genius of Iranian culture is its ability to synthesize and transcend differences.

Yet, in periods of distress, national salvation has seemed to hinge on recapturing some kind of purification, including purifications of language,[9] political ideology, or religion. To face a modern crisis of identity, the Pahlavi regime's pristine nationalism glorifying the pre-Islamic past and the Islamic regime celebrating pristine Islam (Shi'ism or Islam-i-nab-i-Mohammadi) typify such fruitless purification attempts. In periods of history when the dialectics between power and purity have turned into a dualism, cultural creativity has been suppressed by the imposition of a particular secular or religious ideology. In periods during which power has allowed a diversity of utopian and ethical thoughts to coexist, interact, and result in creative syntheses, Iranian culture has flourished and reached new heights. At its highest forms, Iranian culture is eclectic while keeping the moral vision of a pure and perfect world alive.

Dynastic changes with an average longevity of fifty years also introduced into Islamic Iran a land tenure system primarily based on *iqta'*, which paid the military officers by temporary grants of revenues from their land possessions.[10] This was different from European feudalism in which the landowning aristocracy could pass on their property to their offspring through primogeniture. Frequent changes of dynasties and centralized power in Iran allowed the state to confiscate land and grant it to new "owners." This continued to be the practice under the Qajars and the two Pahlavi monarchs, as well as the Islamic Republic. Ashraf has argued that among other factors, this was an impediment to the growth of capitalism in Iran.[11] The negative effect of this land tenure system was that the frequently changing absentee landowners would not care for the land as much as the European feudal lords did, nor would they venture into manufacturing. The positive effect was the absence of a permanent aristocracy and the introduction of a high degree of social mobility in which commoners could acquire land and achieve the highest positions in the state military and civilian bureaucracy. Aristocratic women and clerics were among the beneficiaries of such a system.

Tensions between power and purity in Iranian political culture were thus often mediated by a degree of egalitarianism in which worthy individuals, such as Amir Kabir (the son of a cook) or Reza Khan (a foot soldier) could reach the highest posts. Patrimonial authority of the kings also allowed frequent co-optations of this kind. If the traditional Iranian tolerance for diversity could combine with the modern liberal democratic values of decentralization of power, the prospects for democracy would be encouraging. If, however, the dialectics between power and purity descends into another confrontation between corrupted power and purist visions of power (such as those represented by some current opposition groups), another period of dictatorship cannot be avoided.

Imperial, Conspiratorial, and Patriotic

The longest and most cherished historical memory of nationalist Iranians is the consciousness of a succession of multinational empires interrupted by foreign invasions. The Achaemenids (550–330 BCE) were overthrown by Alexander's Greek invasion and the rise of the Seleucids (312–64 BCE). The Greeks were followed by the Parthians (250 BC–226 CE), and the Sasanids (226–640 CE) were in turn deposed by the Arab invasion and domination (640–1258 CE). Iranian cultural resurgence under Arab domination produced a series of dynasties from the Samanid to the Tahirid, Ghaznavid, and Saljuq that adopted Persian language, culture (*adab*), and imperial style. In 1258, the Abbasid Empire finally came to an end with the Mongolian invasion. Mongolian devastation of Iran eventually led to the rise of the Safavids (1502–1736) and another period of Iranian cultural and political effervescence. The Safavids were finished by yet another tribal invasion, this time from neighboring Afghanistan. Another period of fragmentation followed until the Afshars and Qajars (1794–1925) once again unified the country. Equipped with modern technology and a military, the foreign invasions in the new round were of an entirely different order. Thus, the Western challenge gave rise to the modernist and constitutionalist movements in politics and culture.

Every time it was vanquished, the Iranian phoenix rose once again from the ashes and reconstructed itself, culturally conquering the conquerors while inaugurating yet another round of political and cultural effervescence. Survival and adaptive skills are thus deeply imprinted in the Iranian psyche. However, the political impotence and cultural decay of recent centuries is often contrasted with the old imperial glories of the past. This historical consciousness, together with the realities of an authoritarian and patriarchal society, has produced a dual response to Iran's weakness in world affairs. Every new regime that comes to power, no matter how elitist or populist, attempts to emulate the past imperial mode, both in policies and style. The

Qajars in the nineteenth century, the Pahlavis in the twentieth century, and the Islamic Republic after 1979 have all attempted and failed to extend the borders beyond their present boundaries. As soon as they achieved power, the two monarchies adopted an ostentatious imperial style in court life. Given oil revenues, the second Pahlavi monarch reached for a higher degree of ostentation by extravagantly celebrating the fiftieth anniversary of the dynasty and the 2,500th anniversary of the Persian Empire. For his pretensions, he thus became an object of ridicule abroad and hatred at home. Except for a few years of austerity during the Iran–Iraq War (1980–1988), the Islamic Republic's clerical ruling group has again assumed the imperial style in its personal and political life.

Political culture manifests itself in architectural styles as well as those signatures of power that define an era. The evolving architectural style in Tehran shows distinctly different public spaces in the three periods of Iranian modern history.[12] During the Qajar period, Tehran resembled a traditional Islamic city. The Gulistan Palace and *shamsol-emareh* (the Sun of Buildings) were built close to the Bazaar and the Shah Mosque in what used to be Tehran's downtown.[13] The rise of Reza Shah led to secular nationalism and a revival of pre-Islamic historical memories. The city architecture followed the new political imagination. Moving further north, the new government buildings emulated the Achaemenid imperial style. By contrast, the new royal palaces around Kakh (Palace) Avenue and hotels in Shemiran followed the European models. Thanks to Queen Farah's initiative toward the end of the Pahlavi regime, the architectural style took a new turn. Instead of the style of the Achaemenid Empire, the new architecture emulated that of the Safavid Empire. The best examples of the new turn are Hotel Shah Abbas in Isfahan, built in the fashion of a medieval *caravansary,* and the Iran Center for Management Studies in Tehran, constructed as a medieval *madresseh.* Following the revolution of 1979, the latter was turned into Imam Sadeq University, a theological university devoted to the education of a new cultural and political elite well versed in both Islamic and modern social sciences. However, by the addition of a huge mosque with an eye-catching dome, the university has added its own signature. The regime has generally followed the Islamic period's architectural style by constructing many new mosques and mausoleums, of which Ayatollah Khomeini's tomb is the most prominent.

"People emulate the style of their rulers"—so goes a proverb. The Iranian upper and middle classes have similarly adopted the imperial or Islamic style in their personal homes and consuming identities. In the 1960s, an industrialist who had brought Coca-Cola, television, and Volkswagen to Iran also built the replica of a Versailles palace in the middle of a barren Tehran avenue. It appeared as a sore thumb. North Tehran is replete with houses that resemble the White House in Washington, D.C., or the Elysee Palace in Paris. The imperial style in the interior decoration of such houses often creates in the viewer an impression of anachronistic ostentation. A few recent postmodernist high-rises in Tehran also demonstrate that globalization cannot be stopped by theological borders. However, the growing amount of brick-layered housing also shows that Iran is a meeting ground of tradition and modernity, East and West, to the point of creating an architectural hodgepodge in Tehran.

Imperial pretensions are just one side of the coin. The other side is a theory of conspiracy that runs through the minds of most Iranians from the lowest to the highest ranks. This has inspired a worldview in which everything that happens in Iran is attributed to dark British, Russian, or American forces. Imperialist domination of Iran has produced a colonial mentality in which no Iranian is considered immune from foreign manipulation.[14] With the establishment of the two secret polices under the late shah (SAVAK) and the Islamic regime (SAVAMA), the conspiracy theories have advanced further and sometimes with real justification.[15]

According to the late shah and his followers, the Islamic Revolution was an American or a British plot.[16] According to the Islamists, the shah's 1979 admission by President Carter into a New York hospital for medical attention was part of a conspiracy to return him to Iran as the CIA had done in 1953. Every illusion, of course, creates its own reality. The shah's conspiratorial mind led to his erratic behavior during 1978–1979 and timid expectations of American instructions on how to resolve the revolutionary crisis. The Islamist conspiracy theory led to the university students' takeover of the U.S. embassy in Tehran and a hostage crisis that lasted for 444 days, isolating Iran from the international community.[17] Such responses to domination are fundamentally no different from the oppressive conditions that have produced the colonized mind characterized by subservience, resistance, and revolt. Conspiracy theories provide a simplistic explanation while rationalizing lack of individual or collective responsibility. There *are* conspiracies in history, but history itself cannot be understood as a conspiracy. In the face of complex historical forces at work, to resort to conspiracy theories is tantamount to abdicating understanding and responsibility.

The synthesis of imperialism and conspiratorialism in Iranian political culture has been a deep-seated patriotism characterized by pride in Iranian historical, literary, and artistic achievements. This cultural pride is related to but can be independent of the ideology of nationalism, which is a modern phenomenon. That pride is commonly shared among all the Iranian peoples, including Tajiks, Afghans, Kurds, Azaris, Baluchis, and Persians. It also cuts across the ideological divide among the Islamists,[18] communists,[19] monarchists,[20] Sufi liberals,[21] secular liberals,[22] and postmodernists.[23] Notwithstanding repressive policies, the Zoroastrian, Baha'i, Sunni, Armenian, and Jewish Iranians also manifest the same feelings of pride in the country's cultural heritage.

Messianism, Fundamentalism, and Ecumenicalism

Political cultures, of course, evolve, but only slowly and in response to changes in material conditions. As Iran achieves greater independence and Iranians advance in education, their political culture will hopefully have its pitfalls and pathologies exorcized.[24] But for centuries, the illiterate population in Iran, as illiterates elsewhere, has been steeped in traditions and rules of conduct imposed on them by custom or religious laws. Those traditions and rules have given them a sense of security otherwise unobtainable in a politically and ecologically insecure environment. With the Safavid Dynasty (1502–1736), the Shi'a branch of Islam became the official religion of the country.[25] As a result, the Shi'a clergy became the arbiters of what is religiously mandatory, desirable, undesirable, or forbidden (*wajeb, mostahab, makrooh, haram*). As one of the few able to read and write, the village mulla (clergy) was for centuries the authority with access to the Shari'a (Islamic law) and therefore capable of distinguishing between these ethical categories. Each ayatollah (the highest degree of religious learning in Shi'a Islam) has had to write an extensive treatise consisting of several volumes on legal matters in order to achieve his status. Each ayatollah is considered a source of imitation (*marjae taqlid*) for his imitators (*moqalled*), who pay him their religious taxes consisting of *khoms* (one-fifth of their income), *zakat* (alms), and *sahm-i-imam* (imam's share). In turn, each ayatollah is responsible for the management of the religious institutions and clerical students (*tullab*) within his jurisdiction. In contrast to their Sunni counterparts, the Shi'a clerics have thus enjoyed an unparalleled independence from state authorities. Historically, therefore, the Shi'a religious hierarchy became a counterbalance to the state. The masses often looked to the clerics for defense against the tyranny and oppression of their rulers. In return, the masses gave their religious leaders their absolute obedience and loyalty. In the Islamic Republic, the tradition of parallel religious institutions under temporal and spiritual authorities has continued. The Friday Prayers' Leaders (Imam Jumeh) are appointed by the Supreme Leader (Vali Faqih) for every district; they have ultimate authority over military and civilian governments. By contrast, the autonomous ayatollahs continue to have their own jurisdictions. As with the past secular governments under the Islamic regime, this has produced cooperation and competition between temporal and spiritual authorities.

This religious system has provided a solid basis for the rise of fundamentalism, that is, literal interpretations of the Quran. Some of the rulings have meted out harsh penalties to adulterers (stoning to death) and thieves (cutting off of hands) while imposing inequalities among men and women in marriage and inheritance laws. They have also confined women to *hejab,* which literally means modest clothing but practically has led to women's covering from top to toe (*chador*) and social disablement. The same legal system, however, has

built into the Jafari Shi'a jurisprudence an extraordinary flexibility of interpretation. An ayatollah can exercise his judgment by the rules of *ijtihad* (literally meaning "exertion") to interpret the law in accordance with the exigencies
of changing circumstances. In Twelver Shiism, predominant in Iran, this authority is derived from the Hidden Imam (Imam-i-qaaeb), the twelfth direct
descendant of Prophet Mohammed, who went into occultation in 878 CE. In
order to restore a true and just Islamic government, the believers expect him
to reappear when the world is filled with injustice. In the meantime, the
fuqaha (the Islamic jurists) presume to act on his behalf. Ayatollah Ruhollah
Khomeini employed this authority to put forth his doctrine of Velayat-e-faqih
(Rule of the Jurist) as the ideological basis for the Islamic Revolution in Iran.[26]
Khomeini was rather explicit in his opposition to democracy. "What the nation wants," he opined in 1979, "is an Islamic Republic. Not just a Republic,
not a democratic Republic, not a Democratic Islamic Republic. Do not use the
word 'democratic' to describe it. That is the Western style."[27] His doctrine
of Rule of the Jurists may be thus considered as the Shi'a equivalent of the
Marxist–Leninist doctrine of "dictatorship of the proletariat," assigning to the
jurists the role of professional revolutionaries and political leadership.[28]

The dialectics of fundamentalism and messianism has informed Iranian religious politics for centuries. Since the Islamic Revolution of 1979, however, it
has dominated the scene. Under the Pahlavi regime (1925–1979), the expectation of the Second Coming was celebrated on the birthdays of Imam Mahdi
with such devotion and pageantry that it clearly challenged the secular
regime. Banners would announce the occasion with such defiant slogans as
"we sincerely congratulate the Muslims on the occasion of His Imperial
Majesty the Hidden Imam's birthday." In the months before the Islamic Revolution, thousands of Iranian believers thought that they had seen the face of
Khomeini in the moon.[29] Traditional Shi'a political doctrine of legitimacy
considers all state power ipso facto illegitimate. The Hidden Imam, a messianic figure, is the ultimate authority. From this point of view, the burden of
proof is on the state to demonstrate that it is sufficiently in conformity with
the Islamic principles and laws to be tolerated. This ingenious doctrine gave
the Shi'a ulama extraordinary authority vis-à-vis the state to check and balance its powers. Once the clerical class achieved state power in the Iranian
Revolution of 1979, its moral authority as a force of restraint on the state has
been significantly diminished. Similar to all other ruling classes, the Shi'a clerics have thus become prone to accusations of arrogance and corruption of
power. Moreover, the doctrine of *beyah* (compact), an allegiance reached between the ruler and the ruled, clearly undermines the principle of Velayat-e-
faqih. When in 622 CE, at the invitation of some quarreling Arab tribes,
Prophet Mohammad made an exodus from Mecca to Media, he entered into
beyah with Muslims and non-Muslims (including Jews) for their protection in
return for their loyalty and payment of taxes (*khoms* and *zakat* by Muslims

and *jizyeh* by the People of the Book). The principle became the basis on which the *khulafa* (successors) to the Prophet legitimized their rule. Consent of the governed thus became a fundamental principle of legitimate Islamic rule. Clearly, this principle has been more violated than observed.[30]

For this reason if no other, since the revolution, a debate has raged in Iran on competing doctrines of legitimacy. The religious liberals such as Ali Shariati; Abdolkarim Soroosh; and Mehdi Bazargan, the first prime minister of the Islamic Republic, have argued that sovereignty in Islam belongs to the people, not to the clerics. Some factions of the ulama propose the doctrine of Velayat-e-faqih mashruteh (Conditional Vicarship of the Jurists). They contrast that with the current official view on Velayat-e-faqih mutlaqeh (Absolute Vicarship of the Jurists) that has conferred on Ayatollah Khomeini and his successor, Ayatollah Khameneii, absolute and unconditional authority. The doctrine of the infallibility of the Supreme Leader (Rahbar) has thus left little room for checks and balances. Political theorists such as Abdolkarim Soroosh[31] have warned that the clerical monopoly of power threatens to delegitimize government and undermine Islam itself. In his recently published autobiography,[32] Ayatollah Hossein Ali Montazeri, the first designated but deposed successor to Ayatollah Khomeini, has claimed that the latter did not wish Velayat-e-faqih to be written into the Islamic Constitution.

However, the Constitution of the Islamic Republic contains provisions both for popular sovereignty and clerical hegemony wrapped in complex layers of jurisdiction.[33] While the Supreme Leader and commander-in-chief is elected by a Council of Guardians composed of clerics, the president and the parliament (Majles) are elected by universal suffrage and direct elections. However, the Council also screens the candidates for their Islamic credentials and has veto power over parliamentary legislation. In addition, the Supreme Leader controls about 37 percent of the country's assets concentrated in the so-called charitable organizations (*bonyads*) while holding the power to appoint judges and military officers. This complex system has led to a political stalemate in which the liberal president and parliament pursue policies that are often vetoed by the conservative clerical factions, the Guardian Council, the judiciary, and ultimately the leader himself.

The synthesis of messianism and fundamentalism in Iranian political culture has resulted in ecumenicalism and a high level of tolerance for religious diversity. In contrast to the Achaemenids who patronized all religions, the Sasanids adopted Zoroastrianism as the state religion. Although Islam became the state religion after the Arab conquest, Zoroastrians were added to the Peoples of the Book (Jews and Christians) as worthy of Islamic protection in return for payment of *jizya*. Under the Safavids, Christian Armenians were brought to the capital to establish their own town (Julfa) at Isfahan, to build their own churches, and to practice their own religion with considerable autonomy. The Ottoman *millet* system that gave autonomy to diverse religious communities was also prevalent in Islamic Iran. Religious bigotry has shown its ugly head from time to time, but the tradition of tolerance has been dominant. In fact, Shi'ism itself may be argued to be an expression of Iranian political culture vis-à-vis the domination of Sunni Arabs and Turks.

Cycles and Archetypes

Another possible approach to the understanding of political culture is to consider the role of heroic archetypes. Bateson et al. have done this through a study of Iranian films.[34] Their findings correspond to Thompson's typology of perennial archetypal heroes as "headman, shaman, hunter, and clown."[35] In a brilliant essay, Thompson has persuasively argued that all societies from tribal to agrarian, industrial, and scientific-planetary civilizations reproduce this basic archetypal pattern in increasingly more complex institutional forms. In terms of Iranian political culture, the four archetypes may be named the shah, imam, *luti,* and *rend.* In Iranian political imagination, a just shah or sultan is a ruler and father figure who cares for his flock. The literature on mirrors for the princes, including that of Nizam ul-Mulk's well-known *Siasat-Nameh,*[36] provides a source for the understanding of the cultural roots of the archetype. Since Iranian history has been replete with tyrannical kings, the counterpoint to the unjust ruler has generally been presented as the "innocent imam" (*imam-i-ma'sum*) providing spiritual guidance and resistance against unjust rule. The martyrdom of Imam Hussein and its reenactment in annual passion plays provide the sources of inspiration for this particular myth. However, in pre-Islamic mythology also we can see a parallel episode in the martyrdom of Siavash.[37] *Luti* or *javanmard* (chivalrous man) constitutes another archetypal hero for resistance against the unjust and in support of the oppressed. The epic hero Rustam in Ferdowsi's *Shahnameh* is one such figure. Finally, there is the figure of *rend* (wise fool or jester) in Persian lore and literature. *Rend* has no pretensions to power and leadership. As a wise fool, he may be considered a postmodernist antihero hero deconstructing all ideological pretensions. Mulla Nasser ed-Din[38] in folklore and Hafez in highbrow culture provide embodiments of such heroes.

The five major Iranian political figures of the twentieth century (Reza Shah, Mohammad Reza Shah, Mohammad Mosaddeq, Amir Abbas Hoveyda, and Rouhollah Khomeini) provide apt examples of the four archetypes. The five figures also demonstrate the successes and failures of the Iranian political culture to deal with the complexity of Iran's political, economic, and cultural problems. The four dialectical tensions have expressed themselves in a complex variety of ways in Iran's five major political figures of the twentieth century. What distinguishes the five from each other is a historical process of deepening and broadening of Iranian political culture from its secular and elitist to the religious and populist features. While the two Pahlavi monarchs and Prime Minister Hoveyda represented a complex mix of elitist and populist trends, Mosaddeq and Khomeini articulated the anti-imperialist and populist sentiments, the latter with strong religious casting.

Reza Shah was the embodiment of a conflict between heroism and opportunism. He appeared on the scene at a time when the country was in deep distress. He fulfilled the people's expectation of a mythological *javanmard* or *luti*, the chivalrous strongman who arrives just in time to vanquish the oppressor and uplift the oppressed. He entered Tehran on February 21, 1921, at the head of an army of 3,000 men in a bloodless coup that changed the course of Iranian history. He soon replaced the Qajar dynasty with his own Pahlavi dynasty to hark back to the Iranian pre-Islamic memories. Despite his murky beginnings as a British tool, most Iranians welcomed him as a true patriot who could unify and modernize the country. He was extraordinarily successful in launching an ambitious modernization program, including a revamping of the educational and legal systems and development of transportation as well as military and civilian bureaucracies.[39] Soon, however, he fell victim to greed and self-aggrandizement by murdering his opponents and confiscating some 2,000 villages. From heroism, he had descended to cynicism, paranoia, and tyranny.

Dr. Mosaddeq also represented a heroic and pragmatic political leader in significantly different ways. He was a well-educated doctor of jurisprudence with a pragmatic understanding of what a poor and dependent country such as Iran needed to do in order to rid itself of British domination. He had exceptional political skills and theatrical talents. By dramatizing his patriotic feelings in tearful speeches and appearing as a pajama-clad prime minister receiving visitors in his sickbed, he appealed to an Iranian martyrdom complex, the love of the blameless saints and martyrs. His mystical bond with the Iranian people and fervent wish not to appear less than a devoted patriot led him to ignore the pragmatic need for an oil settlement. He was confronting too many enemies at home (the monarchists, communists, and right-wing clerics) and fighting too many powerful enemies abroad (Britain, the United States, and the oil cartel). At the end, he lost his nationalist cause to his failure to strike a balance between patriotic idealism and political realism. However, he remained faithful to his principles of constitutional democracy. Despite the coup of August 15, 1953, against his democratic government, he requested the shah, through the Court Minister Hossein Ala, to stay on and not leave the country.[40] He also refused to give the communist and National Front parties weapons with which to defend his government. At the end, he seems to have been pleased to be relieved of his responsibilities. As reported by Dr. Seyyed Ali Shayegan,[41] one of Mosaddeq's closest lieutenants, on "August 19, 1953, as Dr. Mosaddeq's house came under attack from General Zahedi's forces, we took refuge to the neighbors by a ladder. From there, we were driven to our hiding place. There was a deadly silence between us for a long time before I broke it to say, 'Sir, what a disaster!' [*Agha, che bad shod!*] To my surprise, Dr. Mosaddeq replied in protest, 'No, Sir, it turned out for the best!' [*Na, agha, che khoob shod!*]"

Mohammad Reza Shah, by contrast, strongly gravitated toward the imperial–conspiratorial axis. According to his autobiography, *Mission for My Country*, he was a sickly boy in his childhood, experiencing apparitions of holy men who saved him and assured him of his future greatness. Standing in the shadow of a tall, willful, and tyrannical father, his life was spent on emulating while trying to distinguish himself from his father's autocracy. For a while in his early years as a young shah, he showed potential to be a democratic monarch. But following the coup of 1953, he assumed dictatorial powers. As a modernizer, he succeeded in raising the oil revenues by skillfully manipulating the international oil markets while launching an ambitious program of industrialization. In fact, by launching a land reform and subduing the tribes without developing modern institutions of political participation, he paved the way for the popular revolution to come. As oil revenues grew and domestic and foreign flatterers bowed to his will, he increasingly covered his inner insecurities with arrogance in speech and behavior that offended both his friends and foes. As his imperial pretensions started to rise, so did his conspiracy theories. In 1975, he went so far as to ask the Iranians who disagreed with him to obtain their passports and get out of the country. Given the fact that poor Iranians did not have anywhere else to go, he was digging his own grave while putting the blame for his own shortcomings on real and presumed domestic and foreign enemies. His last testament, *Response to History*, is a sad account of his own downfall in which he takes no responsibility for his own errors.

In a meeting that we had with the shah in 1975 to report on the findings of a research project, I discovered him to be a profoundly insecure man. Our research findings showed the rise of Islamic ideologies among youth, government employees, and the population at large.[42] He showed little intellectual curiosity about the content of the report and was most anxious to impress his superiority of knowledge and intellect upon a group of technocrats. He often would interrupt the report with long lectures that derailed us from the main topic. He was particularly incensed by the presence of two former Tudeh Party members (Mahmoud Jafarian and Parviz Nikkhah) who had subsequently recanted and joined the services of National Iranian Radio and Television. He spent a significant part of the meeting castigating those who had betrayed their king and country. We were thus unable to convey the central message of the report to him. He showed little intellectual curiosity and clearly lacked a sense of history about his own role in Iran. Although some of this may be attributed to his cancerous conditions by this time, he was clearly more focused on technological rather than cultural and political requirements for Iran's transition to a modern society. He was keen on the latest technological advances in satellite communication. He told us that the physicist Wernher Von Braun had personally informed him that the longevity of satellites was significantly increasing. He decreed that Iran must acquire broadcast satellites for the diffusion of Persian language and culture in the West Asia region.

Prime Minister Hoveyda[43] provides an even more clear-cut example of the complex dialectics of *heroism, opportunism, and pragmatism* as well as *imperialism, conspiratorialism, and patriotism.* As a member of a new Western-educated technocratic class, some with leftist leanings during student days, Hoveyda came into prominence during his collaboration with Prime Minister Hassanali Mansour. Together they formed the Iran Novin Party, which carried out the shah's White Revolution. Following Mansour's assassination in 1965, Hoveyda assumed the premiership and stayed in the post for a period of twelve years. Although Hoveyda always kept a low profile in the shah's haughty shadow, his political influence grew through his political party, which was basically an office-holders' organization. When relatively free elections were conducted in Sari to test the possibilities for fair elections under the shah's dictatorship, Iran Novin Party candidates emerged out of the ballot boxes. Alarmed by Hoveyda's growing power, the shah decided in 1975 to establish a one-party system by abolishing all previous political parties. In a meeting I had with Hoveyda during this critical period, he was visibly shaken by the events. He was subsequently replaced with Jamshid Amouzegar, a technocrat who did not have Hoveyda's political and populist skills. Hoveyda assumed the role of the court minister for a short time until, in response to the Islamic revolutionary movement, the shah dismissed him in 1978. He was arrested later by General Azhari's government. Unlike many others of the shah's ministers, he refused to escape Iran and fell victim to the revolution's wrath. In February 1979, he gave himself up to the revolutionary government. Two months later he was sentenced to death by the Islamic Revolutionary Court and shot the same day. Depending on whose views we accept, he could be considered an opportunist, a pragmatist, or a hero. Following three long meetings I had with Hoveyda in 1975, 1977, and 1978, I came to the conclusion that he was a highly sophisticated, complex, and patriotic man. As the revolution began to threaten the throne, his services to the shah were rewarded by his dismissal from premiership and court ministry, arrest, and execution.

The dialectics between mysticism, nihilism, and skepticism is explicitly manifested in the beliefs and behavior of all five major rulers of Iran during the twentieth century. In all five instances, we can see a dependence on mystical powers while their policies were leading them to the partial defeat of their political projects. When Colonel Reza Khan in 1921–1924 was entertaining the thought of emulating Ataturk by establishing a republic in Iran, he was opposed in this project by the ulama. To allay their fears and in an act of religious piety, the powerful colonel walked several miles from Tehran to the Shi'a shrine of Shah Abdul-Azim barefooted and with straw on his bare head. He soon changed his plans from republicanism to a monarchical change of dynasty. His son, Mohammad Reza Shah,[44] also related childhood mystical visions in his autobiography while often visiting the Imam Reza shrine in Mashhad. However, when the opposition of the ulama to his White Revolution took a violent turn in June 1963, he denounced the "lice-ridden clerics" as reactionary and accused them of a Red–Black alliance with the communists. Nevertheless, when faced with a religious revolt in 1978, he was willing to "hear the revolutionary call" for change if it could only save his crown. Although a secular liberal in orientation, Mosaddeq also portrayed himself as a devout Muslim while pursuing policies that alienated some of his clerical supporters. And finally, Ayatollah Khomeini was known for his mystical love poetry as well as religious learning and political savvy. He initially portrayed himself as a religious scholar who intended to retire in Qom after the fall of the monarchy while letting the politicians manage the government. However, he soon revealed his real scheme by establishing an Islamic Republic under clerical leadership and taking direct charge after the revolution. In all instances, a complex combination of mysticism, nihilism, and skepticism was at work.

Ayatollah Khomeini, another archetypal figure in twentieth-century Iran, best symbolized the contradictions between messianism and fundamentalism. He appeared first as a messianic figure focused on ridding the country of foreign domination and monarchical dictatorship while promising to retire to a life of religious scholarship once the monarchical regime was deposed. However, shortly after his arrival in Tehran in February 1979, he asserted his authority and power against the policies of the liberals and the communists. His austere lifestyle and indomitable will endeared him to a patriarchal society in search of a lost father figure—dictatorial yet benevolent, willful yet protective, single-minded yet accommodating. At the end, his strengths proved to be his weaknesses. Critics view his opposition to popular sovereignty and democratic principles as anachronistic and un-Islamic. His doctrine of Velayat-e-faqih placed sovereignty in God's vicars on earth (the Islamic jurists). Since there is no priesthood in Islam and relations between the believers and God are direct, some other ayatollahs considered his doctrine of vicarship of the jurists un-Islamic. They argued that he introduced a doctrine of sovereignty into the constitution that has been an impediment to the development of civil society. Other critics argued that the Prophet and his four immediate Rightly Guided Successors (Khulaf al-Rashidun) had all received their political legitimacy through their knowledge and personal charisma. Sunni critics further argued that a council of elders of the nascent community had *elected* each of the first four successors. This election also had to be confirmed by *beyah* (compact) with the new ruler, in which each believer and nonbeliever living in the Islamic state would enter into a contractual obligation of rights and responsibilities. In contrast to the doctrine of Velayat-e-faqih mutlaqeh, this contract (*beyah*) was conditional on just rule that could be otherwise revoked. Religious as well as secular critics argued that absolute power by Velayat-e-faqih without checks and balances has led to serious errors in policy. Some critics have charged that Ayatollah Khomeini used summary executions for the opposition groups instead of fair and open trials and thus turned a relatively peaceful and just revolution into revenge and violence.[45] From 1979 to 1981, he endorsed the taking of American diplomats as hostages and thus isolated Iran from the international community. His determination prolonged a war with Iraq for eight years (1980–1988) whereas it could have been possibly settled much earlier to Iran's advantage. The cost was no less than 200,000 Iranians killed and about one million maimed while the country was being destroyed. Nevertheless, Ayatollah Khomeini enjoyed the devotion of millions of followers who bitterly wept at his funeral in 1989.

Pathologies of Political Culture

The dialectics of Iranian political culture can lead the country to creative synthesis as well as pathological self-destruction. Good, Good, and Moradi[46] have argued that at the interpersonal level, depressed Iranian patients show four symptoms: (1) sadness and grief (*gham o ghosseh*); (2) anger (*asabaniyyat*); (3) insecurity and mistrust (*adame amniyyat va sooe zann*); and (4) sensitivity (*hassasiyat*). All four symptoms can be considered, inter alia, as factors responsible for the apparent inability of Iranians to come together for positive (national development, social and political democracy, cultural freedom) rather than negative (anti-imperialism, antidictatorship) national goals. It is said in jest that if two Iranians get together, they form a political party; once the third one joins them, they split! Iranian rugged individualism and a negative attitude toward compromise (pejoratively called *sazesh*) have made it difficult for democratic politics to take root. Although there are other cultural categories for the democratic negotiation of differences (e.g., *kenar amadan, musamehe, musalehe*), the utopian search for power and purity has proved to be an obstacle to democratic politics. The Iranian martyrdom complex demands that a charismatic political leader prove his purity beyond all doubt. That cannot be achieved beyond a shadow of a doubt until the leader is "martyred." As long as a charismatic political leader, such as Mosaddeq or Khomeini, is active, his adoring followers push him to extremist positions guaranteeing his political failure or "martyrdom." Once martyred, the political leader becomes a saint worthy of adoration by succeeding generations. In this perspective, Mosaddeq's failure at reaching an oil agreement and Khomeini's failure at shortening the war with Iraq were attributed not to the domestic politics of extremism but to foreign machinations.

However, the most serious pathology of Iranian political culture in the modern era may be considered to be a kind of cultural schizophrenia leading to political extremism. The multiple cultural personality of Iran, mainly organized around pre-Islamic and post-Islamic identities, has created a vast political schism between the modernist, educated, and professional classes and the lower and lower middle classes. Moderate politicians such as Mosaddeq, Bazargan, Hoveyda, and Khatami who have tried to bridge this cultural chasm by championing a middle road have enjoyed popularity but not effective power. It is often the extremists such as the Pahlavi monarchs, Khomeini, and Khamenei who wield real power while generating the swing to the opposite sides of political pendulum.

The pathologies of Iranian political culture can also be observed in exile politics. The forced and voluntary exile of over two million Iranians after the revolution of 1979 has provided fertile ground for a vast range of political parties and groups in Europe and the United States. Few of these exile groups appear to have a realistic chance of achieving political power at home. While new political struggles have begun to unfold in Iran, in which the younger generation will have the greatest stake and participation, the aging exile groups continue to engage in the old wars. The ferocity and absurdity of some of these political squabbles are not diminishing with time. A fetish of Iranian identity in its positive as well as negative aspects has become prevalent among some of the Iranians abroad. As Naficy observes, "The fetishism of exilic popular culture . . . helps control the terror and the chaos of liminality, but if one submits to the process, these fetishes become controlling agents of themselves."[47] Much of this fetish is conducted publicly through a diversity of exile media (newspapers, radio, and television) in open contestation among competing identity constructions and political loyalties, from monarchist to a variety of secular and religious persuasions. In the meantime, a new hybrid, exilic political culture is also developing among the younger and most astute Iranians abroad seeking economic and political power through engagement with the host countries. Invariably called Tehrangeles or Irangeles, Southern California has become the birthplace of a new Iranian American culture in the production of new Persian food industries, literature, film, newspapers, radio, and television programs.[48] The high-status Iranian immigrant community in the West has allowed for the new efforts to make significant contributions to Iranian culture generally. Some examples are the publication of *Encyclopaedia Iranica*, a traveling exhibition of Qajar paintings, and academic conference publications undertaken by the Society for Iranian Studies and others.

Conclusion

This chapter on Iranian political culture is limited by the fact that it does not address the enormous class, ethnic, and provincial differences in Iran.[49] Many observers share in the chapter's assumption of an Iranian national culture. If

the dialectical perspective presented here makes any sense, similar studies
would have to be made of "language and speech communities," as proposed
by Beeman,[50] to apply to class, ethnic, provincial, gender, and generational differences.

What is ironic in the development of Iranian political culture is that the five
major Iranian political leaders of the twentieth century have all undermined
their own political projects. While the two Pahlavi monarchs contributed to
the demythologization of monarchy, Ayatollah Khomeini started a process of
the demystification of Islam. The unintended consequences of historical developments also hold in the case of Dr. Mosaddeq. While Dr. Mosaddeq was
the embodiment of Iranian aspirations for national independence and constitutional democracy, he dashed both projects by his uncompromising postures
in domestic and international affairs. Hoveyda's pragmatic opportunism did
not pay off either. It generated rampant cynicism among the shah's political
elite.[51] All five leaders demonstrated a fundamental lack of understanding of
the modern democratic political culture that rests upon the principles of political dialogue, negotiation, and compromise. In that respect, however, they
were all victims of a historical tradition that considers compromise as *sazesh*,
meaning in Persian an unprincipled submission, rather than *kenar amadan*,
meaning mutual respect and coexistence with political opponents.

Political culture, as all culture, is a dynamic phenomenon. Its evolution,
however, is constrained by reified historical memories and collective consciousness as well as changing national and global conditions.[52] In the struggle between the state, market, and civil society through the processes of modernization, the Iranian state has so far had the upper hand. However, market
and civil society forces are increasingly making themselves felt. The forces of
materialism and consumerism generated by the market forces are changing
Iranian political culture in ways that are unpredictable. So are the forces of a
civil society of middle and working classes aspiring to political participation.
The two monarchical regimes (1925–1941 and 1953–1979) partially succeeded in economic modernization while failing at political development. The
secular constitutional eras (1905–1925 and 1941–1953) partially succeeded in
political development and failed at economic modernization. Both the
monarchical and republican regimes imposed severe constraints on the ful-
fillment of popular political and economic aspirations. Under the monarchical as well as republican regimes, the state has been fortified by the centraliz-
ing ideologies of monarchy and *velayat-e-faqih* reinforced by oil revenues. Oil
income has made the state in Iran, as in other petroleum exporting countries,
insensitive to the needs for political participation and social justice. By co-
opting the dissident elements, the state has been able to postpone but not resolve its legitimacy crisis. The prognosis for the emergence of a democratic
political culture in Iran is therefore one of greater struggles between the state,
market, and civil society.

Democracy is the art of negotiation and compromise among political opponents without resorting to violence. But there is clearly no purity in compromise. Purity can live only in our moral imagination. It should be held high above the messiness of power politics. If we were angels, power would always be moral and humane. Since we are not, power always needs to be checked and balanced by other autonomous power nodes and the moral imagination of our faith. To fuse power and purity is tantamount to risking corruption on the one hand and cynicism on the other.

It remains to be seen whether a figure such as President Mohammad Khatami, who has championed the cause of liberalization in Iran at the dawn of a new century, can succeed at the institutionalization of democratic politics and rule of law without succumbing to the forces of violence. Whatever happens to his presidency, however, the main challenge remains one of maintaining the creative tension between the moral vision of a free and just society and the practical politics of compromise in a pluralistic society. Centuries of dependency and decay in Iran have created psychohistorical pathologies that stand in the way of economic, political, and cultural modernization. As the nation achieves greater independence and self-confidence, the wounds of impotence will be gradually healed while a political culture of tolerance and compromise emerges. Negotiable identities and ideologies emerge into the foreground while hegemonic and resistance identities recede into the background.

Notes

1. Erik Erikson, *Gandhi's Truth* (New York: Norton, 1969).

2. Gabriel Almond and Sidney Verba, *The Civic Culture* (Boston: Little, Brown, 1963); Nauka Publishers, *Historical Traditions of East and West in Modern Political Culture* (Moscow: Social Science Today 1989); Arjomand Said, *Authority and Political Culture in Shi'ism* (Albany: SUNY Press, 1988).

3. James Morier, *The Adventures of Haji Baba of Isfahan* (London: J. Murray, 1828).

4. Said, *Orientalism* (New York: Vintage, 1979).

5. Khairallah Tuffah, *Three Whom God Should Not Have Created: Persians, Jews, and Flies,* a monograph by Saddam Hussein's uncle published in Baghdad, as reported by Jon Lee Anderson, "Letter from Baghdad," *The New Yorker,* December 11, 2000, p. 88.

6. Ibn Khaldun, *The Muqaddimah; An Introduction to History,* 3 vols., trans. Franz Rosenthal (New York: Pantheon, 1958).

7. Majid Tehranian, "Communication and Revolution in Iran: The Passing of a Paradigm," *Iranian Studies* 13 (Spring 1980): 1–2.

8. Jamshid Gharachedaghi, "Gofteguii darbareye farhang-i-iran" (A Discourse on Iranian Culture), *Rahavard* 48 (1998): 75–79.

9. We have the example of Ferdowsi here.

10. "iqta" *Encyclopædia Britannica Online.* Available at www.members.eb.com/bol/topic?eu=43694&sctn=1 (accessed December 28, 2000).

11. Ahmad Ashraf, "Historical Obstacles to the Development of a Bourgeoisie in Iran," *Iranian Studies* 11 (Spring–Summer 1969): 2–3; Ashraf, *Mavane tarikhi-ye roshd-i-sarmaye dari dar Iran: dowreh qajariyeh* (Tehran: Zamineh, 1980).

12. Takmil Homayoon, *Tarikhe ejtemaii va farhangiye tehran,* 3 vols. (Social and Cultural History of Tehran) (Tehran: Daftar pajouheshaye farhangi, 2000).

13. After the revolution of 1979, the latter was renamed Imam Mosque.

14. Majid Tehranian, "Ettehamat-I-kayhan." Available at www.Iranian.com/MajidTehranian (accessed February 25, 2001).

15. See U.S. government documents on the 1953 CIA intervention, available at www.pak.net/politics/cia-docs (accessed February 25, 2001).

16. Mohammad Reza Pahlavi, *Answer to History*, trans. Michael Joseph Ltd. (New York: Stein and Day, 1980).

17. Majid Tehranian, *Global Communication and World Politics: Domination, Development, Discourse* (Boulder, Colo.: Lynne Rienner Publishers, 1999). See chapter 6.

18. Morteza Mottahari, *Khadamat-I-motaqabel-I-iran va islam* (The Mutual Contributions of Iran and Islam) (Tehran: Ettehad, 1970).

19. Ehsan Tabari, *Barkhi barressiha darbareh jahanbinihay e jonbeshhay e ejtemaii dar Iran* (Some Research Notes on the Worldviews of Social Movements in Iran) (n.p., 1969).

20. Mohammad Reza Pahlavi, *Mission for My Country* (New York: McGraw Hill, 1960); Pahlavi, *Answer to History*; Shoja ed-Din Shafa, *Tavallodi digar: Iran kohan dar hezareh no* (Another Birth: Ancient Iran in the New Millennium) (Nashre farzad, 1999).

21. A. H. Zarrinkoob, *Na sharqi, na gharib, ensani* (Neither Eastern nor Western but Humane) (Tehran: Amir Kabir, 1974).

22. Ali Banuazizi and Shahrokh Meskoob, *Darbareh siasat va farhang* (On Politics and Culture) (Vincenne, France: Khavaran, 1994).

23. Daryush Shayegan, *Asia dar barabare gharb* (Asia Confronting the West) (Tehran: Amir Kabir, 1972).

24. See note 8.

25. Nikki Keddie, ed., *Religion and Politics in Iran: Shism from Quietism to Revolution* (New Haven, Conn.: Yale University Press, 1983).

26. Ruh Allah Khomeini, *Islam and Revolution*, trans. and annotated by Hamid Algar (Berkeley, Calif.: Mizan Press, 1981); Ruh Allah Khomeini, "Imam Khomeini's Last Will and Testament," in *Kayhan International* X: 2446, (Tehran, June 24, 1989): 6.

27. Elaine Sciolino, *Persian Mirrors: The Elusive Face of Iran* (New York: The Free Press, 2000), p. 68.

28. Majid Tehranian, "Khomeini's Doctrine of Legitimacy," in Anthony J. Parel and Ronald C. Keith, eds., *Comparative Political Philosophy* (New Delhi: Sage Publications, 1992).

29. Sattareh Farman-Farmaian and Dona Munker, *Daughter of Persia: A Woman's Journey from Her Father's Harem through the Islamic Revolution* (New York: Crown, 1992).

30. Majid Tehranian, "Rahe sevvom," Iranian.com/MajidTehranian/ (accessed April 9, 2001).

31. Abdolkarim Soroosh, *Farbehtar as Ideology* (More Robust than Ideology) (Tehran: Sarat, 1995).

32. Ayatollah Hossein Ali Montazeri, available at www.montazeri.com (accessed April 9, 2001). Published under Ayatoolah Hosseinali Montazeri, *Khaterat* (Los Angeles: Ketab Corp., 2001).

33. Asghar Schirazi, *The Constitution of Iran: Politics and the State in the Islamic Republic* (London: I. B. Tauris, 1997).

34. M. C. Bateson, J. W. Clinton, J. B. M. Kassarjian, H. Safavi, and M. Sorya, "Safayi Batin: A Study of the Interrelations of a Set of Iranian Ideal Character Types," in L. Carl Brown and N. Itzkowitz, eds., *Psychological Dimensions of Near Eastern Studies* (Princeton, N.J.: The Darwin Press, 1977).

35. William Irwin Thompson, *At the Edge of History: Speculations on the Transformation of Culture* (New York: Harper Torchbooks, 1971), pp. 104–50.

36. Nizam ul-Mulk, *Siasat-Nameh* (Book of Politics) (Tehran: Entesharat-I-Franklin, 1969).

37. Meskoob, Shahrokh, *Sook-I-siavash: dar marg va rastakhiz* (The Passion of Siavash: On Death and Resurrection), (Tehran: Kharazm, 1969).

38. Idries Shah, *The Pleasantries of the Incredible Mulla Nasrudin* (London: Pan Books, 1977).

39. Amin Banani, *The Modernization of Iran* (Stanford, Calif.: Stanford University Press, 1961).

40. Farman-Farmaian and Munker, *Daughter of Persia*.

41. Seyyed Ali Shayegan, personal conversation with author.

42. Majid Tehranian, Farhad Hakimzadeh, and Marcello Vidale, eds., *Communications Policy for National Development: A Comparative Perspective* (London: Routledge & Kegan Paul, 1977).

43. Abbas Milani Hoveyda, *The Persian Sphinx: Amir Abbas Hoveyda and the Riddle of the Iranian Revolution* (Washington, D.C.: Mage Publishers, 2000).

44. Pahlavi, *Mission for My Country*.

45. Montazeri, available at www.montazeri.com (accessed April 9, 2001); see Montazeri, pp. 350–68.

46. Byron J. Good, Mary-Jo DelVecchio Good, and Robert Moradi, "The Interpretation of Iranian Depressive Illness and Dysophoric Affect," in Gilford Weary and Herbert L. Mirels, eds., *Integrations of Clinical and Social Psychology* (New York: Oxford University Press, 1985), p. 395.

47. Hamid Naficy, *The Making of Exile Cultures: Iranian Television in Los Angeles* (Minneapolis: University of Minnesota Press, 1993), p. 128.

48. Ron Kelley, Jonathan Friedlander, and Anita Colby, eds., *Irangeles: Iranians in Los Angeles* (Berkeley: University of California Press, 1993).

49. Beeman, *Culture, Performance, and Communication in Iran* (Tokyo: ICLAA, 1982), pp. 3–23.

50. Ibid.

51. Martin Zonis, *The Political Elite of Iran* (Princeton, N.J.: Princeton University Press, 1971).

52. Jonathan Friedman, *Cultural Identity and Global Processes* (Newbury Park, Calif.: Sage, 1994); Katharine Kia Tehranian, "Global Communication and Pluralization of Identities," *The Futures* 30 (1998): 2–3.

Index

About the Editor and Contributors

Roksana Bahramitash is a faculty member at the Simon de Beauvoir Institute at Concordia University and a research associate at the McGill Institute for Islamic Studies in Montreal, Canada.

Sohrab Behdad is a professor and the John E. Harris Chair in economics at Denison University (Ohio). He is coauthor (with Saeed Rahnema) of *Iran after the Revolution: Crisis of an Islamic State.*

Jamshid Behnam is a sociologist and a former professor at the University of Tehran and Sorbonne University in Paris. He is the author of several books in Persian and French. He is coauthor (with Ramin Jahanbegloo) of *Civilization and Modernity* (published in Tehran, 2003).

Hamid Dabashi is the Hagop Kevorkian Professor of Iranian Studies and the director of graduate studies at the Centre for Comparative Literature and Society at Columbia University. His most recent book is *Close Up: Iranian Cinema, Past, Present, Future* (2001).

Nader Hashemi is a doctoral candidate in political science at the University of Toronto, Canada. He is the author of several articles on Iranian civil society and Islam and democracy.

Ramin Jahanbegloo was born in Tehran, Iran. He received his B.A. and M.A. in philosophy, history, and political science and later his Ph.D. in philosophy from the Sorbonne University. In 1993 he taught at the Academy of Philosophy in Tehran. He has been a researcher at the French Institute for Iranian Studies, a fellow at the Center for Middle Eastern Studies at Harvard University, and a fellow at the National Endowment for Democracy in Washington, D.C. He was also an adjunct professor in political philosophy at the University of Toronto from 1999 to 2001. His is the author of twenty books in English, French, and Persian. His books include *Conversations with Isaiah Berlin* (1991), *Gandhi: aux sources de la nonviolence* (1998), *Penser la nonviolence* (1999), and *The Fourth Wave* (2003). He is also the author of many articles in Iranian, Indian, American, and French journals. Dr. Jahanbegloo is presently Head of the Department for Contemporary Studies at the Cultural Research Bureau, Tehran.

Mazyar Lotfalian is a postdoctoral fellow at the Centre for Religion and Media at New York University. He is the author of a thesis on "Technoscientific Identities: Muslims and the Culture of Curiosity," which will be published in the near future.

Monica M. Ringer is an assistant professor of history at Amherst College in Massachusetts. She is the author of *Education, Religion and the Discourse of Cultural Reform in Qajar Iran* (2001).

Ahmad Sadri is professor and chair of the department of sociology and anthropology at Lake Forest College and writes a regular column for the *Daily Star* of Lebanon. He is the coeditor of *Reason, Freedom, and Democracy in Islam: Essential Writings by Abdolkarim Soroush* (2000) and the author of *Max Weber's Sociology of Intellectuals* (1992).

Sussan Siavoshi is a professor of comparative politics in the Department of Political Science, Trinity University. She is the author of *Liberal Nationalism in Iran: The Failure of a Movement* (1990).

Mohamad Tavakoli-Targhi is an associate professor of history at Illinois State University and a visiting professor in the Department of History at the University of Toronto. He is the author of *Refashioning Iran: Orientalism, Occidentalism and Historiography* (2001).

Majid Tehranian is a professor of international communication at the University of Hawaii and the director of the Toda Institute for Global Peace and Policy Research. His most recent book is *Dialogue of Civilizations: A New Peace Agenda for a New Millennium* (2002).

Farzin Vahdat is a lecturer on social studies at Harvard University. He is the author of *God and Juggernaut: Iran's Intellectual Encounter with Modernity* (2002).